STRIKE BACK

By Ernie Roberts

Forewords by
Tony Benn and Arthur Scargill

ISBN 0 9523929 0 9

Published by Ernie Roberts,
13–15 High Street, St Mary Gray, Orpington BR5 3NL
Tel: 0689 831810

Cover photograph of the Anti-Nazi League carnival and demonstration
in London, May 1994: by Mark Campbell.

Production by Owain Hammonds, Ebeneser, Bont-goch, Talybont, Dyfed SY24 5DP

"The thing one prizes most is life. Life comes to us but once and it should be possible to live one's life in such a way that, looking back, one feels no regret for years lived pointlessly, no shame for a petty, worthless past – so that as one died, one could say: all my life and all my strength have been given to the most beautiful thing in the world – the struggle for the freedom of the human race."

This book is dedicated to all those who fight back against exploitation and for the Socialist alternative.

Contents

Foreword: Tony Benn MP   i

Foreword: Arthur Scargill   ii

Appreciation: Lord Fenner Brockway   iv

1   Childhood under poor law & deportation to Coventry   1

2   Coventry city councillor, wartime actions and Civil Defence   55

3   Elected Assistant General Secretary AEU. Prisoner of the
    Pope of Peckham   94

4   Fight for democracy within the trade unions   126

5   Struggles for Socialism within the Labour Party   164

6   The role of the media and workers' press   200

7   Labour's heresy-hunting, reds in the bed   222

8   Breaking the fascist menace and the spy scandal   248

9   Arrival in Parliament, representing Britain's poorest borough   265

10 Election, re-election, de-selection and first black woman MP   273

Foreword by Arthur Scargill

Ernie Roberts embodies the enduring principles on which the British trade union and Labour movement was built.

This gentle, unfailingly kind, compassionate man is unyielding in his commitment to the working class and its struggles, inflexible in his hatred of all forms of oppression and cannot be deterred from his pursuit of our collective aims.

I've known him for nearly 40 years; at the time we met he was already an established engineering workers' leader and I was still a teenager hungry for inspiration as well as information. Ernie Roberts provided both.

Miners, of course, can claim him as one of us, since he first went to work in the coal industry at the age of 13. That was just before the 1926 General Strike, when, as now, the State was engaged in a ferocious war against effective trade unionism.

Over the past decade, with the National Union of Mineworkers a constant target of State attack, I am among many others who have drawn hope and strength from Ernie's unfailing solidarity.

As an organiser among the employed and unemployed, a trade union official, Labour Party activist (and witch-hunt target), through his time as a Member of Parliament and since, involved in internationalist campaigns and the fight against fascism, Ernie Roberts' utter integrity has helped fuel all facets of our movement for well over half a century.

The publication of his life story is very timely indeed. It serves not just as a vital historical record but a continuing inspiration to us all.

Appreciation by Fenner Brockway

I have known Ernie Roberts for more years than I can recall. We have always seemed to be companions in struggles for freedom, socialism and peace. He has always shown not only dedication but courage. He has not merely urged ideals, but worked in a practical way to realise them. After long years of work for the Trade Union and Labour movements, he has become an MP, and in the Commons has shown the same dedication and application. I pay tribute to him.

Chapter 1

"The right of thinking freely and acting independently, of using our minds without excessive awe of authority, and shaping our lives without unquestioning obedience to custom."
John Viscount Morley

1   Childhood under the Poor Law

2   Deportation to Coventry

3   Entering the Engineering trade

4   Three years unemployment in the 1930s

5   Joining the AEU, 1932

6   Member of the Young Communist League

7   Membership of and expulsion from the Communist Party, 1941

8   Joining the Labour Party

The year of 1912 saw a miners' strike, a dockers' strike and a transport workers' strike. It was the year that Scott reached the South Pole, Woolworths was founded, and the Titanic sank. Amongst the events which caused only a minor ripple in the tide of 1912 was the birth of Ernest Alfred Cecil Roberts, first of 11 children of Alf Roberts, an ostler, and his wife Florence, who had been in service before her marriage.

Nobody knows for certain which is more important to a child's development – his parentage, or the environment he grew up in. So it is interesting to ask ourselves, "What if...?"

What would have happened to Hitler – and to history – if he had been taken at the age of five to live on a kibbutz?

What would have been the result of transplanting the young Winston

Churchill into the East End of London, and leaving him there to make his own way in the world?

And what would have happened to me if a certain wealthy family had succeeded in their attempt to adopt me, a little boy from a Shrewsbury slum who grew up to be a socialist, trade union officer, engineer, Member of Parliament, councillor, writer, public speaker, founder member of innumerable organisations and movements, newspaper editor, chairman of countless meetings, and youth leader?

Before marrying Alf, Florence had been in service in St Ives, and when she took me down to Cornwall to show me off to some relatives there, her former employers – a vicar and his wife – took to me and offered to give me a home. It was clearly an offer to remove me from poverty into plenty, and so must have given my parents food for thought, especially when I was followed at regular intervals by brothers and sisters, until there were eleven children in all.

My father, Alf Roberts, had been born in Aberdare, where he became a soldier, and travelled up to Shrewsbury with his regiment. He came from a respectable family, his father being a baker and his sister a schoolteacher. He had learned something of the bakery trade before opting for the army as a career. However, on arriving in Shrewsbury he met my mother, Florence, and quickly made up his mind to marry her, leaving the army to set up home with her.

He found a civilian job as an ostler, at a time when ostlers were a dying breed. It was the ostler's job to look after horses at an inn, and as horses were superseded by trains and then by cars as a means of transport, ostlers became less and less necessary to society. It was not long after my birth that my father became unemployed.

My mother – 'Floss' – was the daughter of a blacksmith. Her mother was a cook in a Shrewsbury cafe, the Busy Bee, and she herself worked at Singleton & Cole's, the snuff makers, where her job was making cigars. At the age of seventeen, my mother had won a local beauty competition. By nineteen she had married my father, and in spite of the domestic difficulties she had to bear she always maintained that she had a happy life. Gentle, placid, calm and softly-spoken, she kept her family clean and neat, and was house-proud even when there was little to be house-proud with.

We lived at that time in one of those 'picturesque' cottages we are all inclined to admire, so long as we don't actually have to live there. The house was in Frankwell, a poor suburb in the little country town of Shrewsbury. It was a sixteenth-century half-timbered building, close by the Welsh Bridge, and is probably the one mentioned in HE Forrest's book 'The Old Houses of Shrewsbury' as being recently restored by Mr Eldred, and:

> remarkable for the ancient plaster ceiling to the front room (now divided) on the first floor; the cornice has the familiar 'vine' pattern, but the flat part has geometric panels containing roughly-modelled flowers and fruit, the whole evidently moulded by hand.

Country craftsmen of that period introduced a homely beauty into even the simplest of cottages, as this was. But the beauty did not extend into the garret, which was the part of the building tenanted by our family, the remaining living accommodation being let to Mr Wainwright, who was the local rabbit- and mole-catcher.

The room my father rented was poor, sparsely-furnished, and expensive at 2/6d a week. It was also permeated by the smell of Eldred's Ropeworks, which at that time occupied the lower part of the house, below the Wainwrights. The ropeworks was a thriving business and one of its regular commissions was to provide tents and ropes for the annual Shrewsbury Flower Show.

As jobs in small country towns became few and far between, in particular work with horses such as my father was used to, there followed an exodus of poor families into industrial areas. Our family, expanding at the rate of one child per year, joined the exodus, first to Oswestry, then to Welshpool, where my father opened a knitting-machine shop. When he had saturated the wealthier part of the area with knitting-machines, he turned his rented premises into a 'penny bazaar', which my mother helped him to run. By this time there were enough children to warrant some assistance and my mother's sister, Doll, came to stay with the family 'on loan' from her mother to help look after her nephews and nieces. Aunt Doll was herself little more than a child!

She would take the four children – myself, about three years old, walking beside her, the rest in a pram – for walks around the local beauty spots, including the grounds of the Earl of Powys's residence, where I held the gate open for the Earl to ride through on his horse, and the Earl would swing me up on to the saddle in front of him to 'give me a ride'.

After the walk we would go home to the rooms above the 'penny bazaar', which was rather a misnomer since it sold anything which could be bought for under sixpence. This included pots and pans, haberdashery, candles, foodstuffs, and sweets. The sweets were a sore temptation to us, and I, together with as many of my brothers and sisters as could walk, would sneak downstairs at night and steal handfuls of goodies from the jars. If caught in the act we hurriedly stuffed the plunder under the loose carpeting on the stairs and angelically swore that we 'weren't doing anything'.

At Christmas time there would be treats for the children when my father heated up pennies in a saucepan on the gas-ring and threw the hot coins, together with oranges and apples, out of an upstairs window for the kids – his own and everybody else's – to fight for.

The bazaar did not make the family's fortune and before long we were moving on, this time to Aberfan in South Wales, where a further attempt at running a penny bazaar also ended in failure. After this, my father went down the pit in Merthyr. I started school in Aberfan and was taught Welsh. Not that I ever learned it, but I had the lessons! The school in Aberfan was destroyed in October 1966 by the pit spoil mountain with the deaths of 200 children.

During the Great War, 1914–1918, my father left my mother and children to rejoin the Welsh Yeomanry. The family he left behind eventually moved back to Shrewsbury to live in Frankwell again, this time in Bakehouse Passage. The passage opened out into a squalid collection of buildings, of which a prominent feature was a row of outside lavatories with ill-fitting doors and cisterns which often failed to work, giving the whole place a characteristic and nauseating smell. There was a brick-built wash-house common to all the tenants, and a concrete drying-ground. In the wash-house were two 'coppers' and one of my jobs was to collect sacks of woodshavings and offcuts from the sawmill to make a fire under the copper so that my mother could boil up the washing. The woodshavings were also used as fuel for a fire in the living room, as we could not afford coal.

The area was infested with children, who used the outbuildings and drying-ground to play in. The houses were dilapidated, certainly not weatherproof, and never painted. Because they were close to the River Severn the passage would sometimes be flooded in winter, even to the extent that Aunt Doll had to take the children to school in a boat.

My mother lived with her children and her sister Doll in three rooms, one on the ground floor, one immediately above it, and one in the attic. When my dad came home from the war – slightly injured but promoted to Sergeant-Major – he and my mother and the youngest child slept in one bedroom and I with the others slept on the floor in the attic, covered with old coats. Before we went to sleep, we would have a competition to see who could kill the most bugs, by flattening them on the wall with the sole of a shoe. My mother could keep the children clean, but she had no means of dealing with things that crawled out of the woodwork at night! There were often squabbles among us over who should sleep under the places where the roof leaked, and as the number of brothers and sisters grew and the attic became more crowded, it became more and more difficult to avoid the leaks.

The few sheets which the family possessed were never used in the way they were meant to be used, because my mother kept them washed and ironed and they were often taken to 'Uncle's' across the Welsh Bridge to be pawned.

My father returned from the Great War, not to 'homes fit for heroes to live in', but to the filthy slums of Bakehouse Passage, and to unemployment which led to hunger and ill-health. The influenza epidemic which started by 1918 had, by 1920, killed twenty-two million people throughout the world. It was hardly surprising that so many succumbed to the epidemic. The surprising thing was that so many survived. The whole of our family went down with the illness, with the exception of myself who, at the age of six, became nurse to my parents and brothers and sisters, making gruel for them under the direction of my mother from her sick-bed. There was no question of calling a doctor; doctors were too expensive. All the family pulled through on this occasion, but I later had to look on while a young brother, Ivor, died of peritonitis because there was no money to buy him the medical attention.

Family ailments were usually treated with home-made remedies. I used to go to my grandmother's house to get goose-fat to treat my brother's and sister's sore throats, while a mixture of margarine, sugar and vinegar calmed down attacks of 'the croup'. My sister Dot suffered from eczema, which at one time caused her to lose all her hair and for a while left her with sores all over her head. My mother dealt with this by making her a cap from an old handkerchief, and Dot wore this cap filled with a paste of Robin starch and water, until the sores were healed.

Fortunately, my mother was a sensible woman who knew how to handle an emergency. One day while playing football I was kicked on the shin and the dye from my sock ran into the cut. After a few days the smell from the wound became unbearable but still no doctor was called in. Only my mother's conscientiousness efforts with an endless supply of hot bread poultices saved me from losing the leg altogether.

There were of course occasions when expert medical attention had to be bought. For families like ours it was the Poor People's Doctor who supplied the need. One of my earliest memories is of being pinned down by the arms and legs on a table at home, while a white-coated doctor approached me with a scalpel and proceeded to cut an abscess out of my throat, without an anaesthetic. If any further treatment were needed after a home visit, Dr Piggott, the Poor People's Doctor, would issue tickets for medicine from the Poor People's Dispensary.

But these were not the only tickets we needed. Because of my dad's unemployment and the severe poverty of the family, we came under the care of the Shrewsbury Board of Guardians who issued tickets to poor families to buy food from certain shops nominated by the Board. When all else failed there was always the soup kitchen where, with the Board's tickets to prove themselves a needy case, soup could be bought for 2½d a quart, and bread for ½d for half a loaf.

This was better than nothing, but there was still never enough to eat, and there was always another child on the way. We used to collect wild berries and nettle-tops to supplement our diet. The berries were supposed to keep scurvy at bay; they certainly didn't do much to stave off our constant hunger.

Meals included 'cabbage soup' (which consisted of the water in which cabbage had been boiled) and the luxury of 'sop' – bread soaked in tea and (on good days) sugar. As the eldest child, I had the responsibility of collecting food from various sources: I visited cake-shops for two-pennyworth of stale cakes, and the grocer's where I could get bacon bones for a penny or two, redeemed from the sawdust on the floor, and then the family would dine off bacon-bone soup with split-peas in it, which was considered a great treat. Sometimes we stole a potato or a carrot from a market stall, but these were eaten raw before we got home. Our parents were poor but honest!

During the annual Shrewsbury Flower Show we haunted the tea-tents, picking up odd slices of bread and butter after the visitors had left, but the family's bread usually came direct from the bakery, collected by me in a sack at the end of the week. The sack contained about a dozen loaves, but with an ever-growing family these did not last long, especially when, by the time we got down to the last loaf, it was stale and almost uneatable. The bakery which supplied our staple food belonged to the Morris family, relatives of William Morris, socialist writer and artist of the nineteenth century. This family gave excellent premises to the Labour Party in Shrewsbury, in remembrance of their famous kinsman, which they still enjoy.

Another source of food was Shrewsbury Grammar School. My Aunt Doll was now working at the school, and I went there regularly to get leftovers from the school meals, even though I was terrified by the lonely journey across the Quarry, through a graveyard, and round to the back door of the kitchen after dark. It is surprising what I would do for food!

Aunt Doll had left our family and was living in at the school. Following the death of my mother's mother, her youngest sister, Edna, came to live with us in Bakehouse Passage, so my mother still had an extra mouth to feed, and even cold school leftovers were welcome. The grammar school staff were very sympathetic towards Aunt Doll's nephews and nieces, and the music master's wife would pass on secondhand toys to give us as Christmas presents, as well as helping out with food.

But food was not the only thing I collected. My dad smoked, and tobacco was too expensive to buy, so I went scavenging in the gutters for fag-ends. Then followed an evening's 'entertainment', peeling off the old cigarette papers and making up the secondhand tobacco into new cigarettes for my dad.

Relying on the Board of Guardians for food was a sure road to starvation, so other means of raising money had to be found. Tory politicians claimed (in 1920, as they do today) that if you paid a man more when he was unemployed than he could get by working, then that man would choose not to work. Therefore, relief from the Board of Guardians was limited to an amount which would keep a family below the very lowest level to be achieved by working. This effectively meant starvation level. I was sent out to supplement the family income by 'rag-and-boning' with an old pram and some balloons. While I was proud to bring home a few rags for my father to sell, I never got used to the humiliation of being seen in the streets by my friends, pushing the pram and shouting 'rag-bone'.

Another of my jobs after school was hawking a box of cheap tie-pins, collar-studs, pegs and shoe-laces from door to door in the more prosperous parts of town. My dad financed this venture by speculating what little he had on goods from a wholesale warehouse, but he could not be seen hawking them himself, for fear of losing his assistance from the Board.

But life was not all misery. There was sometimes an hour or two spent with Uncle George, husband of my mother's sister Em, who used to take out a coracle on the River Severn to fish for eels. And afterwards I could watch the eels squirming as they cooked in my Aunt's saucepan. Uncle George had a steady job as a dustman, but he also kept ferrets, which he used for poaching rabbits when he got half a chance.

Sometimes the whole family would go to visit Uncle Bill, my mother's cousin, who worked as a caretaker at The Mount – birthplace of Charles Darwin – which was a short distance from Frankwell, and this was almost like going into the country.

I became a choirboy at St Chad's Church, although anybody knowing my religious views, or my singing voice, today would find that difficult to believe. Carol-singing was an annual event for the choir, and one Christmas found me singing in a pub. When my voice gave out because of a sore throat, one of the drinkers gave me half a crown wrapped up in a paper with the word 'IPECACUANHA' written on it, telling me to 'get some of that down me'. But half a crown was a large sum of money, and my mother spent it on food for the family rather than the luxury of medicine.

One of the perks of being a choirboy was the choir's annual outing to the seaside. Like many of my friends, I had never seen the sea, and burned with curiosity for weeks before the excursion. Why, oh why, did they have to choose Southport, where the sea is more often than not three miles offshore? The choir never saw a drop of saltwater that year, and my disillusionment with the choir set in soon afterwards.

St Chad's was not the limit of my religious education, however. Winter evenings were sometimes spent watching Salvation Army lantern-slide shows about stories from the bible, and at the end of the entertainment each child was given a picture-card of 'Daniel in the Lion's Den' or some other religious anecdote to take home.

The lantern-slides were fascinating, but more exciting to the local kids was 'the muckyard', where the filth from the gutters and drains was deposited. It never seemed to occur to anybody that this might possibly be unhealthy, and so the Frankwell lads spent many a happy hour pelting each other with the hardened lumps of 'muck'. Another good place to play was by the woollen mill, where sacks filled with raw wool were used as make-do trampolines. I was less lucky with the woollen mill than with the muckyard, though, because I caught ringworm from the wool, and temporarily lost some of my hair!

At about this time, I had a lucky find, although I had cause to regret it before very long. I came across a purse in the street near my school, and it had tenpence in it. Operating the childhood principles of 'finders, keepers', I bought sweets and treated my mates with this untold wealth. Then came the day of reckoning. The headmaster, Mr Jones, asked the boys if any of them had found a purse belonging to a little girl, and I, cast (for the time being, at least) in the mould of George Washington who could not tell a lie, confessed that I had not only found the purse but spent the contents.

The punishment was to repay the money at the rate of a penny a week. This would have been bearable but for the method of payment: each penny had to be carried into the girl's school, past all the sniggering little girls, and given to the headmistress. It was a nightmare and enough to kill any criminal inclinations in any little thief.

But the same headmaster who inflicted this terrible punishment was a just and caring man, for it was he who, seeing the ragged state of my family, took me to his own house and kitted me out with secondhand clothes and shoes which were fit to wear. Later, I left school with a testimonial from my headmaster, to the effect that this boy was 'not of a giddy or frivolous nature'.

It would be easy to run away with the idea that my father was a wastrel, nothing but a workshy scoundrel, abandoning his family to the pitiless Board of Guardians. But at that time there were a million and a half unemployed, which meant up to 17 per cent unemployment, and he was simply one of the casualties of the recession.

It is true that he drank rather more than was good for him, and this sometimes rebounded on us, who suffered from his foul temper when he was the worse for drink. He would bring oranges and apples home for us, but, being drunk, would throw them to other people's kids in the street and arrive home empty-handed. It was embarrassing for the Roberts children to see our father lying drunk in the gutter, with other children standing about jeering at him.

On one occasion, my sister, Vera, dared to laugh at him, and he retaliated by flinging an earthenware bowl in her face. When Aunt Doll, was unlucky enough to drop a bowl full of milk, he picked up the broken pieces of the bowl and beat her with them. While Doll was still hardly more than a child, in the penny bazaar days, she went out to fetch some candles for the shop, and stopped off on the way home at a children's playground. Swinging on the 'maypole' (a rope with a crossbar handle), she dropped the candles and broke them in pieces, and this too earned her a beating, even though her face and arms were badly cut from falling off the maypole. My brothers were often beaten for quite minor offences, and although some people still believe that corporal punishment is a character-builder, there are few nowadays who would beat a child with a bicycle chain, as they were beaten.

There were only two members of the family who mostly escaped this treatment from my dad – one was my mother, the other me. Mother only once suffered from his bouts of drunken viciousness, and on that occasion he punched her in the face, leaving Doll to take her away, streaming with blood, to stay the rest of that night with a neighbour. The worst I suffered was threats: my father once snatched up a sharp kitchen knife, threatening to cut my throat, but although I was badly frightened, my father never harmed me.

After the war, for long periods of time dad was just an unemployment statistic. He certainly made an effort. He had a succession of jobs, but none of them lasted very long. He took a job navvying for road-makers, but this folded up when the road was finished. He took a job in the 'rathole' in Hanley Colliery, where the seam was so narrow that a man could barely crawl through on his stomach, but this too came to an end. Increasing periods between jobs were spent in the care of the Board of Guardians.

A man of high intelligence, he must have found this life frustrating in the extreme. He was a musically-inclined man, and played the mouth organ and the tin whistle, as well as an 'instrument' which he put together himself, consisting of glass jars filled to varying levels with water and called a 'glass harmonica'. It did not sound as good as the concert-hall versions, but was still quite impressive for a self-taught musician.

He was quite well-read for a man of his station, and my love of reading probably stems from the time when I brought books from the local library for my father to read – mostly detective stories. His writing, learned painstakingly in elementary school in South Wales, was a beautiful copper-plate script.

There is no doubt that, with education, he would have made something of his life. Even in those conditions of poverty and deprivation, he wrote a novel (unpublished: it was said to bear too close a resemblance to Wilkie Collins' 'Lady in White') and was responsible for a number of inventions, some of which were bought for small sums by whichever employer he happened to be working for at the time. Whatever mechanical thing he saw, he could see a way of improving it: one of his inventions was a mechanically-operated traffic indicator for cars, and another was a safety device for pit cages, to prevent them from plummeting down to the bottom of the lift shaft when the cables broke, which was a common pit accident.

Even when he was unemployed, dad would not be idle. My brothers and sisters brought in old woollen pullovers which they unravelled so that he could make tapestry wall hangings with pictures he designed himself, to sell for a few shillings. He made models out of spent matchsticks, including one very impressive model of the Taj Mahal. In fact, he was good at any kind of handicraft, and sometimes managed to make a few shillings from his skills.

When I was ten or eleven years old, Alf turned to the fairground for employment. He made a game consisting of a wooden board with squares painted on it, and the object was to throw pennies on to the board, to land in the middle of the small squares. If the penny touched the edge of a square, it was forfeited to the stallholder. Alf took me with him to the fairgrounds at weekends, and sometimes my pockets would be bursting with pennies at the end of the day. Other times, there would not even be enough money to pay the rent of the pitch, let alone to take lodgings overnight, and father and I would camp out under a hedge, rolled in the canvas cover that was our stall during the daytime.

When the showpeople realised that I was sleeping rough, they took me into one of their caravans, where I was warm and had something to eat and drink, and I have never forgotten their friendliness and generosity. At this time, I also learned the art of palmistry from my father, and this came in handy later on when, as a young unemployed engineer about nineteen years old, I would travel the fairgrounds as I had done as a child, trying to make enough to live on by telling 'fortunes'.

I – scavenger, fairground stallholder, palmist, rag-and-bone boy, hawker – was also, at twelve years old, the school captain, a position which I achieved on my merits as a scholar, although I was also undoubtedly a 'good boy'; unlike my brother Ron who achieved notoriety by flinging an inkwell (full) at his teacher, and running out of the school.

12

Being an avid reader, I would sometimes outsmart my teachers, but that did not seem to injure my reputation with them. The teacher said that water boiled at 100 degrees centigrade. I said it sometimes boiled at a lower temperature. The teacher told me not to be silly. I explained to the teacher that if you took water up a mountain, it would boil at a lower temperature because of the difference in pressure. Exit deflated teacher.

I was by this time in the top class – X7 – which was in the privileged position of getting no real education at all. The reason for this was that boys of all ages occupied the single schoolroom, and were divided into classes roughly according to age, but there were not enough masters to go round. X7 was therefore given 'work' to do, and told to get on with it, alone. In the same year that I was captain of the school, 1924, I won a scholarship to Shrewsbury School of Art. I was not especially talented at art, and this may have been a ploy by his school to enable me to continue in full-time education. But the poverty of my parents made it unthinkable that I should take up a scholarship; the family needed a breadwinner, not a student, so my artistic and academic inclinations fell by the wayside.

1924 was also the year of a General Election. There had been a General Election in 1923, in which the Conservative stronghold of Shrewsbury had fallen to the Liberals. The Liberal candidate, Joe Sunlight, of Sunlight Soap fame, polled 11,097 against the 10,548 of the Tory candidate, Viscount Sandon. The 1923 election had resulted in a minority Conservative government, with 101 fewer seats than the other parties combined, and this made another General Election at an early date unavoidable.

My parents were not very politically inclined, but they had both come from Liberal-supporting families which had switched to Labour when the Labour Party was formed just after the turn of the century. In 1924, Labour contested the Shrewsbury seat for the first time, against the two seasoned campaigners for the Tories and Liberals, and this gave them the chance to vote for the Labour candidate, who was a blind man by the name of Lawley. It was clear that he had no chance of winning. Nevertheless, at twelve years of age I distributed leaflets for him, went to meetings to listen to him, took numbers at the polling station for him, sang for him ('Vote, vote, vote for Mr Lawley' – to the tune of 'Tramp, tramp, tramp the boys are marching') and generally entered into the spirit of the election with an intensity beyond my age. It is not clear whether this was a result of political conviction, even at such an early age, or whether the sum of 7/6d paid to me after the election had a bearing on the matter. Whatever the original motive, in this, my first political activity, I supported the candidate who represented the 'have-nots' against the 'haves', and this is the political stance I have maintained ever since.

The election resulted in the Tory winning back the seat from the Liberal, the Labour candidate coming as expected a very poor third:

Viscount Sandon (Conservative) 13,220
J Sunlight (Liberal)   9,945
D Lawley (Labour)   1,614

My strongest memory of the election was of meeting Lady Sandon, the Tory candidate's wife, in circumstances which were not likely to impress me very favourably. Lady Sandon, canvassing for her husband, was driving through the poorer areas of Shrewsbury, stopping en route to meet the constituents on whose votes her husband depended. Stopping right by where I stood, she rose in the open-topped car to address the crowd. I glanced down and saw in the gutter by the car a pearl necklace which was hardly likely to have fallen from the neck of one of the inhabitants of Frankwell. Bending to pick it up and return it to Lady Sandon, I was surprised to hear the Lady herself rasp, "Where did you get that from?" Snatching the necklace from me, she urged the chauffeur to drive on – presumably to escape from the thieves and rogues of the less inviting parts of the constituency!

Throughout the days of the General Election, life continued as normal for our family, who were keeping their heads just above water with the assistance of the Board of Guardians. The inspector whose responsibility we were was a man called Johnny Heathcote. He was a sympathetic man, who gave us all that he was empowered to give. But the burden of such a family on the Shrewsbury ratepayers was unwelcome, and he was instructed to find a job for dad – anywhere, but not in Shrewsbury.

The job that Heathcote found for him was as a miner in Binley Colliery, near Coventry, and so, for me, the phrase 'sent to Coventry' took on a special meaning: all the children were supplied with new boots for the journey, and travelled to Coventry on the back of a lorry, with our father, together with what bits of furniture were worth taking with them. Mother and the youngest child were given permits to go by train.

Passing under a bridge on the outskirts of the city, I noticed a sign which stuck in my mind as being friendly and inviting: 'Welcome to Coventry, home of the Alvis car'. It was almost like the story of Dick Whittington, for passing under the bridge that day was a future Coventry councillor who would have been Lord Mayor had I stayed in the city a little longer, who would in all probability have been Member of Parliament for one of the Coventry seats, but for the political intriguing that went on behind the scenes, and who became president of 36,000 local engineers.

I was in my thirteenth year, and still bound by law to continue attending school until my fourteenth birthday. But leaving Shrewsbury for Coventry marked the end of an era in my life in more ways than one, because I never went back to school. Instead, I started work with my father in Binley Colliery, for several weeks until the miners General Strike in 1926.

After that brief experience I left the pit, vowing that those who wanted coal could go and get it themselves, because I certainly wasn't going to get it for them. Instead, I left the mining village of Binley to walk five miles or so into Coventry each day to the Terry Road Valve Company, where I started work after leaving the pit. But I left there as soon as I was legally entitled to look for a job, at the age of fourteen, and moved to Armstrong-Siddeley to work in the back-axle section.

The start of this job coincided with the start of the General Strike in 1926. My father was on strike, of course, as a miner in Binley Colliery, and thus the family depended on me for financial support. Armstrong-Siddeley went on strike for a short period, but for most of the General Strike I was the family's breadwinner. Walking five miles to work every morning and home again in the evening not only added a considerable amount of time to the working day, it also made life very uncomfortable for me when the weather was cold or wet, arriving at work in broken boots, without a coat, and then having to work through the day without a change of clothing.

Curiously enough, it was this, rather than the General Strike, which impressed me as being my first experience of comradeship among workers.

The shop steward of my section approached me one day, saying that I would catch my death of cold, and on hearing that my father was on strike, that I had seven brothers and sisters younger than me, and that I didn't possess a mac or decent boots, made an arrangement to meet me after work. I hardly knew what to say when the shop steward took me to buy a pair of new boots (paid for out of the factory's social fund) and I was even more grateful when, for the duration of the strike, the men in my section made a collection each week to help me support my family.

Out of my earnings, I was given 6d pocket-money, and I generally chose to spend it on books. I passed my leisure hours in the quiet colliery village reading Sexton Blake stories, for there was little else for a young boy to do.

After the General Strike was over I moved to Humber – always with a view to better wages – where I worked on a capstan, making small car-parts. To break the monotony of the job, the youngsters played jokes on each other, and of course the old hands played tricks on the new ones, such as sending them to the stores for 'a long stand' or a 'five-thou clearance'. Some of the jokes were not altogether funny. A belt-driven pump would pump out foam coolant on to the job and when the foam stopped, as it occasionally did, the boys would suck the tube until the coolant came through again. It was considered a 'joke' to hold the belt deliberately to stop the coolant, then let it go when some poor lad had his mouth to the tube.

It was a long day broken only by dinner-time, when I dined off a couple of slices of bread and marge. The smell of the margarine reminded me of the axle-grease I worked with, and it was not a pleasant meal. The job itself was humdrum, with no hope of progress, and it was not long before I moved on to Triumph, where I worked in the finishing-shop on the Triumph Super Seven. Here my job was to turn back the milometers after the cars had had a test-run. I quickly found a new way of doing this which did not involve stripping down the milometer, and I was able to make a good bonus on piecework. But the prospects were nil.

The motor industry suffered from seasonal unemployment during the run-up to the Motor Show in the autumn, and employees were either dismissed or put on short time until new orders came in for models on display at the Show. I moved during this period to a new job on electrical wiring at Hillmans, and the family moved at about the same time to a wooden hut in Pinley Gardens. Father had lost his job at the colliery, and the house we had been living in went with the job. During our brief period of prosperity after the General Strike, when both father and I were working, he had redecorated the living room, and bought a three-piece suite on hire purchase. Now, the house was lost, and the suite repossessed.

The wooden hut had two bedrooms. My mother's sister, Edna, had stayed behind in Shrewsbury, as she was a year older than me and had already gone into service by the time we left, so that eased the pressure on accommodation a little. Again, mother, father and baby slept in one room, and we other seven children slept in one bed in the second room. We slept like sardines, four facing one way and three the other, and again came the squabbles about who was to sleep under the leaky parts of the roof.

In 1929, during the Motor Show recession, I left home and cycled to Oxford. I was seventeen. I lodged temporarily with my Aunt Sis (another of Floss's sisters!), although with three children of her own, she was glad when I found a room of my own in the city. At first I worked in the city centre, at an agricultural engineering shop called Curtis and Horne. A few months of this was enough to convince me that I could not make a career of it, so I joined Pressed Steel at Cowley, paintspraying and rubbing down car bodies. The job was so uninteresting (as well as being downright unpleasant) that one or other of the workers would occasionally stop the track deliberately, just to relieve the monotony.

After moving out of my aunt's house to lodgings in Rose Place near St Aldate's, I began to attend public lectures which were held from time to time in the colleges. I went to all kinds of lectures, but was most struck by the absurdity of learned Oxford professors making profound dissertations on metaphysics, in which they proved – to their own satisfaction at least – that there was no such thing as material existence, only sense-perceptions. A lecturer, standing behind a solid oak table, maintained that the table only existed by virtue of the senses of the beholder; a voice from the audience invited him to 'take a step forward, then!'

It was at this time also that I used to visit the daughters of the celebrated Dr Spooner. The Reverend Dr William Spooner had for many years been the warden of New College, Oxford, and became famous for his 'spooner-isms': he was said to have referred to Queen Victoria as 'our queer old Dean', and to have invited an unco-operative student to leave Oxford 'by the next town drain', although some of the sayings attributed to him are no doubt what people would have liked him to say, rather than what he actually said.

I was living in Oxford during 1930, the year of Dr Spooner's death, when his two daughters kept 'open house' for young workers, and gave them instruction in the appreciation of music and the arts. Because of their encouragement, I still have a lingering (if not very knowledgeable) affection for the oboe and the violin.

It seems strange that these essentially Victorian ladies – Victorian even to the long black dresses trimmed with lace – who had been brought up in a privileged and rarified educational atmosphere then reserved only for the moneyed few, should have turned their attention to the labouring classes and attempted to improve their lot in life. Not everybody had the same opinions as the Spooner sisters, however, and at that time there was more animosity than co-operation between the 'upper' and the 'lower' classes in Oxford – an animosity which frequently came to a head in the Town Gown Rags, when young workers and students gave vent to their mutual hatred.

In 1931 I cycled back to Coventry again, landing there in the middle of the seasonal unemployment which had made me leave the city in the first place. I found it impossible to get a job, and impossible to get any relief from the Labour Exchange, where I was told that I must go back to my family and live off the earnings of those of my younger brothers and sisters who were lucky enough to have work. My father was also unemployed, and my family plainly could not afford to keep me, so I told my parents that they must put me out of the house, and then I could claim benefit as I would be independent.

I went into rooms with another unemployed youth, Stan Woodman, and we lived a miserable life, eating when we could afford it, and endlessly looking for jobs that did not exist. Unemployment during 1931 was running at a national average of 21.3 per cent, and was rising steadily.

Nevertheless, I refused to let my standards drop. Always noted for my smart appearance – even when working in a factory – I bought a shirt at a knockdown price (it was so outrageously fashionable, having collar-points nearly five inches long, that not many people would choose to be seen in public in such a garment), and as it was the only one I had, I washed it at night and wore it the following day. My friend Colin Derbyshire recalls that whenever he visited Stan and me, I was always standing at the sink, naked to the waist, washing my shirt!

On one occasion, Stan brought home a loaf which turned out to have been stolen from a doorstep. When I found out where it had come from, I told Stan to stop cutting it up and take it right back where he had found it. This was not because I had a rooted objection to stealing in principle, but because I knew that the loaf must have come from people who were as poor as us, who would suffer from the loss of their bread. That family must have been mildly surprised, to say the least, when they found that their loaf had already been sliced for them.

At the age of about twenty, my horizons of experience were widened still further when I went to prison.

My father, for once in work, had committed a trivial motoring offence for which a fine was imposed. The penalty was about two pounds, which he could not pay, and the alternative was a month in prison. I could not pay the fine either, being unemployed, but I did not have a family to support as my father did, so I took the blame for the offence and elected to go to prison.

I was taken by Black Maria to Winson Green Prison in Birmingham. Once there, I had to strip off, and was given a receipt for the clothes and personal belongings that were taken from me. I had to have a bath and a medical examination, after which I was kitted out with prison uniform.

My first job was scrubbing the floor of the prison chapel. I could not see why I should do the work. After all, I had merely refused to pay a fine, and the penalty was loss of liberty, not hard labour. However, the warden who came to see why I was not working soon convinced me that I should carry on scrubbing. "All right," he said, "you needn't do it. But if you don't scrub this floor, you'll spend every day on your own in your cell instead. Take your pick." As the cell was lonely, and the only reading-matter was a bible, I considered that I was better off working, especially when I asked for alternative books and my request was turned down.

Another job was breaking up stones with a pick. For a man unused to this type of work, it was a backbreaking job, and hard on the hands. One of the older warders, seeing me examining my blistered, bruised and bleeding hands, took pity on me and gave me a barrow instead, telling me to go and pick up loose stones and the other rubbish which was lying around, and generally clean up the quadrangle. But the younger warders were less considerate, and treated the prisoners roughly, making them work until they dropped.

On my first night, the evening meal consisted of two hunks of bread and marge and a cup of cocoa. As I put my mug out through the trap in the cell door, the warder said, "No, no! you'll have to learn better than that. Stand the mug on your plate and put them both out together. You get more that way." And he poured the cocoa into the mug until it came up to the rim and overflowed on to the plate. The food was so poor in quantity and quality that I observed some of the prisoners picking up stray bits of food that were lying about on the floor or outside in the quad – old potatoes, for example, which were only fit for animal feed.

In the cell was ready-cut canvas, with needles and thread. After the convicts were locked up after work, the evening's entertainment consisted of sewing mailbags. When the warder came the next morning to collect my quota of sewing, I protested that I hadn't done any because I didn't know how to sew. I was curtly told that the penalty for not knowing how to sew was a bread and water diet, so I had better learn – fast. The next night I did try – but I told the warder that I had trouble threading the needle, which explained why I had done so little. In fact, I never completed one mailbag.

After ten days or so of my month's sentence, I was called out of parade in the quadrangle. "C3/29 – go to the Governor's office." The Governor told me that my fine had been paid and I was to be released immediately. I protested that I would prefer to finish my sentence, but this was not allowed. A group of my friends, wondering where I had disappeared to, had tracked me down to Winson Green, and made a collection to pay off my fine and get me released.

There followed long periods of unemployment. The months grew into years, and still the unemployed numbered millions, and the millions became more and more demoralised. They looked on their unemployment as an unavoidable misfortune, which they had as little chance of changing as they had of changing the weather.

The unemployed used to congregate in the market square, where various individuals and groups would take the opportunity to harangue their audience on a variety of topics. One of these was 'Gentleman Smith', who apparently came of a good family, spoke with an educated accent, and wore full upper-crust costume, including spats. He addressed impromptu meetings on political, scientific and social matters, and would finish by taking a collection, which he pocketed and used for his living expenses. On being challenged by a sceptical listener who claimed that 'Gentleman Smith' had once been in an asylum, he did not deny the accusation but countered with the remark that he was the only one on the market square with a certificate to say he was sane. To which I replied – with more wit than kindness – "That's because you're the only one there's ever been any doubt about!"

More dangerous than Gentleman Smith was a chameleon-like character by the name of Dolan. He belonged to no organisation, but was active as an individual among the unemployed, addressing his market square audience with muddle-headed ideas which owed their origins in part to socialism but partly also to fascism. One day he appeared on the square sporting a black shirt, knee-breeches and boots, and subsequently became a national organiser in Oswald Moseley's British Union of Fascists. He later became disenchanted with fascism and approached me – I had by then become a member of the Communist Party – with information about the BUF. He handed over information about the organisation, including the secret insignia they used to indicate rank, and also the names and ranks of local

BUF members, which I passed on to the Communist Party, for them to make whatever use they could of it. Dolan dropped out of politics after leaving the BUF and subsequently became a parson.

During months of walking the streets, there was plenty of time for thinking. I began to consider the meaning of money and its relationship to work. I realised that the symbols of pounds, shillings and pence which appeared on goods in shop windows did not represent the value of the goods. I thought it would be more just to have a system in which the 'price' of goods was fixed in terms of the time taken to produce and distribute them, because this was their real value.

Two of the regular market square speakers were George Kingston and Fred Tyrrell, leaders of the National Unemployed Workers' Movement (NUWM) in Coventry, and I began to discuss my theories about money with them. They told me that a man called Karl Marx had already developed these ideas in a book called 'Wages, Price and Profit'. I immediately went off to the library and borrowed this and other books by Marx, and followed them up with works by Engels and Lenin. As a result, I made an important discovery: that I had been a Marxist by conviction without even knowing of the existence of Marx. Many words in the books I read were new to me. I understood the meanings by using a pocket dictionary but I never heard them spoken, so my ideas on how they were pronounced were no more than wild guesses; but it was the meaning that mattered.

As a result of my reading and my talks with the NUWM leaders, I became active in the NUWM, believing that it was just as important to organise the unemployed as the employed. Any unemployed person could join the NUWM for 1d a week; the Movement was fighting for more or less the same things that the unemployed are fighting for now: the abolition of 'task work' schemes, which were no better than slave-labour jobs, the establishment of 'real work' schemes at trade-union rates, the restoration of cuts which had been made in unemployment benefits and the increase of benefits to a point above starvation level.

I began to attend political meetings, as well as reading as many political books as I could lay hands on. One of the earliest meetings I attended was addressed by Captain Strickland, Member of Parliament for Coventry. The

NUWM organiser George Kingston attacked the Tory Strickland for his lack of activity on behalf of the unemployed, and his failure to take up matters in their interests. I also made an attack, from the floor. But my harsh words were directed at George Kingston who, I said, ought to know better than to expect a Tory to have any concern for the unemployed. So vehement was I in my denunciation of Toryism in general and Captain Strickland in particular, that Strickland threatened to come down from his platform and 'deal with' me if I did not shut up.

The first Communist to be elected to Parliament, Saklatvala, used to hold meetings in Coventry, in the Corn Exchange, and it was he who gave me my first opportunity to speak to a large audience. When I confessed that I was nervous, Saklatvala gave me a piece of advice: "Forget that there are people out there – imagine you're in the middle of a field, and you're talking to rows of cabbages!"

From being a public speaker, it was a short step to becoming a chairman. The first meeting I chaired was a debate between the Church and the National Unemployed Workers' Movement. Four of Coventry's 17,000 unemployed took part, and four churchmen. The gentlemen of the cloth took the line that unemployment was nothing to do with them or the Church, and argued that the Church should not get itself involved in such political problems, at which the audience became so incensed that I, the embryo chairman, threatened to close the meeting.

I also attended and spoke at meetings which were addressed by Wal Hannington and Tom Mann, both champions of the cause of the unemployed, and learned a lot from their presentation of the socialist case on the reasons for unemployment.

In 1932 I joined the Young Communist League, and the following year became a member of the Amalgamated Engineering Union, being proposed for membership by Bill Stokes, who was then a Communist Party leader in Coventry. (Stokes later left the CP, became a Divisional Organiser in the AEU, and finally left that job in order to take up a post with the National Steel Board.) At about the same time I was elected to the National Executive of the Young Communist League, along with John Gollan, who went on to become Secretary of the Party. My friends Colin Derbyshire,

Mary Franklin and Stan Woodman were also active in the YCL, and they were also on good terms with members of the Labour League of Youth, including Ted Willis, who afterwards became a successful playwright, and subsequently took a peerage.★

Not all my time was taken up with politics. During 1935 and 1936 I was involved in an activity of quite a different nature. I founded a club called the Coventry Young Workers' Social Club, which became a dramatic success. In those days the idea of young people organising such a club for themselves, or even having a say in what happened in their own lives, was totally novel, and the club grew rapidly, having a membership of about a thousand by the end of the first year. A 'youth club' was such an unusual thing that the police raided the premises one night, to find out what was going on there. They found nothing to object to.

The subscription was 6d a week, paid to one of my sisters, who was the Treasurer, and there was an official printed programme, giving details of the club's activities. We rented premises in Much Park Street, next to the Building Trades Club. A committee met to consider what activities we should engage in to begin with, and we begged old sports equipment and furniture to get us off the ground. We did our own painting and decorating of the premises and when everything was ready, opened with a programme of boxing, cycling, dancing, card-playing, weight-lifting, darts and other sports. The club was open day and evening, to cater for those who were working and those who were not. We practised equality of the sexes which meant, among other things, that the girls could ask the boys to dance, which was considered to be a very daring thing to do.

A noticeboard contained two sheets of paper, one for suggestions for future activities, the other a criticism sheet on which members could raise objections about the conduct of the club, or about the conduct of individuals. These two sheets were taken down each week, and formed the agenda for an open meeting every Thursday, which any member could attend. The forum of open discussion was a useful exercise in self-determination, although of course it had its lighter moments: it can be imagined how

---

★ References will occasionally be made to the elevations of certain persons to various ranks and positions; this is not done with the intention of name-dropping, but to draw the reader's attention to the political position of those elevated!

much useful discussion came out of the comment scrawled on the criticism sheet that "Ernie Roberts' girlfriend Irene looks like a herring tied up in a cloth!" Nevertheless, the members certainly got their 6d-worth, and the growing number of members provided the committee with a lot of work.

So much so that I, prompted on the one hand by the necessity of finding a job as soon as possible, and on the other hand by hints from my YCL friends that maybe I would be better employed if I directed my organisational talents into a political channel, gave up my involvement with the club. Some of my friends felt that the club was not political enough; other members (but not many) did not like the weekly open meetings, and wanted to "take the politics out of it". Finding that it was impossible to please all the people all the time, I resigned and, as so often happens when one live-wire has been responsible for the lion's share of the work, the Coventry Young Workers' Social Club folded up soon afterwards.

Twenty-one years later, when I had become Assistant General Secretary of the Engineers' Union, I received an invitation to attend the 21st birthday celebrations of the Coventry Cycling Club. On my arrival at the function I was told that this cycling club was the sole surviving section of the Social Club which I had founded as a young man so many years before.

So in 1936, at the age of twenty-four, I put all my eggs into a political basket, where they have been ever since. It was the year of the Spanish Civil War, when joint meetings of the Young Communist League and the Labour League of Youth discussed fascism and the possibility of similar wars in other countries, and also made collections to pay for food and medical supplies in the fight against Franco. Several of their number were not content with this: they also gave their lives in Spain.

In 1937 I helped to organise a Left Book Club branch in Coventry. The Left Book Club published a series of political books, and the Left Book Club branches met to discuss these books and their wider political implications. Among the prime movers in setting up the branch were Bill Callow, Steve Pearson, Frank White and George Hodgkinson, who were all members of the Labour Party, and one time or another City Councillors in Coventry. The meetings were well-attended, drawing members from the Labour Party, the Communist Party and the trade union movement, and the Club's activities nationally probably helped in some measure to bring about the Labour victory in the 1945 General Election.

George Hodgkinson, writing about the Left Book Club in his autobiography 'Sent to Coventry', has some interesting remarks to make, especially in view of my later experiences as a nominee for the Coventry parliamentary seats in 1945. The Left Book Club branch of which Hodgkinson was secretary attracted a wide spectrum of political viewpoints, ranging from left to right in the labour movement, and accordingly Hodgkinson found himself chairing a meeting at which Victor Gollancz (the Left Book Club publisher) and Harry Pollitt (General Secretary of the Communist Party) were the speakers. Hodgkinson:

> Some kind friend who did not like to see any member of the Labour Party fraternising with a member of the Communist Party, sent a copy of the leaflet advertising the meeting to the Head Office of the Labour Party. George Shepherd, National Agent, later Lord Shepherd, wrote to enquire all about it.... To be quizzed by headquarters on a matter like this disgusted me because I believe the Labour movement ought to be all-embracing. The attitude they took savoured of social apartheid and did not square with my ideas of human brotherhood.

As well as this more general political involvement, I kept up my youth movement contacts, even after the Social Club had folded up. I was instrumental in founding the AEU Youth Fellowship in the City – a forerunner of the Junior Workers' Committees, which are today a part of the constitution of the Engineers' Union. I took part in the Apprentices' Strike marches (although it is worth pointing out that because of the unusual circumstances of my early years of working life, I never 'served my time' as an apprentice, and struggled into the toolmaking trade by dint of pulling myself up by my bootstraps, having had no formal training.) The apprentices were asking for a wage increase of 1/- a week, and for the trade unions to have the right to negotiate for them, as they did for all other engineers, and after a long fight both these points were conceded.

On many occasions workers met together in the open to discuss the issues of the day. Invariably they were 'moved on' by police, or, if the numbers were large enough, were told that they were breaking the law by assembling in this way. Even the largest of public open spaces – the parks – were not allowed as meeting places. I was one of a deputation to see the

Liberal Mayor of the day, Mr Payne, and we asked him to raise in the Council the matter of setting aside a certain area in each local park which could be used as a Speakers' Corner. This was one example of the success of direct action, since the Council agreed to the suggestion, and so there are to this day 'legal' areas in Coventry parks where those who wish to hold a meeting can do so unchallenged.

There was one other major activity involving young people in which I was involved at this time: the Coventry Youth Peace Council. By 1938 there was plenty of employment, especially in an engineering city such as Coventry, where preparations for the 'war effort' were growing. I was working at Baginton at that time, on the production of Whitley bombers, and the workers there were beginning to question the motives behind the production of these aircraft: how were they to be used, and against whom?

It seems strange that I, totally opposed to war, should be involved in the production of bombers, whose only object was destruction. Indeed, a young lady of my acquaintance wrote to ask how I, with my avowed political principles, could do such a job. My answer was simple: whatever job I did, from ploughing fields to serving in the army, would be of assistance to the war effort. Any job in Britain at that time was directed towards the war effort, if only by releasing another person to go as a soldier, so I might as well be doing an engineering job as any other. In any case, my hatred of war was exceeded by my hatred of fascism, and by 1938 it was becoming apparent that if force were used to impose fascism on the world, it would have to be met with force.

When the idea of fascism was relatively new in the mind of the man-in-the-street, my friend Colin Derbyshire, using an amateur printing kit, printed thousands of leaflets bearing the simple slogan 'FASCISM MEANS WAR'. Colin and I, with other YCL members carried pocketfuls of these and went about the city sticking them on lamp-posts and walls. Then Colin had a marvellous idea: Sir Alan Cobham's Air Circus was coming to Coventry, and one of the features of the event was to be joy-rides for members of the public at 10/- a time. Colin thought he would sink 10/- of his wages in an air-ticket, and distribute his leaflets in an entirely novel way, by throwing them over the open sides of the little aeroplane. As the time drew nearer he got more and more nervous, and was more than relieved when the flights were cancelled following the death of one of the Cobham pilots in an air stunt. After that the YCL stuck to more conventional methods of distributing handbills.

The Coventry Youth Peace Council, however, did much more than hand out leaflets. There were many organisations involved, and all were active: in addition to the Labour League of Youth, the Young Communists, and the Woodcraft Folk (the youth section of the Co-operative Movement), there was representation from the Independent Labour Party Guild of Youth, the League of Nations Union, and church youth organisations.

There were a good many meetings and demonstrations, and one in which I took part was a 'lobby' of Coventry City football ground – one place where we could be sure of getting a mass audience. They stood on rising ground near the gates to the pitch, drawing the attention of fans to the threat of war with sandwich boards and posters painted with slogans. The most striking part of the demonstration was that the participants wore 'gas-masks' – home-made with goggles and lengths of hose-pipe – as a warning of what could happen in Britain in the event of war. Many of the fans jeered at the masks, and looked upon the whole thing as scare-mongering put about by cranks, but others passed by more thoughtfully, and some joined the Peace Council.

One year, the Council applied to have a float in the Coventry Carnival. The Carnival Committee 'received information' that the proposed float would constitute a 'political demonstration', and sent for the principal organisers. I argued that, far from being a political demonstration, our float would promote peace – a prominent part of the design, I said, was a dove with an olive-branch in its mouth. What I didn't mention was that there would be a 'bomb' dangling from the olive-branch, labelled 'FOR INDIA'. The committee decided to give permission for us to go ahead.

The float was to consist of two halves – one side of the lorry would represent 'war', and would consist of soldiers, barbed wire and blood; the other half, 'peace', would feature nurses tending the wounded. The whole thing was to be prominently named 'WORLD PEACE'. The biggest snag was that they had no soldiers' uniforms, and I was pressed into service again to remedy this. I paid a visit to the local army drill hall, and explained that I was involved in preparing a carnival float illustrating 'the role of the armed forces'. The army was delighted to oblige, and kitted me out with an officer's uniform there and then, and sent me away with a selection of other uniforms for my friends. As I was leaving, the sergeant remembered something else: "Oh, do you need any guns?" I declined, but I did not turn down the offer of kitbags. On the day of the Carnival, the kitbags were filled with propaganda leaflets, each one in its own envelope, and these were handed out to the crowds along the route. The envelopes were expensive, but a necessity, as we were not supposed to use the Carnival for propaganda purposes. By the time the organisers found out what was happening, the leaflets had gone! The float was a great success: as we passed the local hospital, the watching nurses, seeing 'their' side of the lorry, with nurses' uniforms prominent, began to clap and cheer; then, as the float went by and they saw more clearly what the nurses were doing, the clapping faded away, and the nurses were left open-mouthed and speechless.

The Coventry Youth Peace Council also set up a Peace Shop in disused premises in Broadgate. In the window of the shop were pictures of the destruction caused in the 1914–1918 war: the faces and bodies of the injured, the damaged buildings of France and Germany. With the pictures was the message: "This could be Coventry in the next war". The Peace Shop was prophetic, for Broadgate was completely wiped out in the 'coventrating' of the city during the Second World War. (The term 'coventrating' was said to have been coined by Hitler, when he threatened to destroy other cities in the same way that he had destroyed Coventry during the Blitz.) But some people, even in 1938, were not convinced of the need to take action to avert the coming war: one day an observer saw a figure approach the window of the Peace Shop and attach a message which read "Cowards flinch and run away". The person who left this message was, it was reported, a reverend gentleman who afterwards "flinched and ran away" in the direction of Holy Trinity Church, adjacent to the shop premises. He did not sign his name.

In 1939 war came to Coventry from an unexpected source. Five passers-by were killed by a bomb, planted by the Irish Republican Army in a bicycle-pannier in a busy shopping area. I joined in a march of 2,000 workers from Armstrong-Whitworth's to the police station in protest against the murder of innocent people.

The only full-scale war that the British had been schooled to expect, however, was not with the Irish, nor even the Germans but with the Soviet Union. We had been taught that Russia was the enemy, but when war came, expectation was turned on its head – the Soviet Union was our ally. Britain was busy supplying Germany with armaments, and these supplies continued until hostilities were declared; at the very moment when the war officially started, ships were at sea carrying weapons to Germany. Coventry, a city already devoted to engineering in a big way, found itself converted very quickly to military preparations. All the major plants which had been producing cars were turned over to aircraft production, and this made Coventry a prime target for bombing raids throughout the war. But life carried on as normally as possible. Trade union meetings were frequently conducted with the members sitting under the table rather than round it, but the meetings went on just the same.

One night, returning to Coventry after a meeting in London, my colleagues and I were nearing the city when we saw people in the streets gazing anxiously at the sky, then flattening themselves on the ground. We jumped out of the car, diving on to the pavement to avoid becoming sitting targets for Hitler's bombers. It was on this occasion that the Rex cinema in Corporation Street was destroyed. Fortunately it was empty, otherwise the destruction in terms of human life would have been horrific. The film showing that week was, appropriately enough, 'Gone with the Wind'.

The Rex fell in the raid of 25th August 1940, but the really serious attacks were still to come, the principal ones being on 14th November 1940, and 10th and 12th April 1941. To those who experienced these attacks, the memory will live on; but there are now many millions of people whose only knowledge of the war comes from books and films, and finally anecdotes. Kenneth Richardson's account of the air-raid of 14th November 1940 (taken from his book 'Twentieth Century Coventry') fills in the frightening details:

The raid followed a pattern which was to become all too familiar. First, to light up the target area, flares were dropped by parachute; this was followed by incendiary bombs with explosive charges, and then by attack with high explosive bombs. The Central Control at Coventry received the yellow warning at seven o'clock, the red warning ten minutes later, and fourteen minutes after that the first fires in the city were reported. By the time the 'raiders passed' signal was received at 6.16pm on the following morning, 400 enemy aircraft had appeared over the city. They had dropped 500 tons of bombs and landmines, and 30,000 incendiaries, which proved in many ways the most dangerous weapon of all....

As the raiders withdrew and the weary men and women on the ground savoured the rare pleasure of being alive, the work began of assessing the damage and doing something about it. In terms of human life, 554 people had been killed and 865 seriously injured.... According to a later estimate of Lord Rootes, nearly 75% of the city's industry had been seriously damaged and so had 46,000 houses.... The city lacked telephones and water, as it lacked shops and food.

On that occasion, the cathedral was almost totally destroyed – a fact which everyone remembers – and 15,500 people were thrown out of work – a statistic which is for some reason considered less important.

Each factory was responsible for its own safety during air-raids, and groups of workers were put on duty throughout the night to watch for raids, and in particular to keep an eye open for incendiary bombs. Incendiaries were a bit like fireworks – if they did not cause a fire on impact, people were inclined to think they were 'safe'. I, who ought to have known better, carried one home, unscrewed to top, threw away the powder, and kept the case as a souvenir!

I employed the long hours of fire-watching usefully by organising a discussion group which talked about the war, fascism, capitalism and the operation of society in general. Inevitably, the cornerstone of the discussions was socialism. The men were interested and the group was a success – until somebody squealed to the management. I was sent for and told that, since I was so busy with my trade union and political activities, the management was sure that I could spend my time more usefully outside the factory than inside it, and therefore in future I was to be exempted from fire-watching. When the others complained that I was in a privileged position, I told them that all they had to do to get out of fire-watching was to start a discussion group on socialism.

It is not difficult to see why a trade unionist like me got under the employers' skin. Wherever I saw an injustice I would fight until I saw that justice was done, and this inevitably led me into trouble, especially when my reputation spread, and AEU members began to bring their problems to me in increasing numbers.

One or two of the difficulties which cropped up at Armstrong-Whitworth's at Baginton will serve to illustrate the kind of matters which were brought to a shop steward to deal with. The outcome of such difficulties depended to a large extent on the type of shop steward the workers had elected to represent them.

There was a tool-thief at work in the Baginton monocoque shop, where the aeroplane bodies were assembled. Theft of tools is the worst crime you can commit in a factory, because the workers need their tools to earn their bread and butter. The victims had discovered the identity of the thief, and asked me to approach the management to get him dismissed from his job. I, however, persuaded the workers to take a different line: getting the man sacked, I said, would not help them to get their tools back, and would not necessarily stop the thief from stealing more tools. I suggested that the man should be tackled with the theft, and told that if he returned the stolen items, or paid for any that were no longer in his possession, then the management would not get to hear of the incident. This solution was agreed, and the problem was resolved.

Armstrong-Whitworth had always been a well-organised factory, and as a result, wages and conditions there were among the best in the city. A small group of men – about ten in all – steadfastly refused to join the union. Not because they were anti-Socialist, but because they were members of the Socialist Party of Great Britain, which was firmly anti-union. They claimed that trade union leaders were the lieutenants of capitalism – saddling the workers so that the boss could ride them better. Finally, the other workers decided to take some action against the SPGB members for breaking the closed shop, and they approached their shop stewards with the problem. The solution was a fairly amicable one: the non-union men agreed that they would pay a contribution equivalent to their union subscription to a charity of their choice, so that there could be no question of their opting out of membership for financial reasons, and the rest of the shop then let them hold on to their anti-union principles in peace.

Another closed-shop incident ended in a less friendly way. A man had refused to join the AEU, although he had apparently no real reason for doing so – except perhaps that he was a bit of a lone wolf. The management refused to sack him, and the rest of the workforce went on strike for several hours, until it struck them that it was foolish to allow one man to stop them from earning their wages. A manager came up to me, out of breath with running, begging me to stop what was going on "before the fellow gets lynched, or the planes are smashed". I went with him to the scene of the trouble, where I found hundreds of workers arranged in a semi-circle round an aircraft body, slowly closing in on the non-union man, who was standing high up in the doorway of the plane, clutching his toolbox, too petrified to move. I called for the men to stop shouting abuse, to give me a chance to talk to the fellow; "you can see what the position is: will you join the union, or go now before any damage is done?" The man decided to go, and the men cleared a path for him to walk out of the shop.

Baginton was also the scene of an industrial 'first' in Britain: factories had been occupied in other European countries, but not over here. Until a dispute came to a head and the workers decided that, instead of walking out they would sit in for a change. They sent out a party to make arrangements for the food and other supplies necessary for a siege, but the things were never used: management settled before the end of the day!

At the beginning of the war, when all hands and materials were being turned over to the war effort, a worker at Baginton Aircraft was sacked for doing a 'foreigner' – making something for himself, during the company's time and using the company's materials. He asked me to take up his case for him. With the convenor and the shop steward, I met management to discuss the reinstatement of the sacked man, but the employers refused to have him back. I – a life-long non-smoker – asked if I could borrow the works' superintendent's cigarette lighter, and offered it to one of my colleagues, who had taken out a cigarette.

Looking at the lighter, I said casually:

This is a foreigner. In fact, the management have a number of them, which they asked workers to make, using materials which were meant for the war effort. It's not a very good example to the workers, is it?

The sacked man was reinstated.

I myself was involved in making a foreigner which caused some comment, while working at Hobson's. The head of the Design Department produced some drawings of a curiously-shaped piece of equipment which was to be made in copper, and then chromium-plated. He stressed that it should have no sharp corners and all its surfaces and edges were to be smooth. I had never seen anything like it before, but, following the drawings, made the instrument precisely according to instructions. When my friend, Henry Brennan, passed by the workbench, he eyed the unusual contours with some scepticism, and asked me what on earth I was making. For once, I was at a loss for an answer. When the chap who had commissioned the job came to pick it up, however, all became clear, as he held the rounded receptacle against his hip joint and pronounced it a perfect fit – he had had a colostomy operation, and needed a 'cup' to collect the contents of his stomach via a tube which fitted into the neck of the copper bottle.

I quickly became known, wherever I worked, as a good fellow to have on your side in an argument. A typical case was that of a trade unionist who had been suspended from his job at Nuffield Mechanisations, and who I felt had been victimised for his trade union activity. At the tribunal the chairman was the City Coroner, a Mr Iliffe, and there were representatives present from the employers and the union. I questioned the labour manager:

"Did you hire this worker?"

"Yes, I did."

"Did you interview him in your office?"

"Yes."

"Have you got on your wall a copy of the rules and conditions of service for your employees?"

"No. What's that got to do with it?"

"Did you give this man a copy of any conditions of service when you took him on?"

"No."

"Where did you get the right to suspend this worker?"

"From the Essential Work Order."

"No, you didn't. The Essential Work Order simply limits the length of suspension where the right to suspend already exists by contract or agreement with the company. Nuffield Mechanisations has no agreement on suspension."

Mr Iliffe said that this was the first time he had heard this contention made in court, and he adjourned to consult the Ministry. When the court reconvened a few days later, the tribunal agreed that the worker had been unjustly suspended, and should be reinstated and paid for his time out of work. But no ruling was given on my interpretation of the Essential Work Order.

During 1939 and 1940, I myself was on Essential Work, making aero-engines for Armstrong-Siddeley. Men had been called up into the armed forces, and women were fast taking their place in the factories. Employers were taking advantage of their inexperience of industry to use them as cheap labour. I could see that these women were doing the same work as the men had done before them, and were being exploited by the employers. I therefore attempted to organise the women to take some sort of action although I had no support from my union: (the AEU did not establish a women's section until 1942). As shop steward in the aero-engine fitting shop, I raised the matter with the employers, insisting that there should be no de-skilling or de-rating of men's jobs which were at present being done by women. In fact, I was calling for equal pay for equal work – a battle-cry which was still being raised 35 years later, when the Equal Pay Act came into force.

Later in the war, Coventry established a committee to defend women's rights, chaired by Kit Suddick. I was the only male member.

While I was working in the fitting shop, the war was making itself felt in Coventry in the form of air-raids, day and night. The Trades Council was making demands for deep bomb-proof shelters; what they got were brick and corrugated iron shelters. Some of them were said to have collapsed in the bad weather, without waiting for a bomb! I attended a Council meeting where this issue was being raised, and sat in the public gallery, taking notes which I intended to pass on to the 'Daily Worker'. The Mayor stopped the meeting and told me to stop taking notes, and the Town Clerk demanded to see what I had written. I asked whether he would be asking the other reporters what they had written, to which the answer was no. So I invited them to look in the 'Daily Worker' if they wanted to see my comments. The article duly appeared, and was critical of the line taken by the Council over shelters. The Trades Council called a meeting on the issue, and invited Alderman Hodgkinson to present the Council's point of view, but when I arrived at the hall, Hodgkinson declared: "Either he goes, or I go." It was Hodgkinson who went – without addressing the meeting.

At Armstrong-Siddeley (now part of Rolls-Royce), corrugated iron shelters were put up in the fitting shop, and when the sirens sounded the workers were supposed to go into them until the all-clear came through. The firm even sent a director in, to persuade the sceptical workers that the shelters were safe, but I was contemptuous of them, knowing that they were an absurdity in a room full of machines, for if a bomb made a direct hit, flying pieces of machinery would cut through the corrugated iron like knives through butter. Instead I made my way over the road when the siren went, and came back to the factory after the all-clear. A works' superintendent challenged me about this, wanting to know why I was always late back to work after a raid. I answered solemnly that I went across to the cemetery, because I knew that the Germans wouldn't waste their bombs on people who were already dead. In any case, I added, if by some misfortune I did get hit, I would save everybody a lot of trouble by already being in the cemetery.

My visits to the cemetery were cut short when I was sacked from Armstrong-Siddeley because of my trade union activities on behalf of the women workers. This came about when half a dozen men approached the superintendent of the section, claiming that I was putting pressure on them to go on strike in support of the women. I had no backing from the AEU in my attempts to get my job back, as the union was not then in sympathy with the demand for equal pay. The AEU took the shortsighted view that if women were paid as much as men, they would want to continue working after the war was over, thus overloading the labour market and causing unemployment. In any case, the union did not want any trouble to interrupt the war effort.

My next job was at Rootes, making parts for aero-engines. During 1940 King George VI was scheduled to make a visit to the factory to 'encourage the workers', and extensive preparations were made to entertain him. His route was to take him through the section where I, well-known in the factory as a republican, was working. This led to jokes from my mates, who wanted to know what I would do when the king came by. I said that I would tell the king that his loyal subjects were making a bloody fool of him: the components which they were displaying for him to admire were in fact so much scrap – highly-polished to make them look good, but only fit to be thrown away after the king's visit, since true precision components are never polished. But I had no opportunity to say anything at all to His Majesty, for about twenty minutes before he was due to arrive, a young worker approached me and asked me to take a look at his work – in another part of the shop. I was working as a fitting inspector at the time, but did not cover the section where the young man worked, so I told the youth to go back and find his own inspector to do the job. The same fellow reappeared at about twenty-past two – now only ten minutes before the king's arrival – and once again asked me to come and inspect his work, as he could not continue until it had been checked, and his own inspector was nowhere to be found. I again refused, and the young man went away.

Five minutes later, the unhappy apprentice returned yet again, pleading with me to come over to his section immediately, and explaining that the manager had told him to "get Roberts across to his bench and keep him there until after the king had gone."

I did not want to cause any trouble for a fellow worker, and in any case I had no desire to put on any public demonstration of my feelings, so I accompanied the young man to his bench and stayed there until The Visit was over. I noticed two men looking curiously out of place nearby – out of place because they were wearing good suits in the middle of the factory floor, and yet were not part of the Royal Progress. A mate afterwards said to me:

37

"You were highly honoured, weren't you?"

"Highly honoured? What do you mean?"

"Those two men near your bench – they were plain-cloths men from Scotland Yard, making sure you didn't try anything on."

But I had no intention of trying anything on. I had my own ideas about disposing of royalty, and they did not include hitting the king over the head in the middle of a factory.

It was not long before I was sacked from Rootes, again for my trade union activities. The shop stewards were not prepared to take any action to support me, so I placed a box outside the factory gates, and used it as a platform from which to address the workers as they arrived for work and again as they left at the end of a shift. I told them the facts about my dismissal and asked them to support my demand for reinstatement.

While I was on my orange-box, the management sent out a messenger with a copy of the Official Secrets Act which all workers had to sign on entering employment at Rootes, as they were engaged in military work. I, they said, was rendering myself liable to fourteen years' imprisonment by my actions, as I was breaking the Official Secrets Act. I sent the Act and the messenger back with the reply that, if they **could** get me fourteen years in prison, I had no doubt they would do so – without bothering to warn me.

Undeterred, I continued my harangue for about a week, and as a result pressure was put on the shop stewards to take action to get me reinstated. But when I was taken back on the job, I found that a wire cage was being erected in my department. It was about ten feet by six, in the middle of the floor. The others joked about it, saying that it was for me, to curtail my union activities.

Many a true word is spoken in jest. I was informed that there was an AID (Aeronautical Inspectorate Directorate) job to be done, top secret, and I had been specially selected to do it (I who had been threatened with imprisonment for breaking the Official Secrets Act only days before!) The job would involve working in the cage, which I must on no account leave. The object of the exercise was plain: 'keep me in my place'. But I found a way round my captivity and took part in strike action on wages problems while I was supposed to be locked in my cage. As a result, I was sacked again, and this time there was no reinstatement.

I was by now an experienced toolmaker – although I had never been through an apprenticeship – and toolmakers were an increasingly important sector of the engineering industry. Machine tools were a method of increasing production without increasing costs, and were therefore very valuable to employers. The toolmaker was a highly skilled worker who designed and made tools which could then be used to produce thousands of identical components. This made mass production a viable proposition, instead of producing each item on a one-off basis.

The start of the war upset the toolmaking sector of the industry, and involved me in the establishment of a new agreement – the Coventry Toolroom Agreement – which was of enormous benefit to toolmakers until 1975. My book, 'Workers Control', explains how the Agreement came into existence in 1941:

> Previously, toolmakers' wages were based on a national agreement, reached in 1940, which was made in order to get toolmakers producing the tools required for the war effort, because many had left the toolrooms (where they were paid on low day-rates) to work on piecework production, where the wages were much higher. Under the national agreement of 1940, the toolmakers' rate in any given factory was the average of the skilled production workers' wages in that factory. But in the Coventry district, the centre of the arms industry, the national agreement did not solve the problem, because a number of workers, both on production and in the toolrooms, were already getting much higher wages than some other factories in the district. Therefore the tendency was for toolmakers to gravitate towards the plants where the production earnings were highest.

The differences between various factories were substantial. At Nuffield Mechanisations, for example, where the Bofors gun was being made, skilled production workers were making 5/- an hour, compared with the 3/- an hour of workers elsewhere. It was hardly surprising that everyone wanted to work at Nuffield Mech.

As a result of threats of strike action, three Coventry toolmakers travelled down to London to meet the Executive of the AEU. They were mandated to say that the Coventry District Committee would declare a strike of all members in the district unless Coventry could have its own local agreement. The three negotiators were Dick Eaves, Charlie Worrard and me. 'Workers' Control' continues:

> For the first time to my knowledge, the Executive Council agreed to meet the delegates on equal terms, in the Council Chamber, and also agreed to the negotiation of a district agreement.

> The Coventry Toolroom Agreement was based on the weighted average of the skilled production workers' earnings in twenty-two firms in the area.... These rates are provided monthly by the employers themselves, on the basis of their own calculations of the average wage of skilled production workers; the Coventry toolmakers' district average has therefore become a barometer for all the workers in the engineering industry in their demand for parity of earnings.

At the time of writing 'Workers' Control' in 1973, the fight was on to retain the agreement, after the Coventry Engineering Employers' Association had given notice to terminate it. Some workers took action to defend the agreement, but they did not get the necessary back-up from their District Committee or from the National Executive of the union, and the Coventry Toolroom Agreement, having served the engineers well for thirty-four years, came to an end in 1975.

After being sacked for my activities while in the cage at Rootes, I went again to the Rover, working on Lancaster bombers. Both England and Germany had put up barrage balloons over major towns and cities – enormous air-ships, tethered to the ground by steel cables – so that enemy aircraft would be forced to fly at higher altitudes and would find it more difficult to home in on their targets. My job was on wing-components for the Lancasters. The wings were designed so that the leading edge would, if it came into contact with a barrage balloon hawser, cause a small explosion – enough to snap the hawser – so that the plane would not be brought down by the balloon. I was not on the job for long. My struggle on wages – both in the toolroom (which was not paying the correct toolroom rate) and for women workers – led to my dismissal from the factory. My case was taken up by the union's solicitors – in fact, by Mr WH Thompson himself, the senior partner in the firm – under the Essential Work Order, which was meant to safeguard workers from wrongful dismissal.

Old Mr Thompson told me that the barrister taking up the case on behalf of the employers was a Labour Member of Parliament, and he

(Thompson) did not consider that a very principled way for a socialist to behave! However, Thompson got his own back when he went off to have his lunch and a 'quiet read'; as he told me, he had picked up his opponent's brief 'by mistake', and would hand it back to him after the lunch-hour. The judge, summing up the case, criticised me for my impudent and disrespectful behaviour in the witness box (I was the last person you could expect to be respectful to the establishment), but directed that my dismissal had been unfair, and I was to be reinstated and paid for the time I had lost.

Representatives of the Rover plant told me to be at the factory first thing the following Monday morning, and when I presented myself for work I was escorted to the manager's office by two Home Guard officers with rifles, who stood on guard outside the office until the boss arrived. I was told that I was not wanted in the factory, and my wages would be sent to me at home, by post. I received my wages as promised each week, but this in my opinion did not amount to 'reinstatement'.

It was then that I got in touch with the Minister of Labour, Ernie Bevin, and stated my case: that I was not allowed to do the job, even though I had skills which were vital to the war effort, nor was I called up for active service, because the National Service authorities claimed that my personal records had been lost, and there was therefore no question of my being called up.

The Essential Work Order prevented a worker from leaving a job without the agreement of the National Service Officer. A worker could be put in prison for leaving a job without permission, and the employer could be fined for sacking an employee wrongfully. However, the operation of these provisions was rather one-sided: up to March 1942, 91 employees had been imprisoned for leaving their jobs, but only three employers had been fined (£10 each) for wrongful dismissal.

Furthermore, some employers had found an additional let-out by agreeing to reinstate a worker, then sending him home and paying his wages. This was done in cases where the employer disliked the employee's trade union activities, and it amounted to no more nor less than victimisation. It was not only me who suffered in this way. In fact, the Minister of Labour was obliged to clarify the position to the House of Commons in June 1943, and it was reported in the press:

Mr Bevin's statement on the Essential Work Order in Parliament makes it quite clear that where a worker has been dismissed and the employer is directed to reinstate him, he must be given his job back and not merely paid wages for doing nothing. If the employer claims he has no work for the reinstated person, the Ministry of Labour will make enquiries and, if necessary, transfer other workers as redundant. Thus the Minister has blocked the loophole by which many reactionary employers have tried to evade the 'no victimisation' provisions of the Order.

In my case, the Minister made arrangements for me to go to the Jaguar plant. I was given time off to do trade union work (as I held offices outside my job – for example, on the Ministry of Information Committee and the Food Control Committee), and I was also elected shop steward for my section in Jaguar.

But, as George Hodgkinson points out in 'Sent to Coventry', the shop steward:

> was a marked man and he ran the risk of being labelled 'blackballed' by members of the Employers' Association. The quality of his work had to be first class, his private life unimpeachable, and above all, his resolve firm against the management's attempts to compromise his case, either through the subtle blandishments of smoke and drink or the devious wordplay acquired from practice and superior education. As JT Murphy says in the pamphlet 'Workers' Committee', the one-time agitator when put into office of responsibility ceases to fight; he gets caught in the meshes of the establishment and becomes a different animal altogether.... The nature and nurture of shop stewards was part of management techniques to split the shop steward from his working-class loyalties by shifting him from the climate of the workshop to the cosiness of the office.

In me, any would-be operator of such techniques had a tough subject. To begin with, I was proof against the "subtle blandishments of smoke and drink" by being a non-smoker and total abstainer. And my time spent in the library as a youth stood me in good stead as far as the "devious wordplay" went – I could give as good as I got, and often better, in an argument. In fact, I was not to be bought, and this made me extremely unpopular.

A few months after Bevin had found me the Jaguar job, I was told that my presence was no longer required. The Minister, management claimed, had only asked for 'temporary employment' for me, and the time had come for me to leave. Intervention by Bevin convinced the Jaguar that he did

not intend this employment to be temporary, and I was taken back again. But not for long. One day, the works' superintendent told me to pack up my tools and go. I said that I was on my way out to a union meeting and would continue the discussion the next morning. The next morning I found that my bench had been cleared and my tool-box taken down to the factory gate.

"But it's got company tools in it – gauges and instruments that I've signed out for, for my job."

"Never mind about that – take them with you and go."

I went, making sure that I had papers to prove that I had not stolen any tools before I left.

There followed a succession of jobs which got more and more absurd.

I was taken on at Bramble Engineering, but told to leave after only a few months. Again I said to the labour manager, "I'll discuss it with you in the morning." But I hadn't reckoned with air-raids. When I arrived at work the next day, the factory had gone. All I could see was the manager walking about amid the rubble. Unfortunately, my toolbox had gone up in smoke with the rest of the factory, and I wished I had taken my cards the night before!

When I started work at the Alvis, my mind went back to the sign on the bridge, "Welcome to Coventry, home of the Alvis car." The job, however, was distinctly less welcoming than the sign.

I started work in the morning, and word quickly got round that I was in the factory, since it was by this time well known that I was active in trade union circles. At various times during the morning workers came up to me to wish me well in my new job, and a number brought problems to me. The head of the department where I was working, seeing the procession, approached the convenor, George Rowley (who later became a District Secretary of the AEU), and asked him, "Who is that new man? Is he a member of Coventry City football team?"

Rowley answered: "Don't you know him? That's Roberts the Red." At lunchtime 'Roberts the Red' was given the sack.

At a local conference between employers and union officers, the Director of the Employers' Association said that I had got the Alvis job under false pretences, as I had used a false name. In fact, I had given my name as Cecil Ernest Roberts (Cecil was my third name), which in itself was no crime. It only went to prove that if I had used my first name I would never even have got a start at the factory, and that the employers' claim that there was no blacklist of trade union activists was nonsense.

On another occasion I got a toolroom job at Cornercrofts, a small firm employing only a few hundred workers. At the interview I was asked for details of my skill and experience, and when I offered to start on the following Monday, I was told they needed someone immediately, so I agreed to start the next morning. When I arrived for work as arranged I was met at the head of the department's office and told to go back to the gate.

"But I have to wait here for my working instructions."

Whereupon the messenger picked up my toolbox and marched off with it to the factory-gate, where the departmental head was waiting. He explained to me that a mistake had been made – there was no job available, even though he had been so keen for me to make a start only the evening before.

I wanted proof that I had been employed, and claimed the right to an hour's notice. The head of the department put his hand into his pocket there and then and counted enough money to cover an hour's wages for a toolmaker, which I took as evidence that I had been employed and then sacked without even making a start on the job.

At the Humber factory I had an appointment to see the labour manager at about 4.30pm. The labour manager agreed to start me first thing next morning. But at eight o'clock next day, that same manager told me that the job no longer existed and I was handed my cards. I sent for the convenor, who promised to take the matter up for me. I met that convenor, Bro Danny Maher, thirty years later, when Maher was a workers' representative on the Manor House Hospital Committee in London. Maher said that after I had been sacked on that occasion, the union members refused to allow any other worker to use the machine that I was to have used. As a result, that machine stood idle for some years, but obviously that was better for the management than allowing me to work in the factory.

The union also took up my case when British Thomson Houston promised me a job then suddenly found that they had made a mistake and there really wasn't a job at all. The shop stewards extracted a promise from BTH management that they would offer me the very next toolmaking job that came vacant. I am still waiting for the offer.

The time between my being taken on and being sacked was getting shorter and shorter, culminating in the boss of Rover at Clay Lane calling at my home one night, claiming that there had been an error, and they really didn't want any more toolroom workers at present, even though he had been convinced earlier the same day that they did. By this time, the requirement of an hour's notice had been stepped up to a week, so I claimed my week's pay in lieu of notice and also demanded a stamp on my card – again to use as evidence that I had had a job and been sacked from it, even though in this case I had never set foot in the factory.

It was obvious that the much-denied blacklist was in operation among engineering employers in the city. I went to the Labour Exchange, where I was given introduction cards to factory after factory where labour was wanted; but on arrival at the factory I would be told that there was no job for me. I made a collection of these green cards, and my diary for 1942 lists forty-seven of the companies where I tried to get a start and was refused.

This victimisation extended over a period of several years, including three years' unemployment after the war. To add insult to injury, a letter from the AEU Executive Council threatened to 'take action' against me if I did not get a job (as if I hadn't been trying!), even if it meant leaving Coventry. I therefore tried Birmingham, and got a start at the Rover there, working as an investigating inspector. After a week at work, the inevitable happened: the head of the department invited me into his office, and there followed a surprising conversation:

> I want to have a private chat with you, but if any of it is repeated I shall have to deny that it ever took place, because it's in your own interests that I have this talk.
> I don't understand it – your work is good and I have no complaints about you, but the manager has told me to give you the sack. Why? Have you been in prison?

I explained. The poor head of department, who was clearly carrying out an instruction that he did not like too much, apologised for sacking me, but said, "When you get a place, come to me for a reference, because you've been a good worker and behaved quite properly while you've been here."

These events, condensed here into a few pages, were the events of years, beginning during my membership of the Communist Party and carrying on long afterwards. While all this was going on, I was also facing other conflicts.

The year 1942 was significant for me personally in that it marked a turning point in my life, being the year when I joined the Labour Party.

I had joined the Young Communist League in 1932, at the age of 20, and during my two years' membership served on the YCL Midlands District Committee and the National Committee, as well as doing the more humdrum tasks, like distributing the 'Daily Worker'. Many retailers refused to handle the paper, but even the ones who would take it had problems, because the wholesalers refused to deal with it, too. The paper was therefore distributed to those retailers who were willing by a rota of volunteers, who got up in the middle of the night to meet the London train at about 4am, to pick up the 'Daily Worker' and pedal with it, on a machine known as 'The Party Bike', to the local newsagents.

In 1934, I became a member of the Communist Party, but over the period of seven years up to 1941, became increasingly unhappy about the way the Party operated and also the direction it was taking over the war.

As an unemployed youth, before becoming associated with the CP, I had spent a great deal of my time in the public library, reading a wide range of books on philosophy, many of which would have been beyond my comprehension but for the pocket dictionary I carried about with me to help me over the difficult words. So when I joined the CP my political **education** was quite advanced compared with my political **experience**. The notebooks I kept at the time of my CP membership – which were later condemned by the Party leadership as being "inimical to the Party" – are therefore of great interest.

I begin with a series of philosophical statements, some quoted from books, others from lectures, but as the notes develop they get further away from political philosophy and much more involved with the 'Party line'.

The oldest notebook to survive, dated 1937, begins with quotations from Spinoza, Hegel, Kant, Schelling and others, some of which I remember and quote freely, more than forty years later:

"Without impediment we should not have progress."

"Proof is never coercive."

"We step and do not step into the same river."

"An idea completes itself in action."

Next come lecture notes, and again the points I considered worth writing down in 1937 have stayed with me, absorbed into my own philosophy of life:

Strikes: it is not the immediate result that is important but the resultant widening unity and intelligence of the workers.

Revolutionaries **do** fight for the immediate demands of workers (reforms) but lead this struggle for immediate concessions to the complete abolition of capitalism as the only ultimate and complete cure for their troubles.

There are also some brief notes on capitalist economics, fore-runners of the Common Market food-mountains:

Anarchy of production – over production – under-consumption – destruction of food – loss of life and health.

The later notes are much more concerned with Party discipline, and foreshadow the differences between myself and the CP which were shortly to come to a head. In 1939 I wrote:

The Party must be a highly-disciplined organisation, one with a central authority, each member pursuing the same course, everyone subservient to its policy and principles.

This Party: factions and friction – open discussion only, full exhaustive discussion first, then decision of majority, finally everyone disciplined and applying this direction.

How should a comrade be treated who opposes the line of the Party? So long as he expresses his opinions in the Party and does not consistently and persistently oppose the fundamentals of Party policy, he can remain in the Party.

The final extract from the notebook is the most illuminating of all, because it outlines a procedure which I later followed to the letter in my argument with the Party; furthermore, the change from 'you' to 'I' in the middle of the note rather suggests a child learning its catechism:

What to do if you are still not convinced: firstly, discuss and campaign for your viewpoint. Failing, then take it to the district leadership, then study and consider my viewpoint again. If I am still convinced that I am correct, take it to the Central Committee.

I was something of an individualist, and never one to let myself, or anyone else, be pushed and bullied without putting up a fight. I was already blacklisted among Coventry employers as a 'troublemaker'. But in trade unions, activists don't **make** trouble – they only highlight the trouble which already exists and persuade others to fight against it with them. Among the Communists I was also branded as a troublemaker, because I carried my trade union principles into the Party. I could not understand 'Party discipline', or at least not when it was interpreted as 'blind faith'. It seemed obvious to me that the questioning and probing in which I engaged in industrial life should be extended into the Party, because criticism is necessary to healthy growth. Yet 'good' Party members, active and alert **outside** the Party, never opened their mouths in criticism **within** it, but accepted decisions without question.

I believed that membership of an organisation involved agreement with the broad principles of that organisation, but not necessarily 100 per cent belief in its decisions, right or wrong. Many other members came round to this conclusion after Hungary in 1956, leading to massive losses of membership for the Party at that time. Consequently, I was inclined to agitate rather more than the Party approved of, to fight for my own ideas instead of accepting the ideas of others automatically, and to engage in industrial struggle outside the Party which did not always have Party approval.

But the biggest political division between myself and the CP after 1939 was on the question of war. The Party took the line that while the war against fascism continued, the class struggle should be in abeyance. I, seeing that the employers were taking advantage of the war to engage in profiteering and exploitation, believed that the class war should be fought alongside the fascist war, otherwise the workers would suffer setbacks which would take years to overcome once the war had ended. This of course was why, during the war years, I received so little support in my many industrial struggles on behalf of my fellow workers, because the union and the CP believed that industry should be as far as possible at peace until the war against fascism was over. The fight for equal pay was a case in point: the union and the CP were content to allow the situation to ride for the duration of the war, under the illusion that afterwards women would take up their unskilled jobs once more, and the returning soldiers would resume their former skilled work in the factories. It did not seem to occur to them that the employers would wherever possible continue to employ women at lower rates, and that it was in everyone's interests that women should get the rate for the job right from the start.

This was the background of my CP membership which led up to my expulsion in 1941. After a long exchange of letters between the Branch, the Midlands District Party Committee (DPC), and myself, I was finally expelled in August of that year, and immediately appealed to the Central Committee against that decision, which had been taken by the Midlands DPC.

The Central Committee demanded a copy of the DPC statement giving reasons for the expulsion, but by the middle of November the DPC had still not complied with that demand. The DPC eventually wrote to me on 25th November (after I had put considerable pressure on the Party to review the case), saying that the case against me had been destroyed immediately after the decision to expel had been made, but they had written a new statement which was substantially the same as the original one. This was a ten-point statement, which I forwarded to the Central Committee, together with a twelve-page letter answering each point in turn.

The DPC's statement was new to me. I had been investigated and had attended a DPC meeting to defend myself, without ever hearing the details of the allegations made against me. The District Party Committee claimed:

that I lacked discipline;

that I organised groupings outside the Party;

that I could not work in a team, and had made attacks on a comrade which had caused problems in the Party;

that I made mountains out of molehills;

that my own sackings had led to others being sacked, and disrupted Party work on the industrial front;

that I had presented a recruitment form, purporting to be an application from a person who later denied applying to join the Party;

that I collected information about the Party with unwarranted eagerness;

that my personal life did not bear examination – the only example being offered was the fact that I could run a car, even though unemployed;

that information had been received that I had had associations with the police;

that I had challenged comrades to bring proof of their allegations in a very matter-of-fact way;

that my work was damaging to the Party.

The statement is peppered with uncomplimentary adjectives – individualistic, disruptive, egotistical, viciously personal, to name but a few. But on several occasions the Committee was obliged to point out that there was no conclusive evidence against me, and that they had not been able to check up on certain allegations, notably the claim about the police. I had already written a sixteen-page letter to the Central Committee, although I had not at that stage seen the charges which had been made against me. Now another lengthy letter was necessary, to answer the precise charges.

I pointed out that since first joining the Party in 1934 I had been elected three times to the Midlands District Party Committee, and had regularly been on the Coventry local committee. On two occasions I had been a member of a political commission set up by the District to investigate problems which were holding up the development of the Party locally, and had been secretary of this commission, with the job of reporting back on its findings to the Coventry branch. So much for not being willing "to work in a team"!

Admitting that I could probably be considered 'individualistic' in the sense that I always fought strenuously for my point of view, I went on to say that I had conducted these struggles only on issues on which no Party decision had yet been taken, and always "at the proper time and in the proper place" (that is, not outside the Party).

My industrial record showed the considerable support I enjoyed among the members of the AEU: I missed election to the National Committee in 1940 by only one vote, I missed getting into the second ballot for District President by fourteen votes in 1940, and had missed again – this time by twenty votes – in 1941, although this was because it was claimed that some branch returns had been sent in too late. In quoting these near-misses, I am trying to show that for a 'disrupter' I enjoyed considerable popularity in my union. The fact that I failed to be elected on these occasions sounds as though my popularity was not all it might have been, but it must be remembered that I was a young man – still under thirty years old – and even 'nearly' getting into the second ballot for District President was quite an achievement. In fact, I went on to become Coventry's youngest ever District President not long afterwards.

The letter of defence to the Central Committee continues with a brief record of my sackings: "....so it is obvious that on occasion I have not even been at the firm long enough to do anything wrong or right, but that their minds were made up to discharge me as soon as they found out who I was.... The fact that often workers have supported me is proof that I have not lost their support.... I don't ever remember any other Party members or shop stewards being discharged with me over any issue that I have raised." My 'worst fault', I admitted, was my failure to bring recruits into the Party, but the fellow who denied having joined the Party had in fact applied to join, together with his brother, at a Party group meeting.

The likelihood of my allowing other workers to be dismissed with me or putting up false names to the Party as new members is very remote. In all my trials and tribulations in industry, I was the one to carry burdens for others, losing my job in their defence. I fought more strongly against other people's wrongs than against those done to myself. There was no evidence brought to support any of these claims, and I remained steady in my denials – challenging them to bring proof, knowing that none could be brought.

Although the DPC statement claimed that the decision to expel me from the Party had been unanimous, I said that this had not been so. I had been invited to the Committee meeting at which the decision was taken, and gave the following account of the proceedings:

> Comrade Blackwell spoke at great length.... He said he had to leave early to catch a bus back to Birmingham, so it left very little time to discuss the matter.... 3 voted for, 3 voted against. Comrade Cohen, who had just come into the district to take over the local organiser's job said he was going to vote for my expulsion in order to be loyal to those who had already taken the decision to expel.

The rooted dislike of note-taking and storing of information seems to be widespread in the Communist Party, so I, with my squirrel-like tendency to hoard every scrap of paper that came into my possession, must have been a worry to the Party leaders. Hence the DPC's accusation that I collected information about the Party with unwarranted eagerness. But the Party's animosity against note-takers did not deter me from taking notes at the DPC meeting at which I was expelled, and I was therefore able to quote in some detail what the members of the Committee had said about me. Comrade Warman had said that I had "always genuinely tried to get an understanding between the AEU and the T&GWU", and that I was "very sincere and not an agent provocateur"; also that there was "nothing wrong in taking extensive notes". Comrade Blackwell on the other hand had argued that I "was of an ivy-clinging nature" and "not nice". He said that it was "better to take a chance on making a mistake than leave a possible disrupter in the Party". Two local members, Comrades Lucas and Brown,

> stated that I was generally liked for my good TU work, but people disliked my politics. Is this not the position generally with many Party members who take an active part in the trade unions in many parts of the country, and is it not because we – the Party – have failed to convince the trade unionists of the correctness of Party policy, and not just a personal failing on my part?

The allegations about associating with the police, I answered as follows:

> I consider this to be the most serious accusation, and about which I have been told practically nothing. Such as how or through whom I am supposed to have had these associations, or who has made the charge, or precisely what the charge was.... I was led to understand by a statement made by Comrade Blackwell at the Committee meeting that I last attended that the information had come from the publican or someone using the pub named 'The Nag's Head' in Nuneaton, that I was a police agent and that I was in touch with the Nuneaton police. This is absolutely untrue. I have never had anything to do with the police either in Nuneaton or Coventry or anywhere else. In fact, whenever the suggestion has made that the Party branch asks the police permission to do certain things, I have opposed it as being incorrect.

Again, charges without substantiation. Perhaps the most hurtful part of the allegation about the police was that it appeared to have come from someone (unnamed) who was not a Party member, and that the DPC was prepared to take his word against mine. Anyone knowing me would say that it was unthinkable that I could ever be "an agent of the police", in any way or for any reason.

The remaining charges against me were trifling in comparison with the others, but they were still dealt with seriously; I was accused of being 'matter-of-fact' in my replies to the questions of my comrades:

> What else could I do but be matter-of-fact in my replies to them, for it is by fact that they can be refuted.... Of course I asked for proof – is it wrong to do so? I was asked to give proof of my honesty and integrity, so I ask for proof which will prove otherwise....
>
> I do not pretend to be free from error or to have always done the correct thing, but rather I have attempted to do much, therefore I have made more mistakes.... Whatever the verdict now, I shall prove myself in the future and vindicate myself from past allegations.

This long letter was written in December 1941. I waited patiently until 31st May 1942 before writing again:

> I have let this matter stand over until now because I realised that the investigations would take some time, but I have not received any reply at all to my statement.

The Central Organisation Department promised (on 4th June 1942) to hurry the matter up and let him know the decision as quickly as possible. I did not write again until 18th May 1943. This letter mentions for the first time an interesting development in my political career:

> Nearly twelve months have elapsed – I have not received any further communication from you. I know the passage of time proves many statements to be true or false. I have been certain that I have been stating the truth, therefore I did not mind waiting for time and events to prove my words. Very much has happened in my life in the political and trade union movement in these last twelve months. I have become active in the local Labour Party, and am a member of the Coventry Executive Committee, also Coventry's representative on the West Midlands Regional Council and the Warwickshire representative on the Executive Committee of the West Midlands Regional Council, and I still hold offices in the trade union movement, so you see I have not been inactive during my period outside the Party.
>
> I am still anxious to clear the whole matter up. May I be permitted to suggest that I come to London in order to come before you and/or the Committee very soon?

After much to-ing and fro-ing of correspondence, a meeting was fixed for 28th August 1943, and at this meeting the whole performance of allegation and refutation was repeated yet again, after which the proceedings of that session went before the Executive Committee of the Party, and the upshot was a letter from Harry Pollitt, secretary of the Executive Committee, two years after my expulsion:

> At its meeting on September 19th, the Executive Committee decided to uphold your appeal against expulsion, and that you should be readmitted to the Party immediately and credited with uninterrupted membership.

On the surface, it seems strange that I should go to such lengths to bring my appeal to a successful conclusion, when I had joined the Labour Party in 1942, and had no intention of going back to the Communist Party, even if cleared of all charges against me. There was, however, the important issue of political integrity to be considered. I wished to vindicate my actions, and demonstrate to anyone who cared to investigate the matter that I had done nothing to be ashamed of. It was very important to me that I did not leave the CP under a cloud. It became increasingly obvious that the CP wanted to drop the case and let it sink into oblivion, but they were obliged by my persistence to re-open it in 1943. It was unfortunate that I never formally resigned from the CP but simply broke communications with them after the clearing of my name, as this had serious repercussions later on.

I had long been convinced that, while I still believed in many of the principles of the Communist Party – with regard to public ownership, for example – I could not fall into line with the Party's central control, organisational and disciplinary procedures, which were totally alien to my nature. Yet it was also alien to my nature to be without a political party whose colours I could nail to my mast. I found my own political principles embodied in Clause 4 of the Labour Party Constitution, and it was this which led me into the Labour Party, and started me on a path from which I have not veered in over fifty years.

My parting words to the Midland District Committee of the Communist Party were typical of my commitment to the labour movement:

> You can expel me from the Communist Party, but you can't expel me from the working class – it doesn't belong to you.

Chapter 2

Yes, my dear brethren in criticism, take my word for it, our judgements are too much of a single piece; we should learn to bring more freedom into them. We ought to inspire ourselves with more of that clearest result of all the lessons of life, that everything even amongst the greatest of all the sons of men is incomplete, mixed, relative; everything is possible in the way of contradictions and limits; every virtue neighbours elements of uncongenial alloy, all heroism may hide points of littleness, all genius has its days of shortened vision.

Diderot

1   Wartime activities and blacklisting
2   Coventry City Councillor 1949–1957. Municipal Socialism
3   Banning of Civil Defence
4   Elected District President for 30,000 engineers
5   Elected Assistant General Secretary AEU

A cting in accordance with my thoughts led me into one scrape after another, until at one stage in 1942 I was at odds with my employers, my union, and with the Communist Party which had expelled me, all at the same time.

It was in 1942 that I found a job with Wafford & Salt, a small tool-making business with fewer than a dozen employees, operating from one of the buildings at the Brandon race-track, which was commandeered for industrial use during the war. Before long, I was elected shop steward there.

One day, while Mr Wafford was off the premises, I pinned a cartoon to his door, showing a boss on the golf-course saying to his partner, "I'll just phone the factory to see if there are any absentees today." Wafford threatened to sack the man responsible for this outrage but, although he may have had his suspicions, I retained my job, on that occasion.

But it was not long before I was down to my 'ninth life'. In June, with the annual holiday approaching, a dispute arose over holiday pay. I contended – with the full backing of the workers, as it later turned out – that holiday pay should be based on the District Average rate for toolmakers, which was what they normally earned, and that overtime pay should also be based on this rate. These very reasonably demands were conceded by the management within a month – but not before they had raised a hornet's nest for me.

On 30th June the workers received their holiday pay: paid at the lower base-rate, not at their normal District Average rate. Every man handed back his holiday pay untouched. After discussing the matter with Mr Cocking the works manager, it appeared that Mr Wafford and Mr Cocking had paid a visit to the AEU District Secretary Bro Taylor, on 27th June, and had been advised that the shop steward was in the wrong, and the firm need only pay holiday pay and overtime on the base-rate.

On the following day, 1st July, all the workers received holiday pay based on the normal wage-rate, the District Average. About three weeks later, after the holiday, I heard from a colleague, Bro Measures, that some of the Wafford & Salt management had again visited the District Secretary, on 18th July, this time to discuss my dismissal. Six days after the alleged visit, I got my discharge notice along with my pay packet.

I immediately got in touch with Bro Stokes, the AEU Divisional Organiser, who was the next man up from Bro Taylor in the hierarchy, and Stokes advised me to get statements in writing, signed by the men who had witnessed what had been said. Accordingly, I and four other workers signed to the effect that Mr Cocking had told us of the visit to the District Secretary, and two men joined with me in corroborating what they had heard from Measures about my dismissal. When this was done, Stokes, Taylor and I paid a visit to Mr Wafford. Wafford agreed that the first statement was true: he had visited Taylor together with the works manager, and they had been advised that they need not pay the District Average rate. Bro Taylor was not happy with the word 'advised', but could do no other than agree that the meeting had taken place. Wafford denied that he had met Taylor on the second occasion, to secure my dismissal. However, the information supplied by Bro Measures did not name Mr Wafford; it merely claimed that 'members of the management' had met Taylor, so Wafford's personal denial did not make the statement false.

The Coventry District Committee then elected a sub-committee to investigate the case, which they said constituted a charge against Bro Taylor in the execution of his duties. Those who had signed the two statements were interviewed, and stood by what they had signed. Another colleague, Bro Peace, who had also been a witness on both occasions, took time off work to attend the sub-committee hearing, but was refused permission to give evidence. He later signed and submitted to the District Committee statements similar to those of his colleagues, and made a formal complaint about the treatment he had received from the sub-committee.

The dispute, which had started as a simple matter of rates of pay, had developed into a struggle between the District Committee, who ranged themselves on the side of Wafford & Salt in their efforts to discredit me, and myself defending not only my integrity as a workers' representative, but – yet again! – my job.

As regards rates of pay, I was entirely in the right. There was no reason why holidays and overtime should be paid at a rate lower than normal. But now Bro Taylor was anxious to protect himself against what he regarded as a personal attack by me. At the very least, the statements made showed him in a bad light as a trade unionist, although the original intention of them had only been to protect me against unfair dismissal.

The sub-committee put its findings before the District Committee. They agreed that:

Bro Roberts is unfit to hold office in this Society.

and that

the other members be censured for signing statements.

The fact that all the members had signed statements only at the instigation of the Divisional Organiser was overlooked!

The District Committee put these recommendations up to the Executive Council for a final decision. The EC found in favour of the

District Committee, and I was suspended from all offices in the union for a period of twelve months from October 1942. At that time I was a member of the General Purposes Committee and the District Committee, the AEU representative on the Ministry of Information Committee and on the Joint District Production Committee, of which I was also on the Executive, and I was secretary of Coventry Central Branch. Most seriously, the suspension prevented me from standing in the annual election for District President, for which I had been nominated.

There was only one course left open and that was to take the case to the union's Final Appeal Court. The FAC sat in July 1943, when the suspension had already run nine months of its course. Meanwhile I was without a job, and debarred from taking office in the union. The Final Appeal Court was decisive: they found in my favour by nine votes to one, and the suspension was overruled.

I had, however, suffered three-quarters of the penalty already, and had missed a chance of contesting the District Presidency. And there was one more blow to follow. Found 'not guilty' by the highest judicial body in the union, I was then told by the Executive that I would not be reinstated in my old positions: if I wanted them back, I would have to stand for election again. In one of my letters to the Executive Council at this time, I wrote bitterly: "They bait Jews in Germany; they bait active trade unionists here."

It never took me long to bounce back. In October 1943, I was nominated for District President, and on 4th January 1944 the result of the second ballot was declared:

Roberts   1196
Hanson   870

Thus I became the youngest-ever District President in the union, at the age of 32, with responsibilities ranging over a wide area throughout the Midlands, and covering 25,000 members. Nobody could say that I did not take my job seriously. Every year of my presidency, I took care to visit each one of the AEU branches, in addition to all my other duties. However, my load was lighter in one respect than most other District Presidents': I was nearly always unemployed!

Being for once in a job, in early 1944, I was responsible for initiating an experiment which is only now beginning to be taken seriously in the Labour Party. While all my trials were going on in the union in 1942/43, I had of course continued enthusiastic membership of the Party. I had been a contracted-in member through the AEU since 1933, and an individual member since 1942. The Labour Party was viewing with some concern a significant drop in membership during the war years, partly due to the fact that working hours were long, and in any case few people felt like braving air-raids to go out to evening meetings, even if they were not working.

While employed at the Daimler in Browns Lane, I sought permission from the Coventry Labour Party and the West Midlands Regional Council (of which I was on the Executive) to start a factory branch on an experimental basis. Very soon the branch had a hundred or more members. I collected Party subscriptions along with the trade union subs. It was too much to expect management to supply a room for the branch to use, but that problem was quickly solved. The members met in one of the buses that brought the workers to the factory. We held weekly lunch-time meetings, with 'standing-room only' – the forty-five seats occupied, and about ten in the gangway. The branch had no representation in the Coventry Labour Party, but could put up resolutions to the CLP. The experiment continued successfully until, inevitably, I was sacked, and shortly afterwards the branch folded up.

The Labour Party Conference has recently breathed new life into the proposal for formalised links between constituency parties and workplace branches. I, who have never given up the idea that parliamentary and municipal elections can be won for Labour in the factories, still feel strongly that elections are not won in a brief campaign before the poll. I have always argued that there should be no rigid separation between election campaigns and ordinary Party activities: the election is simply a harvest-period for seeds the Party has sown in preceding years. Why not, then, continually put politics before the people, through the medium of workplace branches? I spelled out my ideas on how such an idea could work, based on my own previous experience, in 'Labour Weekly' (20th June 1980):

> Workplace-branch officers would be responsible for collecting subs, which would be paid into the constituency party in which the workplace was situated. Such a

branch would elect delegates to the CLP in the same way as union branches do, and they could send resolutions to the constituency party, MP or NEC like other constituent bodies of the party.

This means that a workplace branch would send delegates to the constituency to represent members who worked in the constituency but did not live there; but there is a precedent for this in affiliated union branches, whose membership may be drawn from a number of constituencies, and no harm appears to have come from that.

There is no reason, either, for friction between the constituency where the workplace is situated (which would be receiving the subs) and the various constituencies where the workplace-branch members actually lived (which would get no financial contribution).

The new member would be notified to his local Labour Party, where he would have full membership rights. While his own constituency party would carry him as a 'free' member, they would also gain from the affiliation of other workplace branches whose members in fact lived in another constituency.

It would be a case of swings and roundabouts. Even if a few non-industrial constituencies found themselves marginally losing by this arrangement, the party would gain immeasurably by the acquisition of new members who probably would not have joined the party in the traditional way....

The party should not be afraid of members being too active, but rather encourage it. We could have thousands of workplace branches, with millions of active members, in factories, shops and offices, in schools and in hospitals. This would be real democracy in action within the party, and nobody need then complain about trade union versus constituency votes in Conference.

After my brief stay at the Daimler Shadow Factory in 1944, I got on with my trade union and political work alongside the ever-present worry of finding another job. Re-elected to the District Presidency in January 1945, I went on to receive in the same year an award of which I have always been justifiably proud.

One of the sons of Coventry was Tom Mann, a trade unionist who always lived up to his Marxist principles. A member of the Independent Labour Party before becoming a Communists, Mann helped to build the trade union movement not only in Coventry, nor even in Britain, but worldwide. He was the earliest advocate of the eight-hour day, and one of his final achievements was in helping to bring about the amalgamation of various engineering societies into the Amalgamated Engineering Union in 1920.

The Coventry Tom Mann Memorial Trades and Labour Hall Fund Committee met in the summer of 1945, and as a result of their deliberations awarded the Tom Mann Medal to me in recognition of my work in the trade union movement. The award must have been but grudgingly made in some respects, since the trustees and sponsors of the Fund included some who would not have put themselves out to help me, but there were also some whom I was proud to number among my friends, including Wal Hannington and Jack Jones (who was later to become General Secretary of the Transport and General Workers' Union). The secretary wrote to say that, because of wartime difficulties, it would be some time before the presentation could be made "at an appropriate public gathering of trade unionists". When the medal was finally presented, it came with a further apology: because of shortage of materials, the award had been struck in silver. The gold version was to follow. It never arrived, but I still treasure my Tom Mann Medal – as far as is known, the only one that was ever awarded.

With me, it has ever been true that as Fortune gave with one hand, she took away with the other. The Tom Mann Medal episode took place at precisely the same time that I was being denied the opportunity to stand as a Labour candidate in Coventry in the 1945 General Election. And two of those involved in the Tom Mann Fund were also instrumental in making sure that I would never be a Coventry MP: Alderman George Hodgkinson and the AEU Divisional Organiser Bill Stokes both gave evidence against me in the Labour Party enquiry into my suitability as a Labour candidate.

My defeat in the matter of the Labour candidature injured my campaign for the District Presidency, which I nevertheless won again in 1946, although with a majority of only 215, against 427 the preceding year. I was also successful in 1947, but by this time the strain of constant battles against the engineering employers, the union and the Labour Party was beginning to tell, and in the early part of 1947 I became very ill, suffering from a near breakdown, complicated by pneumonia. Towards the latter end of my three months' illness, during which I was treated at home, I went to recuperate at the Coventry and Warwickshire Convalescent Home in Dawlish. My stay there was paid for by the Coventry Hospital Saturday Fund, to which most workers contributed weekly as a voluntary insurance scheme (the NHS was not established until the following year). After a short stay in Dawlish, I decided that 'mind over matter' was the only way of dealing with my illness. I told myself that I was better, and returned to Coventry.

My tenure of the District Presidency had never been trouble-free. Only five weeks after my first being elected in 1944, I was writing to the Executive Council about the obstacles which were being placed in my way:

> If all a District President is expected to do is to follow on the tail of a full-time official and chair meetings of the District Committee and sub-committees, then I would prefer to make it clear to the membership.... that it is better to have someone who is only a figurehead with no responsibilities.

Most of my difficulties arose from the fact that I was a left-wing District President of a right-wing District Committee, and I was obliged to do my job in spite of them, whereas I should have been able to rely on their assistance.

In 1947 and 1948, the attacks upon me built up into a crescendo, gaining strength from my problems with the Labour Party, where stories of my being a 'secret Communist' had started. Although I won a great deal of support from rank-and-file members, both in the union and in the Labour Party, I did not help my cause among the hierarchy of either body by announcing the wrongs done to me loudly and in every quarter. My enemies said I made a martyr of myself deliberately and had developed a persecution complex. They did not allow themselves to consider that I might in fact be being persecuted.

Putting aside the difficulties with the Labour Party, the 'persecution' came from two sources, from the engineering employers en masse, and from certain parts of the union. Although not, it must be said, from the grass roots, as I kept on winning elections: I won the District Presidency for the fifth time in 1948, against George Rowley.

The blacklist operated against me now in every Coventry factory, and by early 1950 my union branch had to put out a statement in my defence, saying that I had not been offered a job during the previous three years, although I had presented myself every other day to sign the 'vacant book' and go after any job that was on offer. The Executive took the view that it was my own fault that I had not found employment, and advised me to leave Coventry. I replied that I was good at my job, and in a city where the engineering population was expanding rapidly, I should have no difficulty in finding work in normal circumstances, so I could not see why I should be forced out of the area. On the one occasion when I tried to get a job outside Coventry, I had been sacked after only a week.

The District Committee blew hot and cold in their efforts to help me to get a job, but they too believed that it was all my own fault, and they were bored with the whole situation. The branches were mostly on my side, but one branch – No 12 – took every possible opportunity to find fault with my work as District President, and the correspondence of 1947 and 1948 is littered with exchanges of letters between the District Committee and No 12 branch, concerning their accusations.

By November 1948, the 'whispers' about my 'secret Communism' had become too serious to ignore any longer and I inserted a public notice in the 'Coventry Evening Telegraph':

> I, Ernest Roberts.... desire to warn those persons who persist in alleging that I am a member of the Communist Party that a continuance of such action will result in my taking legal proceedings against them, as such statements are obviously made in order to damage my position in the Labour movement.

The 'Telegraph', intrigued by the advertisement, printed a story the following week headlined 'Jobless, he fights whisper'. In an article (which does not seem to have been published), I wrote about the election for the District Presidency, which had just finished:

> I have been elected on five previous occasions, but on this occasion reports have reached me from factories, shop stewards and branches of a lying campaign alleging that I am a Communist Party member and am acting as a Trojan Horse inside the AEU and the Labour Party.

I was not surprised by what employers did to me. My political convictions led me to expect activism to be suppressed. But my union was a different matter, and I wrote at the time, "I can understand victimisation by the employers, but not by the trade union." I had by experience learned that no support would be forthcoming from the Executive Council and the rest of the union hierarchy, but it was a terrible blow when after five years the membership also turned against me temporarily, in response to the smears, and George Rowley was elected District President. The extent of the campaign waged against me can be seen in the voting figures, for Rowley rustled up an extra 336 votes from somewhere, suddenly improving the right-wing vote by 32 per cent, while the left-wing vote dropped only three per cent:

17th February 1948
Roberts   1230
Rowley   1069
7th December 1948
Roberts   1189
Rowley   1405

Five months after my defeat for the District Presidency, I was elected on to Coventry City Council, representing Holbrooks Ward.

I had already had a taste of the life, and liked what I tasted, as a representative of the union or the trades council on various committees, such as the Ministry of Information Committee. My role on this committee was to report on 'morale' among the workers during the war. Being rather a good dancer, I attended a local 'hop', where I must have looked conspicuously odd among the uniformed soldiers. Asking a girl to dance, I followed up with what I thought were subtle questions about her attitude to her work and to the war, with a view to using the information in my next report to the Ministry of Information Committee. The young lady, however, had been listening to the 'Walls have ears' warnings, and reported her dancing partner as a possible spy to a military officer at the dance. I was questioned closely about my motives before I was allowed to leave. Subtlety was never one of my strong points.

Another investigation I was involved in when a member of the District Committee was in an attempt to nip in the bud the spread of private employment agencies. It was the opinion of the union that such agencies were a pernicious development, by-passing the Labour Exchanges and charging the workers a fee for the 'service' of putting them in touch with employers. I was to be the guinea-pig, to collect evidence. I registered with an agency, paid my fee and was referred to an employer. Needless to say, I did not get the job! The District Committee presented its case to the

Minister of Labour, demonstrating that such agencies were conning workers into paying fees for jobs which they could get free through the local Labour Exchange, and they were thus performing no useful service and providing not one useful job in the community. The Minister, Isaacs, agreed to 'look into' the matter, and then presumably forgot all about it. Private employment agencies still flourish, making fat profits for which the workers and consumers ultimately pay, and contributing nothing of any value to society. In fact, it is in their interests to keep workers dissatisfied with their employment, since the more people change jobs, the more profit there is for the agencies. It was a Labour Government which passed over the chance to stamp out this parasitic growth in its infancy in the 1940s.

One subject which everyone was interested in during, and for some years after, the war was food, especially since there was little of it about. I had registered myself as a vegetarian early on in the war, realising that the meat ration was going to be thoroughly inadequate. Never very fond of meat, I preferred to have a pocketful of nuts and dried fruit to nibble at in the course of the day. As a member of the Food Control Committee, I was in part responsible for the licensing of shops, for rationing and the allocation of coupons.

The quality of wartime food left a lot to be desired, as anybody who suffered it will remember. Dried eggs and saccharine were bad enough, but even fresh food was often so poor as to be inedible. Complaints were made to the Committee about the supply of potatoes. It was claimed that the potatoes sold for pigswill at ½d a pound were better than those for human consumption at 4d. The Mayor of Coventry, another member of the Food Control Committee, and I arranged to meet the Area Head of the Food Control Department, Mr Perrott, to discuss potatoes. I produced from a pocket a few specimen potatoes and, holding them in the palm of my hand, stated the consumers' case. Perrott stared at the potatoes, and said they looked alright to him. Whereupon I agreed, and turned them over to show the blue denaturisation mark, which indicated that these were for animal feed. I then produced from another pocket the poor, blighted specimens which were intended for human consumption. "He's got you there!" chirped in the Mayor excitedly, "What have you got to say about that?"

Perrott had nothing to say, except – like Isaacs at the Ministry of Labour – that he would "look into it'.

Not much could be done to improve quality during the lean years of rationing, but there was a lot to be done about hygiene and cleanliness. As Trades Council representative on the Food Control Committee, I spearheaded a campaign in the local press and in the trade unions to improve conditions in restaurants and food shops. I made my own investigations and published the results, and in doing so fell foul of the 'Coventry Evening Telegraph', which used a complete editorial to defend the food trade, saying that I had made a statement which "would lead to the belief that Coventry restaurants and cafes are deplorably unhygienic", whereas "most catering establishments are well-conducted, and the conditions in which food is served and eaten are not unhygienic". My campaign was also condemned by the Midland Branch of the Caterers' Association; they approved much more of Coventry's Deputy Medical Officer of Health, who had congratulated caterers on their 'co-operation' during the Food Safety Campaign.

I was hamstrung. I had been condemned for making generalisations but I was not in a position to expose details of the facts I had uncovered for fear of prosecution. The private notes I had made were much more specific than the press reports.

In the 'Geisha' snack bar, I had found cakes and sandwiches on an exposed counter where patrons could cough and smoke over them, and the waitresses handled customers' money and then went on to serve food directly afterwards. The 'Opera House' snack bar boasted a chef with a "black, greasy, filthy overall and hat", the tables were dirty, plates used as ashtrays, and a bucket of milk stood open to the elements on a plush-covered chair which was matted with milk- and tea-stains. At the 'Rex' snack bar, no tongs were used to handle the food, which was served on cracked, chipped crockery.

I compared these in my notes with the 'Cadena' cafe in Oxford, where tongs were used, the waitresses wore clean uniforms and caps, and the floor was kept clean. The lavatory doors bore signs saying 'Now wash your hands' and 'Dirt breeds diseases'. I noted with disgust that Woolworths put a glass cover over the toy counter, but not over food. Mothers sat their children on the counter next to open food, and women rubbed their shopping bags against unprotected food on shop counters.

All in all, the public's response to my campaign was very favourable, and the 'Telegraph' printed a number of letters from readers quoting examples of unhygienic conditions they had seen. I was not claiming every restaurant and food shop was at fault, but that local bye-laws needed to be strengthened to enable action to be taken against offenders. At that time, once a licence had been granted, the Food Control Committee had no powers to take action against shops which failed to meet adequate hygiene conditions. Certainly the campaign I initiated helped to raise the level of awareness of the public by calling on people to be observant, and pointing out the horrifying statistic that as many people died of food poisoning in a year as died in road accidents (about 5,000 at that time), while eight times as many suffered serious illness through food poisoning.

I did not suddenly turn to local politics 'on the rebound', as it were, from losing the District Presidency. After my wartime experiences on the Ministry of Information and Food Control Committees, I had fought, and lost, a bye-election in Whoberley Ward in 1948, when my election address announced me as "a representative who would add zest to the Labour Group on the City Council". My approach recognised that most voters are non-political most of the time, and appealed to their self-interest:

Dear Elector,

You may not be interested in politics, but do you want a good education for your children? A house for those who need one? Good social services of all kinds? These are the things your City Council provides....

Contesting Holbrooks Ward in 1949, I was able to point to things the Labour Government had achieved in the previous four years – the national health service, better educational opportunities ("the Labour Party believes that brains are not the monopoly of a social class"), and full employment. I explained the City Council's policy of building four out of every five houses for rent, saying that the Council "is not against home ownership, but feels there is a special responsibility to those in need who have got the money to buy". And finally I made reference to the rebuilding of the City, the aspect of Council life which was going to occupy me most fully in the years to come: "Labour intends to build a city of which future generations may be proud."

As a councillor over a period of nine years, my service was wide and varied. All councillors were expected to take on membership of a number of committees; I took on more than most, and attacked my commitments with a zeal which was not always appreciated by my colleagues. Numerically speaking, my chief commitments were in the field of education, and at the time I left the Council in 1958, I held the following positions in addition to being a member of the Education Committee itself:

Finance & General Purposes Sub-Committee (Chairman)
Further Education Sub-Committee (Vice-Chairman)
Further Education Administrative Sub-Committee
East District Governing Body
City of Coventry Training College (Governor)
Technical College & College of Art (Vice-Chairman of Governors)
School Government Sub-Committee
School Government Administrative Sub-Committee
Teachers' Joint Consultative Committee
Birmingham University (Governor)
Allesley School (Manager)
St Osburg's School (Manager)

In addition, I was at various times on the Health and Housing Committees, and some of their attendant sub-committees, on the General Purposes Committee, and – my two main interests – on the Planning and Redevelopment Committee, and the Finance Committee, of which I became Vice-Chairman and eventually Chairman. There were also various sidelines like the Post Office Advisory Committee, the Joint Contributions Committee, Coventry Employment Committee, and of course the Food Control Committee, on which I remained the Trades Council's representative. A note in my 1954 diary shows the assiduity with which I tackled my Council work: out of 249 possible committees and sub-committees, I had attended 210, and some of the remainder I failed to attend only because they clashed with other engagements.

The job of councillor had its perks, some of which aroused bitter complaints in the press, such as a twelve-day trip to Sarajevo (Coventry's twin town in Yugoslavia). As far as I was concerned, these were a drop in the ocean of meetings which always threatened to engulf me, and the kind of events which ratepayers indignantly protested about were to me the least important and most dispensable element of my life on the Council.

I had developed the knack of turning any social occasion which I attended into a political event; any person that I spoke to would quickly find himself involved in a political argument, and any speeches I had to make carried a political message, however non-political the gathering. I was not given to telling after-dinner jokes in my speeches, but any that I used I tried to make both witty and political, such as the dispute between those who argue for participation and consultation by workers with their management as opposed to those who demand real control of the company. I told the following story:

> There was a farmer who treated his animals so well that they decided to give him a present to show their appreciation. At a meeting of all the animals, they agreed to give him a bacon-and-egg breakfast every morning. The next day, the pigs approached the hens, and announced that they wanted to back out of the deal. "You see," they explained, "for you it's only participation, but for us it's total involvement."

One aspect of socialising which I disliked was the formal dinner. I never wore formal dress. Even if I conceded to the extent of wearing a navy suit, it would be embellished with a coloured shirt and a red tie. The conventions of these occasions were beyond my comprehension, especially in a gathering of supposed Socialists. As Chairman of the Finance Committee, I found that it was my duty to host a dinner, attended by men in dinner dress and ladies in satin and sequins. Before they sat down, the Lord Mayor, Alderman Pearl Hyde, reminded me that I would have to propose a loyal toast to the Queen, after which I should say, "Gentlemen, you may smoke". Snorting in contempt, I flatly refused, and suggested that if anybody proposed a toast, it would have to be the Lord Mayor, who was the Queen's official representative. I also declined to say 'Gentlemen, you may smoke".

"But you have to say it, otherwise they won't be able to smoke."

"They can go up in flames for all I care. I'm not saying it!"

I could never understand how Socialists could go along with this kind of nonsense. No more could I understand the willingness of some Labour people to touch their forelocks to royalty. In the factory, I had been prevented from meeting the king; on the Council, I could not be kept out of royalty's way so easily, so perhaps it was just as well, and saved embarrassment all round, that I actively shunned royal occasions.

When Princess Margaret was to make a visit to the City, I, as Chairman of the Finance Committee, recommended that the proposed expenditure for the occasion should not be approved. I was supported in this by the Finance Committee, but when the matter came before a full Council Meeting, I bore the brunt of the councillors' wrath, and the Committee's decision was reversed so that the Princess could be entertained in the manner to which she was accustomed. I made my protest in my own way, by refusing to be present when the money was spent.

In February 1958, when the Duchess of Kent was invited to the opening of the Belgrade Theatre, I was there as one of the Trustees of the theatre. The production was 'Half in Earnest', a musical version of Oscar Wilde's play 'The Importance of Being Earnest'. As one of the forelock-tuggers approached with the Duchess in tow, murmuring "I don't think you've been introduced, have you?", I bluntly replied, as I turned on my heel and walked away, "No, and I don't want to be, either." Such rudeness was frowned upon even by some of those who called themselves Socialists, but it was quite intolerable to the Tory contingent, one of whom threatened to 'take me outside'.

I was unrepentant. I would have no truck with any non-elected body which set itself up above the common people in privilege and position, and royalty fell firmly within that category. I felt that they had earned none of the privileges and attention lavished upon them, and the sycophancy with which they were treated was sickening to me.

The dinners, social functions and visits were the icing on the cake of civic life. They did not keep the wheels of local government turning – it was the machinery of decision-making which did that, and I made sure that I played my full part in it. When that machinery was stripped down to its essentials, finance was the ultimate driving-force, and to be Chairman of the Finance Committee was therefore to hold a key position in the life of the city.

For most citizens, the finance of the city came down to one word: rates. The population at large saw rates as an unwarranted imposition on their freedom to dispose of their income. I saw rates as a fund which enabled the city to look after the needs of all its residents. I suffered no pangs of conscience when the rates were put up, so long as the ratepayers were getting value for money. The 'Coventry Evening Telegraph' saw things in a different light, writing in their editorial of 27th February 1957:

> Rates are bound to be a heavy burden, and therefore it behoves every council, no matter what its political complexion, to exercise the utmost prudence. Such exhortations are time-honoured, but they are needed, particularly so in places like Coventry, where for years local government has appeared to be conducted on the assumption that money does not matter.

Coventry was undoubtedly a high-spending authority. There had been by then a Labour administration in the city for twenty years, and the extent of services provided was exceptional. Added to that was the necessary expenditure involved in rebuilding a city devastated by war.

As Chairman of the Finance Committee in 1957, I presented the case to the ratepayers in a very simple form: do you want the services to continue? If so, then the rates must go up, since the Tory Government of the day had cut subsidies in several areas of spending. On my suggestion, the Council issued a leaflet to all households. Headed 'The Truth about the Rates', it explained how the Conservative Government had slashed Coventry's grant aid from £193,000 to nothing; how industrial and commercial rates had been reduced by the Tories to help the employers, leaving domestic rate-payers to bear the burden; how the Tories cut housing subsidies, intending local authorities to put up rents, which Coventry City Council had refused to do. Along with colleagues on the Council, I attended meetings of local ratepayers and residents, to explain the theory behind the Council's rating policy. But when all the arguments were over, the final choice was a simple one: do you want the services or not? The Labour majority was re-elected.

One of my chief hobby-horses when it came to expenditure was municipalisation. Convinced that the Council could beat private suppliers hands down in terms of cost-effectiveness, I made thorough investigations of certain types of municipal enterprise, and saw some of my efforts come to fruition. One of the most notable was the supply of meat to schools, hospitals, canteens, municipal restaurants and other publicly-run undertakings. Asking for tenders from the city's butchers in the usual way, I found that all the tenders were roughly the same, and that the competition which is said to exist in private enterprise was a myth. I approached the Labour Group on the Council with the idea of opening a municipal butchery. The Council already owned farms, and ran its own abattoir; it would be a simple matter to breed the animals for their own use, butcher them, and provide the city's schools and other outlets with meat supplies without involving any private interests. Weathering the opposition of local private butchers, I steered the whole thing from its planning stage into production, under the slogan 'From the Grass to the Class'. The start of the enterprise coincided with my leaving the City Council to take up my job with the AEU in London. On returning to the city, I made enquiries about how the scheme was working out, and learned from the City Treasurer that, in addition to supplying better quality meat than they had previously obtained, the municipal butchery had saved the Council £30,000 during its first three months' operation.

Another municipal scheme which came to a less satisfactory ending was for milk. The price of milk had reached such a level that even the Tories were dismayed by it, and gave local authorities permission to refuse to buy milk at the high private-enterprise prices, and to give schoolchildren – to whom they had a statutory obligation – milk tablets instead of fresh milk.

The Coventry City Council invited tenders for the supply of milk, and all the private dairies submitted tenders for roughly the same amount. I, whose job it was as Chairman of the Finance Committee to open the tenders, was disgusted to find that even the Co-op had tendered the same price. In order to force the situation out into the open, the contract was given wholly to private suppliers, which produced howls of rage from the Co-op members of the Labour Party (especially Alderman Stringer, who was Chairman of Coventry Co-op). As a result, the Co-op put in a significantly lower tender, and obtained the next contract.

Meanwhile, I was investigating another line of supply. Along with Councillor Arthur Waugh, I made enquiries about the possibility of a municipal milk supply. We went into the cost of buying equipment, and buying the waxed cartons necessary to supply 8,000,000 units of milk a year, and decided that it was an economic proposition. We met the Minister concerned, Vosper, and put to him the financial impossibility of supplying milk to schools at the prices charged by private dairies. Making sympathetic noises, the Minister promised "to do anything that could be done". So the two councillors came straight to the point: would the Government allow the Milk Marketing Board to supply the Council with milk to run a municipal dairy? Suddenly the Minister was no longer prepared to do everything that could be done. "I couldn't possibly agree to a thing like that," he spluttered. "Are you forgetting what Party I represent? It's more than my job's worth...."

The Tory Government put another spoke in my wheel over the question of making municipal car-parks pay their way. With a large traffic-free precinct in the course of being built, the local authority was obliged to provide enough parking space near the city centre to satisfy the needs of shoppers. The price of land meant that car-parks were virtually being built on gold-dust. It cost more for the space to park a car than it did for the car itself! Seeing that private filling-stations were coining money, why not, I argued, put petrol stations on municipal car-parks, and use the profit to pay for the park? Once again, the stumbling block was the need for central government permission for the scheme, and the relationship between the Conservative Government and one of the most progressive local authorities in the country left a lot to be desired. Permission was not forthcoming.

One of the ideas which seems to have foundered on the rocks of City Council apathy was a municipal printing scheme, to cope with the tons of paperwork generated by a large local authority. I visited Bristol, where such a scheme was already successfully operating, to learn the ins and outs of it, but I never managed to convince my fellow councillors of the benefits of do-it-yourself in this sphere.

The most ambitious plan for municipal ownership was in banking, and I asked the City Treasurer, Dr AH Marshall, to do a feasibility study on it.

The only municipal bank in existence was in Birmingham, where there were (said Marshall) 'exceptional circumstances'. He had doubts about governments of any political complexion giving local authorities powers to run such banks. The banking business of a country is so delicate, Marshall concluded, that he could not envisage local authorities being entrusted with it. One wonders why a body of elected representatives, with a staff of highly-qualified local government officers at their disposal, should be considered less able to run a bank than to run a city! However, I left Coventry a short time afterwards, and did not pursue this plan any further.

In my quest for loans on lower rates of interest to finance the city's needs, I made contact with an organisation in Italy named 'Comunita Europea Di Credito Communale'. In February 1957 I received the following letter from them:

Councillor Roberts, Chairman of Coventry Finance Committee:

Sir,

I have the honour to inform you that on Friday, 1st March next, at the Madama Palace of Turin, will take place the inauguration of the new administratif Seat of the European Community for Municipal Credit, which is a new Institution deriving from the Council of European Municipalities.

In the meantime the Bureau of the Community, of which I have been elected President at Geneva, on 1st December last, with the full votes of the Italian, French, German, Austrian, Swiss and Belgian Delegates, will be officially installed.

On the occasion the Representatives of ten Western-European Countries will meet in Turin, and during these sittings they will discuss the most important problems on Municipal Credit, in accordance with the proposal for European scheme of loans to Local Authorities.

As I had the possibility of appreciating your interest in the debates about the most important problems on Municipal Credit, and in order to obtain concrete collaboration on the subject, I have the honour to invite you to attend these Meetings of the Bureau of the European Community for Municipal Credit at Turin, as observer.

So you will be in such a position as to be able to debate the problems which have interested you so much, and to examine carefully the ends to which the European Community for Municipal Credit aims.

This was before the setting up of the EEC. I saw the possibilities of local authorities in Europe helping one another with local government finance.

When I arrived at the Conference, representing Coventry, I found I was the only British representative to attend. Consequently, I was asked to speak from the platform to put a British point of view which I gladly accepted. This was the only time in my life I was asked to speak for Britain. This effort by European local authorities to help their citizens was baulked by powerful international financial interests and it failed.

As a member of the Housing Committee, I was involved in the housing problems of the 11,710 families on the housing list in 1949. At the Council's then current rate of building it would have taken three years to house these families, but new ones were adding themselves to the list at the alarming rate of 260 a month. The City Council was faced with the double problem of rebuilding vast numbers of houses destroyed in air-raids and clearing the slums which naturally appear in the course of time, and of rebuilding the commercial heart of the city, laid waste by bombs. An additional complication was that Coventry was a city of engineers, and its builders and civil engineering workers accounted for only 1½ per cent of the workforce, compared with the 6½ per cent which was the national average. There was a long way to go before the spacious attractive housing estates which ring Coventry, within its green belt of grass and woodland, would be ready for occupation.

There was one point on which I saw eye to eye with Winston Churchill. Churchill had said: "I am an expert on experts." After experiencing some of the 'experts' in the Planning Department, I could only agree with him. The experts thought that the shopping precinct should be decorated with areas of cobble-stones, which would be an interesting architectural feature; the Planning Committee thought that pedestrians, especially women in high heels, would prefer ease of passage to architectural features, and put a stop to the cobbles. Another 'architectural feature' was the sunken garden planned for the upper precinct, which the Committee scotched when they realised that it would be at just such a level as to blow dust and debris from the surrounding pavement into the eyes of anyone unfortunate enough to be sitting in it. The 'experts' even pontificated on the amount of decoration allowed on private houses, and decreed that owners of houses in Bell Green should not be allowed to alter their front doors or rebuild their porches, as this would spoil the effect of the rows of identical houses. The Committee over-ruled this, as they could not see why residents should not alter their houses in this way if they wished; the Committee was far more concerned with the rights of the many Coventry residents who were not fortunate enough to have their own homes to alter.

During the war, Coventry's working population had expanded massively, with engineers drafted in by the government to help the war effort. Long after the war, large numbers of these workers remained, still working in the city, and living in the only homes they knew – the hastily-built hostels put up by the Government on local authority land. In the early '50s, the Government decided to close some of the Coventry hostels – occupied by Italian workers – and dispose of them. The City Council's offer to buy the hostels for use as accommodation for single persons was turned down: the price they offered was not high enough. I led a deputation of councillors to see officials at the Ministry of Housing. Before we went into the meeting, I warned my colleagues that I might say some strange things, but on no account were they to contradict or interrupt me. Typically, I kept the trump-card up my sleeve, and did not even tell my fellow councillors what the card was. I put my case bluntly: the local authority was withdrawing its offer to buy the hostels. We had decided to pay only for the hardcore. The land belonged to the Council, and the Government held it on lease. Coventry Corporation wanted the land back to use for housing, so the Government would have to take away the hostels. This would mean reducing them to rubble, which the Council was prepared to pay for at an appropriate rate. Also, I threw in as a parting shot, the Government would then be responsible for making the Italians homeless, and would therefore have to take on the responsibility of rehousing them. The Ministry agreed to sell the hostels on the terms that the Council had originally suggested.

By the time of the 1949 municipal election, the rebuilding of central Coventry had already started, in an area which the Tories on the Council referred to as 'the agricultural development', the traffic island in Broadgate, which was to be covered with grass and planted with the shrubs and bulbs which were a gift from the Netherlands.

76

It was also intended that the rural life should spill over into the shopping centre in the forms of trees and waterfalls, and there was to be sculpture and art to add to the cultural experiences of the shoppers. This was to be a shopping area such as had never before been seen in Britain. One of its features, at that time unique and untried, was that it was designed for pedestrians only. The commercial interests were up in arms, believing that unless the public could bring their cars to the shops, they would prefer to drive into Birmingham. Trade would collapse. The original idea of an entirely traffic-free precinct was shelved, and in 1945 a new plan emerged, in which the shopping area was cut in two by a road. One of the crusades in which I joined was for a reversion to the original plan, but this was not achieved until 1955, when the Broadgate half of the precinct had been completed and the traders could see that an area without traffic brought benefits instead of the expected fall in trade.

From the outset, there was conflict over how much of the precinct was to be municipally-owned. Even within the Labour Group agreement could not be reached, and on the Council opinions ranged from the Tories' view that the whole thing should be turned over to private enterprise, to my view that all the buildings should be built and owned by the local authority, with all shades of opinion in between. The Council had early in the struggle bowed to right-wing pressure, and conceded that the Leofric Hotel, which I and others on the Planning Committee felt certain could have been run profitably as a municipal enterprise, must be built by a private company. Once the Leofric was started, the same company suggested that they might also develop two further blocks in the top half of the precinct. This would blow a big hole in any idea of building the city centre wholly as a Corporation development, so that rents would be paid into the public purse for the benefit of the community. With some of the larger chain stores already building on land leased from the Corporation, and the Hotel Leofric also in progress, the Ministry of Housing and Local Government refused a loan for the remainder of the work on the upper precinct to be undertaken by the local authority, and thus the private developers had their way. But their run of luck went no further.

The remainder of the precinct was developed municipally, so that the ratepayers of Coventry are still reaping the benefits of the rents, and part of the upper precinct became the Bridge Restaurant, owned and run by the local authority, after private offers to use the premises for other purposes had been resisted.

With such massive building programmes on hand to house all those in need and revive the city commercially, a large number of councillors felt that this was not the right time to start building a new cathedral. Bishop Neville Gorton and other clerics of the city, working through the Cathedral Reconstruction Committee, had already drafted a Bill to put before Parliament to enable the work to go ahead, but they were obliged to get the permission of the local planning authority, which was the City Council. The Planning Committee, despite the efforts of its chairman, Alderman Hodgkinson, proposed that the start of the cathedral should be delayed for ten years. Their argument was that, although the main fabric of the cathedral was to be stone, massive quantities of wood and cement, were in very short supply, so the normal programme to replace 60,000 damaged houses and rebuild schools and a hospital would be bound to suffer. Also, the country could not afford to devote so much time and labour to such a project, especially in Coventry, which was already short of builders of all types. The opposing pressures of the Planning Committee and the Cathedral Reconstruction Committee seemed like the immovable force and the irresistible object. the Minister of Works, David Eccles, adjudicated.

At a meeting with Eccles, the Planning Committee deputation, consisting of George Hodgkinson, Sidney Stringer, the Town Clerk and I, put forward a strong case. We reminded the Minister that, during a visit to Coventry two years previously, he had visited a partially-built school; that school had still not been completed. Of a group of twenty houses contracted to be built in 1951, only fourteen had been finished – three years later. Finally, we threw at the Minister of Works a statement made by his colleague, the Minister of Housing, only five weeks previously:

> The Government have made it clear that, although the output of bricks and cement has been considerably increased, supplies are not yet available for a housing programme of more than 300,000 houses a year, particularly bearing in mind the necessity for making a start on slum clearance throughout the country,

and to devoting a greater share of the nation's resources to the improvement of existing houses.

Those of us on the deputation were a motley collection. Alderman Hodgkinson was more on the side of the Cathedral Reconstruction Committee than otherwise, but had to go along with he Planning Committee's decision. Stringer most nearly represented the views of the bulk of the Planning Committee, which was not against the building of the cathedral, nor against the proposed site, but was firmly of the opinion that the timing was wrong – there was more important work to do first. I atheist that I am, opposed the cathedral because of its siting, since it was going to occupy a prime position which could be much better used for other purposes; if I had had my way, the cathedral project would have been shelved and forgotten for good. Like Hodgkinson, however, I was bound to follow the line of the Planning Committee. I did point out to the Minister that religious needs were already being catered for, not only in several churches remaining in the city centre, but also in new churches which were being built on the new housing estates, and in any case, I concluded, it seemed more Christian to me to house the homeless than to build a cathedral. Eccles turned on me, saying, "Who do you think you are? God?" "Oh, no," came my reply. "**You** are God – you will be making the decision."

The Minister's written reply to the deputation made great play of the fact that building restrictions had been eased, and materials were more readily available than at any time since the war. But his decision to allow the cathedral to go ahead seemed to be based in part upon mysticism:

Can we be sure that a Cathedral would be so useless?

Is it always right to prefer things seen to things unseen?

The building licence was granted the following month, and shortly afterwards the 'Coventry Evening Telegraph' published an editorial claiming that the Planning Committee now believed that the new cathedral would **not** impede work on housing and school building, and that they were satisfied on this point now that the decision had been made to go ahead. I wrote a letter to the paper, correcting their statements and giving the majority view of the Planning Committee; the 'Telegraph' printed my letter, with a footnote explaining that I was only a member of the Planning Committee, whereas their comments had been based on a statement made by Alderman Hodgkinson, who was the Committee's Chairman.

The Planning Committee was not always engaged in such lofty considerations. In 1949, the committee proposed that Coventry should have a new railway station. It was a city of some size and importance, growing all the time, yet its rail facilities were far inferior to those of smaller towns nearby. British Rail put in a planning application for an extension to the Parcels Office. The Committee countered with the suggestion of a completely new station. In the end, the Committee had the upper hand, insisting that no planning application would be considered for a new Parcels Office unless it came as part of a package deal for a new station. Thus did Coventry get a railway station befitting its growing importance.

There was another aspect of the transport system which bothered me even more than the station. After nationalisation, the railways had become a public responsibility, subsidised by public money. Yet there were still three travelling classes, with the 1st Class being virtually empty and the 3rd Class permanently cramped. I proposed in a Party meeting that pressure should be applied to establish a single class of travel – and to level **up**, not down. Surprisingly, the vote was lost by 27 votes to 26, and even now, more than thirty years later, our 'nationalised' rail service still gives better treatment to those with money to pay for it.

Anyone who knew me in my ragged days as a Shrewsbury schoolboy might have smiled to see the posts I held in the field of education in Coventry. Perhaps memories of my own education, prematurely terminated when I was thirteen, spurred me on to greater efforts to improve educational opportunities for others. I was a natural champion of comprehensive education (Coventry had a full complement of purpose-built comprehensive schools while other local authorities were still wondering what 'comprehensive' meant), and I fought vigorously against any cuts in the education service, from whatever source they came. In the mid-fifties, I was causing havoc in the Education Committee by initiating a debate on education standards which, I said, were bound to suffer in primary schools where some classes had as many as 60 pupils, and in secondary schools classes of 50. My demands were quite moderate (I suggested classes of 40 in primary, and 30 in secondary schools), but my attacks on the Tory Government which had imposed these conditions through cuts in the school building programme were anything but moderate, and they led to a row about 'using the Committee for political purposes.' I was among those who did not much mind how I used the Committee, as long as the children of the city got a better deal through it.

There were naturally objections to a mere engineer with no educational qualifications presuming to pontificate about educational methods, and similar charges were made against others who ended up as school governors and in other positions of power. After all, what would a man like me know about educating children? I had only one pre-eminent qualification: I had been a child myself! Apart from that, my only claim was that I was a fighter for justice and equality, and that applied to children as much as to adults. I made some enemies in the world of teaching, but I made more friends.

At a school where I was Chairman of the Board of Governors, there were murmurs of discontent about the headmistress, who was said to be inadequate for the job. Both parents and teachers approached the Governors on this matter, and in desperation thirteen out of the sixteen teachers at the school signed a protest, in which they asked either to change their jobs, or change the headmistress. As a result of my pressure, the headmistress was removed from her post and found work elsewhere. I was not surprised to get threats of legal action from her, but was prepared to withstand the onslaught, since I had the backing of the remaining staff and parents. No legal action was taken.

The Director of Education, Mr WL Chinn, got on well with me, although on one occasion he remarked, "Councillor Roberts' logic is impeccable, but unfortunately the situation does not answer to a logical solution." I invariably believed that there were logical solutions to all situations. Mr Chinn wrote, when I was leaving the Council to go to London, that it had been "a great pleasure to work with one who has brought to all problems a keen intelligence and a detached viewpoint."

The 'detached viewpoint' is a matter of opinion. Perhaps what Chinn meant was a viewpoint far removed from the world of educationalists! It was certainly true that, whatever job I was elected to do on the Council, I approached it from the standpoint of Socialism, and refused to allow myself to be cowed by paid Council officials who claimed to be the 'experts' on the job. I felt very often that the elected Councillors bowed to the 'superior knowledge' of the officials, and did not apply their own Party politics to the running of the Council, with the result that policies were often those of town hall bureaucrats rather than those of the elected representatives of the people. This was a general criticism which I applied to most local councils; it was in general less true of Coventry City Council at this time than it was of other administrations.

One matter to which I certainly did not bring a detached viewpoint was that of Civil Defence, in which I was openly and unashamedly biased.

1949 saw the establishment of Civil Defence on a serious scale in Britain. The object was, according to half-page advertisements in the press, to "show any aggressor that Britain has the will to survive." Men and women were urged to join a civilian force, and train to "save the trapped, give first aid to the injured and fight the fires." A Civil Defence Officer was appointed in Coventry, and recruitment started in November 1949. After three days, "few volunteers" were forthcoming, but a month later Coventry was said to have "one of the best recruiting records in the area."

There had been Civil Defence volunteers during the war a few years previously, and in conditions of conventional warfare they had been able to do a useful job. However, with the explosion of the atom bomb by the USA on Hiroshima and then on Nagasaki in 1945, conventional warfare began to grow into something altogether different, and talk of the development of an even more deadly hydrogen bomb meant a further radical change in the concept of war. Civil Defence recruitment paid lip-service to the existence of the A-bomb, and later the H-bomb, but continued to train people in conventional methods of rescue techniques, teaching them to believe that the aftermath of a nuclear war could be faced in the same way as before, by digging people out of collapsed buildings and dressing their wounds.

The Government in the early Fifties issued Civil Defence publicity which emphasised that the techniques which would be "essential in war" would also be "useful in peace", in combating rail-crashes, fires and floods. The Central Office of Information produced a booklet called 'Civil Defence is Common Sense', which contained the memorable line: "a fire, whether caused by a careless match or the heat from an H-bomb, is still fought in the same way." The next page of the booklet goes on to describe an area two miles in radius which would be "totally destroyed" by such a bomb, a further large area of "irreparable damage", and "widespread fires up to about 6½ miles away and isolated fires as far as about 9 miles." To paraphrase Churchill – some fire, some careless match! The danger of radiation is dealt with in the following two complacent pages, showing a map of radiation extending from well inside the Welsh border right over and beyond the east coast, and on the facing page a happy family barricaded into "a groundfloor room with one outer wall", and a sandbagged window. The statistics of devastation they quoted were based on the effects of a 2-megaton bomb, although already a 10-megaton bomb was in the pipeline.

No matter, explains the booklet. If you increase the size of the first atom bomb 500 times, the area of damage only increases by a factor of 64. So that was all right. Until you looked at the figures: the first atom bomb was equivalent to a mere 20,000 tons of high explosives, but the new hydrogen bombs were 10 megatons (that is, equivalent to 10,000,000 tons of high explosives), which is exactly 500 times as much as the 20,000 tons dropped on Hiroshima, and a million times more powerful than the biggest bomb dropped on London during the 1939–45 war.

Talking in these terms, Civil Defence is a cruel deception, and the cynics among the Coventry City Councillors began a campaign to expose Civil Defence as the con-trick they believed it to be. Instead of encouraging the population to resist the development of such horrific means of mass destruction, the Government was teaching the public to believe that they were necessary, and that, with the right wartime spirit, Britain could withstand a nuclear attack. Yet a leaflet put out only a couple of years later quoted a Defence White Paper which said: "It must be admitted that there is at present no means of providing adequate protection against the consequences of a nuclear attack." Even if the effect were as 'limited' as suggested by the Government's own figures, two bombs could wipe out the whole of London, and one would be enough for Coventry, since the intensity of the radiation would finish off those who were unfortunate enough to survive the initial blast. Those outside the immediate vicinity would be in no state to help anybody, and in any case they would be unable to approach the bomb-blasted area until those within it were dead.

Convinced as the majority of Coventry City Councillors were that Civil Defence was a con-trick, they set about exposing it to the citizens of Coventry. The Government's contention that the skills learned for Civil Defence would prove useful in any type of disaster was also exposed; if the Government was seriously concerned to protect the people, why were they cutting back on funds for the essential services – fire, ambulance, hospital and welfare services – on a plea of poverty?

It was in these circumstances that the City Council, in April 1954, carried a resolution:

> That.... the Council decide to send no more delegates to Civil Defence conferences and that they decide, in view of recent reports in regard to the explosion of the hydrogen bomb and its devastating effects, to inform the Home Secretary that it is a waste of public time and money to carry on with the Civil Defence Committee: therefore it is the Council's intention to take steps to terminate its existence.

The event which tipped the scales against Civil Defence in Coventry was the testing of the H-bomb, which had been carried out first by the USA and then by the Soviet Union. The Council asked the Home Secretary to receive a deputation on the issue, and this he unwillingly agreed to do.

The Right Honourable Sir David Maxwell-Fyfe saw a deputation consisting of Alderman Stringer, Alderman Hodgkinson, Councillors Callow, Loosley, McGarry, Coventry's three MPs, Richard Crossman, Maurice Edelman and Elaine Burton, and myself.

Sidney Stringer, leader of the Council's Labour Group, outlined the Council's views, and suggested that a local organisation could not possibly undertake defence on the scale necessary to overcome "the devastating effects (of the H-bomb) which had been indicated by the President of the USA". Coventry was not being deliberately obstructive, he said. What they would like to see was a meeting of "the four great statesmen of the world" to agree on the banning of nuclear weapons.

I had come armed with six questions for the Home Secretary to answer:

1 In the event of an H-bomb dropping on our city, do you believe that the Civil Defence Organisation can save our citizens? If so, how?

2 Are you satisfied with the adequacy of the present Civil Defence Organisation?

3 Are you prepared to persuade our citizens that the Civil Defence Organisation is satisfactory against H-bomb warfare?

4 Are you willing to make an assessment of the effects of an H-bomb dropped on a city and the action that should be taken by Civil Defence in all its aspects i.e. Medical, Fire, Radio-activity, Food, Water, Sewage, Public Services etc., and what would be the situation if ten were dropped on key centres in various parts of Britain?

5 Do you consider that Civil Defence would be better organised if the National Government took direct and complete responsibility instead of the Local Authorities? If so, why would it be so?

6 Are you prepared to ask the Government to make international approaches to the other great powers to bring about the abolition of the H-bomb by international agreement?

The Home Secretary replied that he thought there had been some exaggeration of the possible effects of an H-bomb attack, although the problem was being re-examined in the light of the latest evidence available; there would in any case be the 'fringe problem' of areas outside the vicinity of the immediate attack, where Civil Defence would be valuable. Specifically answering the questions put by me, he said that there could be no defence against a direct hit from a hydrogen bomb, but "the effect of hydrogen bomb explosions over our cities was now being studied". He was not satisfied with present levels of civil defence measures, but would try as he had always done to make improvements.

The deputation was unconvinced by his arguments, and at a subsequent meeting of the full Council, the resolution agreed in April 1954 was put into effect, and the Home Secretary was informed that the Civil Defence Committee in Coventry had been disbanded. Maxwell-Fyfe responded by appointing three Commissioners to take over Coventry's Civil Defence commitment, but when they arrived, they were politely told that the

Council would not co-operate with them. Coventry, as a centre of the armaments industry producing guided missiles and jet aircraft, was sure to be a strategic target in the event of a nuclear attack. The Council wanted the people of Coventry, who had survived the blitzes of the Second War, to be under no illusions about their chances of surviving a nuclear attack. The only defence against such an attack was the banning of nuclear weapons worldwide.

It was reported in one paper that I had asked Civil Defence Officer Dickinson if any special measures were being taken to meet an H-bomb attack:

> "Yes," replied Mr Dickinson. "Arrangements have been made to take over the City's football ground and Butt's stadium for the purpose of laying out the dead."

In fact, cardboard coffins were provided for the purpose!

Coventry led the country in its reaction to the Civil Defence movement. Other local authorities began to be questioned about the effectiveness of their Civil Defence measures, and the answers were not reassuring. The Civil Defence Officer in Islington gave typical answers; questioned by two councillors, he reported that there was no public information leaflet about what to do in the event of a nuclear war, there were no shelters in the borough, and no special protective clothing against radioactivity. He would expect only three to five minutes' warning of an attack, and, asked what Civil Defence could do if a bomb dropped in the area, he replied, "We could do nothing."

The 'Coventry Evening Telegraph' lambasted the Council for their stand, using the 'fringe problem' as its main argument: Coventry might be on the outside edge of an attack, in which case Civil Defence measures would be of some value. In a reply to their editorial, I wrote:

> Do you know that if 10 H-bombs were dropped on this country, approximately 20 million would be killed? Of course, there would be approximately 30 million left, many of whom would be maimed and injured and who would need care and attention. Do you call this sanity not to cry out against this horrible butchery that is to be launched upon the common people of the world? Is it not more sane and honest to expose this to the citizens and not kid or cheat them into believing that they are being defended? We on the City Council are not prepared to lie to our electors in order to keep up so-called public morale, which according to Sir Frank

Newsam, Permanent Secretary at the Home Office, is the reason for Civil Defence.

It was not only the local papers that picked up the issue. All the national papers were either violently pro-Coventry or violently against it. Mostly against. The 'News Chronicle' was opposed to Coventry's stand, but even they were obliged to admit that all but a few of the letters they had received on the issue "attacked the 'News Chronicle' because it has condemned what the Coventry councillors are trying to do." Cassandra of the 'Daily Mirror', however, wrote that "Coventry Council did a notable political service in refusing sunshades against the H-bomb", the 'sunshades' referring to paper contraptions designed to "ward off blasts, burns and gamma rays on a prodigious scale."

The people of Coventry agreed with Cassandra. Some of the right-wing Labour councillors had been concerned about the possible reaction of the electorate on the Civil Defence question; they seemed to be more concerned about losing votes than losing lives. But the Labour majority was re-elected in 1955, despite the red 'warning' leaflets put out by Coventry Tories. In order to combat the propaganda from various sources which was denouncing the Council in general, and the Labour Group in particular, the Labour councillors took to the streets. I joined Sidney Stringer, George Hodgkinson, Pearl Hyde, Bill Callow and Emily Allen, who were among those who organised street meetings to inform the public about the futility of Civil Defence.

The City Council had to suffer the Home Office's Civil Defence exercises, carried out in the city despite their opposition, but they put up a brave counter-attack. When volunteers were drafted in to demonstrate how to rescue those trapped in blasted buildings, Councillor Stringer and his band of supporters took it in turns to supply an alternative commentary to the proceedings, in opposition to the official one, to which they took grave exception. The 'real' commentary accused the Council of negligence and irresponsibility:

> The public-spirited volunteers of Coventry are disappointed by this action of the Council, and many of them have come forward as individuals and are taking part in the role of casualties etc.

> ....We must appreciate that, if this were the real thing and there were no local

workers, a long time would elapse before those sufferers you can see and hear, together with others too badly hurt to be moved, could be rescued.

The Council had asked for the commentary to be altered, deleting the parts derogatory to themselves, but the officer in charge had refused, later saying to a 'Telegraph' reporter:

> They wanted me to change the script to say that the reason why Coventry forces were not taking part was they had all been killed.... it is ridiculous.

So the councillors rigged up microphones and gave their own running commentary, through amplifying apparatus considerably more powerful than the Home Office's own. The result was an hour-long battle of words, which drew attention away from the farce of the mock rescue.

In October 1954, I spoke at the Labour Party Conference, and was reproved by Margaret Herbison, speaking on behalf of the NEC, for my suggestion that Civil Defence should be a national, not a local responsibility. The 'fringe problem' argument was trotted out again, and local authorities urged to keep up their Civil Defence commitments. Yet Margaret Herbison was herself a leading member of a Labour Party committee which announced that:

> We have a civil defence system utterly deficient in the manpower and equipment required to deal with a hydrogen bomb attack, and completely lacking in guidance from the Government in matters such as evacuation and shelter policy.

Despite this, the Party was still anxious to keep up the illusion in the minds of the public that Civil Defence could be adequate in the face of a nuclear attack.

Supporting Coventry's struggle, 'Coventry Labour's Voice' published a report in February 1955 that an impressive new Civil Defence Control Centre had been built three miles out of the city, although "according to the Government's own estimate, the area of total devastation from an H-bomb is a six-mile radius."

Even as those words were written, the end of Coventry's efforts was approaching. In July 1955, after a year of struggle, the Council reversed its decision and resumed its Civil Defence responsibilities. The motion to resume was proposed by the minority Tory Group, who carried with them enough of the right-wing of the Labour Group, discouraged by the lack of response of other local authorities to Coventry's lead, to overturn the previous decision.

In my diary on that day, I wrote: "Father, forgive them, for they know not what they do."

1955 was the year of a General Election, and I had fought and lost Stockport South at the same time as campaigning on Civil Defence, and winning Holbrooks Ward on the City Council for the third time. Some of my colleagues on the Council undoubtedly wished me far enough, and not only among the Tory opposition, either. I was inclined to make a habit of being a thorn in people's flesh, but I always had a good reason for it, even if others did not appreciate it at the time.

Take the matter of the bosses. I had always opposed bosses as a matter of principle, and one night found myself in a Council meeting which devoted itself to a lengthy discussion of them. The bosses they were talking about were the wooden ones in the ceiling of the fourteenth-century St Mary's Guildhall, and the discussion over whether they should be gilded, painted, cleaned or left as they were, was heated and – in my opinion – interminable. Finally, exasperated, I broke into the argument, pointing out that there were a lot more important issues to talk about instead of wasting time on bosses:

I don't care what you do with them. I've always been in favour of tarring and feathering the bosses myself....

The rest of my utterance was drowned in uproar from the Tories, which culminated in a shout of "That's just the sort of rubbish we expect to get from you, Roberts!" But it had the desired effect of bringing the subject to a speedy conclusion.

A suggestion I made at a conference which I attended as a member of the Executive of the Labour Party Regional Council was treated with equal scorn, although it had an element of common sense in it which all the other proposals lacked. As Mr Chinn had said, my logic was impeccable. Two separate problems had been raised. One was the disfiguring appearance of pit slag heaps, the other one the danger of marl holes, which were caused by the quarrying of marl – a lime-impregnated clay soil, which was used as a fertiliser. Replying to the debate on behalf of the Regional Executive, I suggested that the movers of the two resolutions should get together, with a view to filling the marl holes from the one with the slag heaps from the other. I was accused of being facetious, but I really wasn't being facetious at all!

Two matters which could not be construed at all facetiously arose in the early part of 1955. One of these started with rumours of a colour-bar operating in a pub called the General Wolfe in Foleshill Road. One evening, I visited the pub with some members of Coventry Trades Council, including some Indians. One was Atvar Singh, an Indian who had fought for Britain in the war and had been decorated for valour. When we ordered our drinks, we were told that the Indians would not be served in that bar, and in the end the publican called in the police. He denied that he was operating a colour bar, since there were only two of his rooms which coloured people were not allowed to drink in.

Three of the Trades Council group – Singh, the Labour Party agent, RB Ritchie, and I – declared our intention of opposing the renewal of the publican's licence at the next Brewster Sessions, the following month. The 'Coventry Evening Telegraph' printed the story prior to the sessions, as a result of which I received abusive and threatening letters, addressed to 'The Nigger-Lover'.

When the sessions took place, the atmosphere was electric. Normally, little interest was shown, since renewal of licences was usually a formality, but on this occasion the room was packed with publicans who sneered and hissed at me and my companions as we came in to give evidence. The solicitor who presented our case was Bill Wilson, who later became Member of Parliament for Coventry South-East. The publican got the renewal of his licence, getting away with a warning "not to do it again".

My most serious personal problem at that time was over my own housing. My wife and I had been living for two years previously in a caravan, and had put down our name on the housing list in 1953. Then some flats were built over shops in Much Park Street, and these were to be let by the Council at 'economic rents' – that is, much higher than most families could afford. Certain families were selected from the housing list by the Housing Superintendent, and these were put to the Housing Committee as being "people likely to meet the requirements of a high-rent tenancy". The Housing Committee made the final choice from this list, which was as usual presented anonymously, using numbers instead of names. Although I, being a member of the Housing Committee, was present when the flats were allocated, I did not take part in, nor vote on, the allocations, and nobody knew until afterwards that I was involved.

Our tenancy began on 3rd January 1955, and so did the rumours. As well as anonymous letters accusing me of string-pulling, there were reports in the local and national press, saying that both Conservative and Labour councillors were making criticisms of me. The leader of the Labour Group, Sidney Stringer, made a public statement that, while a small number of members from both parties had complained, neither the Tory nor the Labour Group as a whole would support the criticisms, as they knew that the flat had been allocated fairly. Of course, both Tory and Labour groups were represented on the Committee at which the allocation had been made.

I refused to listen to friends who advised me to stay put and weather the storm. I knew that I could not justify myself to **all** those who had heard the accusations, and the only way to deal with the matter was to give up the tenancy, which we did only six weeks after moving into the flat. We returned to the caravan.

By 1957, I had already been involved in seven attempts to join the AEU full-time staff at Peckham Road, either as an Assistant General Secretary, or as an Executive Council member. My eighth election, in which my chief opponent was the man who afterwards became the union's General Secretary, Jim Conway, reached a successful conclusion in the second ballot, when I polled 32,914 compared with Conway's 27,459.

I moved down to London to take up my new post in November 1957, and for the next five months commuted between the two cities in an effort to keep up my Council commitments, before resigning my seat in Holbrooks Ward prior to the 1958 municipal elections. I valued highly the tributes I received from certain of my colleagues on my departure from the Council, although I knew that there were many in the Labour Group who would not willingly have subscribed to the opinion of the Group's secretary, Tom Locksley, when he wrote:

> Coventry Labour Council Group is losing not only a loyal and able member but a colleague for whom we have great respect and much affection.

Reg Underhill, West Midlands Regional Organiser of the Labour Party (then National Agent of the Party, and subsequently Lord Underhill) perhaps had his tongue in his cheek when he wrote that he felt sure,

> that your Labour Party association will be of great value in further developing the close relationship of the AEU with the Labour Party.

This close relationship, forged between the right-wing leaderships of both bodies, was hardly likely to receive any assistance from me, who would vastly have preferred links which would have led to Socialism.

Perhaps the most surprising of the tributes came from the 'Coventry Standard', a newspaper which had not previously fallen over itself to praise me:

> Some years ago a young Coventry man was to be seen in almost every strike procession in the city. He almost fell into the category of being a strike leader, and so ubiquitous at industrial disputes did he become, that reporters from this newspaper regularly approached him to get details of the men's case. he always gave this information with the greatest courtesy.... He certainly appeared to have the men's interests at heart....

> Coun. Roberts' career has been meteoric, as they say, for he is Vice-Chairman of the Housing Committee and Chairman of several sub-committees of the Education Committee, a member of the local Employment Committee, the Ministry of Labour, the Hospital Management Committee and the Coventry Executive Council. Moreover, he is a Parliamentary Candidate for the Labour Party.

> In fact, although he is an engineer tool-maker in Coventry, most of his time must have been spent in recent years in public service.

> Although there are many people in Coventry who disagree emphatically with his political views, no-one can deny that he has gone right ahead in pursuing his political career, and that he has set out steadfastly to do things he believes to be right.

Nobody is universally loved. I never tried to be. Indeed, I would have felt a sense of failure if those whom I opposed so bitterly (on my own benches as well as among the opposition!) had ended up actually **liking** me. I kept a copy of a poem by the nineteenth century poet Charles Mackay which summed up my attitude entirely:

You have no enemies, you say?
Alas! my friend, the boast is poor –
He who has mingled in the fray
Of duty, that the brave endure,
Must have made foes! If you have none
Small is the work that you have done;
You've hit no traitor on the hip;
You've dashed no cup from perjured lip;
You've never turned the wrong to right –
You've been a coward in the fight!

I remember meeting, on one of my frequent returns to Coventry, Gilbert Richards, leader of the Tory Group on the Council, who, with something close to panic in his expression, said "You're not coming back, are you? We were glad to get rid of you!"

But I had to wait more than twenty years for my favourite accolade. Sitting in an almost deserted coffee bar in Brighton during Party Conference week in the late Seventies, I saw a lady approaching from the other end of the room:

You're Ernie Roberts, aren't you?

That's right

I remember you well. We were living in Coventry when you were on the Council, and my husband often talked about you.

Indeed? [politely, but with an inner glow of satisfaction.]

Oh, yes, he was always saying, 'That bloody Roberts!'

Chapter 3

He who would be free, must not conform.

1   Commenced work as Assistant General Secretary, AEU
2   Prisoner of the 'Pope of Peckham'
3   Dirty works in union headquarters
4   'In my personal capacity'
5   Carron's Law
6   Voice of the Unions and IRIS News

As the newly elected Assistant General Secretary of the AEU I took up my post on 4th November 1957. I had already learned that not everyone who called me 'brother' was a friend, but even the bitterness of my previous exchanges with the inmates of Peckham Road had not prepared me for the events of the next twenty years.

On arrival at the General Office, I found no-one expecting me, no-one to tell me where I was to work, no-one to say what I should be doing. Late in the morning, the Office Manager showed me to my office, which contained little but an empty desk. There was no work to do. About an hour later, a member of staff deposited some office circulars on the empty desk-top, and shortly afterwards the other Assistant General Secretary, Walter Baxter, popped in and suggested that I should read the circulars "to give me something to do". There was no word about what portion of the Assistant General Secretaries' duties I was to be allocated, and no question of picking up where the former AGS had left off.

Tuesday was the regular meeting day of the Executive Council, and the EC meetings were normally attended by the General Secretary and the two

Assistant General Secretaries. On 26th November, I, about to go up to the Council Chamber to the EC meeting, was stopped by Baxter, who said that I should not go into the meeting until called by the Executive. Baxter himself went in as usual, and after a couple of hours' hanging about, I was summoned, and informed about the allocation of duties which the EC had agreed for Baxter and myself. I was permitted to remain in the EC meeting on that occasion, although it was made clear that my continued attendance would be reviewed at the end of the year.

The allocation of duties to the two Assistants was absurd:

Assistant General Secretary No. 1 – Bro WC Baxter

Political work

Educational work

National Committee Report

Final Appeal Court

Representative on NCLC

TUC Conference of Unions catering for women workers

NCLC Annual Conference

Super Reserve Department

Filing Department

Assistant General Secretary No. 2 – Bro EA Roberts

Audit Department

Technical Department

Finance Department

Typists' Department

Enquiry Department

Outgoing Department

Packing Department

Proposition and Registration Department

Motor retail and repair JIC

Although the sharing of work looks pretty even-handed on paper, a closer look reveals that the 'meat' of the jobs belong to Baxter, leaving me with the bare bones. Furthermore, the bulk of my allocation was really the work of the General Secretary under the Union's Rules, and had been given to me to provide me with something uncontroversial to do. Baxter got all the work with any political or propaganda content, whereas I was almost totally confined to office routine.

This brought me into my first conflict with the EC. Writing to the General Secretary, and asking that my letter be placed before the EC, I made a case which I was to fall back on time and again in years to come, based on the interpretation of Rule 16, Clause 1, which specified the duties of Assistant General Secretaries.

Before the establishment of the National Health Service, the duties of each AGS had been laid down and clearly defined under Rule, so that one AGS took responsibility for the Health Insurance Scheme for members, and the other did 'the rest'. This meant that when a member stood for election for AGS, he knew exactly what his duties would be if elected. With the appearance of the National Health Service in 1948, the role of the NHI Assistant General Secretary became redundant, and Rule 16, Clause 1, about division of labour was re-written in a way which was rather ambiguous – although custom and practice had so far divided the work in a reasonable and just manner.

In the 1957 Rulebook, Rule 16 Clause 1 provided that the two Assistant General Secretaries should "be allocated to such duties including political and educational as defined by the Executive Council". I maintained that the spirit and intent of this Rule was that one AGS should be responsible for political work, the other for educational work, since these were the two most important and time-consuming tasks they were required to do.

In the past, the work had been shared between the AGSs in this way, and they had also shared National Committee and Final Appeal Court work, and representation on outside bodies. I simply asked for previous custom and practice to be continued, so that (I wrote to General Secretary, Cecil Hallett) "both AGSs will be fully employed and neither of them overburdened with the majority of the duties." This appeal to the better nature of the EC fell on deaf ears. I was to be kept out of political and educational work, and anything else which I might contaminate with my politics. The reason given was that the political and educational work went to the 'senior' (i.e. the longest-serving) Assistant General Secretary (even though this had not been a criterion before I was elected, and the principal of seniority was denied when I became 'senior' myself.)

I was not the sort of man to take this lying down. Instead I organised a campaign among members to get Rule 16 Clause 1 amended. Writing privately to friends in branches all over the country, I explained:

> I feel completely hamstrung and unable to do a useful job for our Union.... There have been many changes in attitude towards Assistant General Secretaries since I was elected.... Will you do all you can to get support for this amendment in your branch and area?

The proposed Rule as amended read:

Rule 16, Clause 1

There shall be a General Secretary, who shall also be the General Treasurer, and two Assistant General Secretaries, who shall be elected by the members. The Assistant General Secretaries shall be allocated duties, one to political and the other to educational, and such other duties as defined by the Executive Council. The Assistant General Secretaries shall attend normal meetings of the Executive Council, but they shall have no vote and may speak only with the permission of the Executive Council.

About a hundred branches submitted this amendment to the Rules Revision Committee as a result of this campaign – which also had the support of the other AGS at the time, Walter Baxter – but the Executive opposed it, and a majority right-wing caucus on the Rules Revision Committee rejected it, in spite of the fact that more branches supported this amendment than any other put forward that year.

Following the death of Walter Baxter in 1961, an old adversary of mine – Jim Conway – was elected to replace him. The allocation of duties then looked even more odd:

Bro EA Roberts

Technical Department (not Central Conference)

Finance Department

Typists Department

Enquiry Department

Outgoing Department

Packing Department

Prop & Registration Department

Super Reserve Department
Filing Department
National Committee Report
Final Appeal Court
Bro J Conway
Audit Department

My quarrel with the list was not that I had too much to do, but that I had too little. It was the sting in the tail that mattered, added almost as an afterthought to the basic list: Bro Conway was to deal with political matters, under the supervision of Bro Boyd, and also educational matters, under the supervision of Bro Hanley.

Political and educational work to be the responsibility of Bro Conway! 'Seniority' suddenly stopped being a criterion in the allocation of duties, when I became the 'senior'. And when Bill Cockin was elected to replace Jim Conway (Conway being elevated to the General Secretaryship), he retained the political and educational work held by his predecessor. No wonder that I kept among my personal possessions a card printed with the words: "Looking for someone with a little authority? I have as little as anyone."

Cockin, however, elected in 1965, had to stand for re-election in 1968, and suffered a surprise defeat at the hands of Ken Brett. This put the EC in a difficult position, because, like it or not – and they didn't! – they were obliged to hand over the political work to me. Not because of a sudden reversion to the principle of seniority, but because Ken Brett was a member of the Communist Party and therefore ineligible to handle the political affairs of a union affiliated to the Labour Party.

The duties of the officer overseeing the political work in the AEU – the duties which now unexpectedly fell on my shoulders – extended from signing parliamentary candidates' expenses forms to organising 'schools' at which prospective MPs received political 'training'.

As a union affiliated to the Labour Party, at that time on the basis of 850,000 affiliated members, the AEU dedicates part of its membership fees to political uses. Members of the union are not obliged to pay this political levy, and can opt out if they wish, but those who elect to pay are, for most practical purposes, members of the Labour Party. (Although in some respects they are treated as 'second-class members'.)

The union pays part of its political levy directly to the central Labour Party. Another portion is paid to the union's own District Committees, where it is used in a variety of ways. It is the responsibility of the union's political officer to ensure that all the money is used for Labour Party political activities, and not in any way which might be detrimental to the Party. Part of the District Committees' money usually goes towards paying the union's affiliation fees to the local constituency parties. The remainder of the political levy is spent (by Head Office) on various central expenses, including the major expense of running a Parliamentary Panel.

The Panel consists of AEU members who wish to stand as parliamentary candidates, sponsored by the union. There are usually more than thirty on the panel, but there are more applications than there are places vacant. Many apply, but few are chosen! One of the political officer's chief duties each year is to organise an examination for students who wish to join the Panel. Each year, the old Panel is disbanded, and a new one established as a result of the examination, so that prospective candidates have to prove their worth from time to time, and are not automatically kept on the Panel.

The examination is thorough, lasting a week. All the nominees must go through the full procedure: they write answers to questions, and an essay on a given topic under examination conditions; they answer a 'letter from a constituent', posing a typical constituency problem; they go through an interview like the one they might expect if nominated for a constituency; and they make a ten minute speech, which is possibly the most gruelling test of all. This speech is given before an audience which as far as possible simulates 'the real thing', with hecklers drafted in – from the local Young Conservatives or Liberals – to try out the nominees' quick responses and ability to handle a potential disturbance in a meeting.

The participants are rated in each task according to performance (the marking is mostly done by members of the union's parliamentary group, who have already jumped the same hurdles themselves on the way to the House of Commons), and the top scorers form the new Parliamentary panel.

The political officer keeps a constant eye on the state of Parliament, watching for seats falling vacant, and for nominations being called for replacements where an MP proposes to retire at the end of the session. When a potentially winnable seat falls vacant, he urges branches of the union within the constituency to select three from the Parliamentary Panel, who will go before a union selection meeting called by the District Committee, to choose one representative who will be the union's nominee for the constituency. The delegates at the selection meeting must of course be members who pay the political levy.

The political officer then completes a nomination form on behalf of the chosen candidate, including a declaration that the union will sponsor that candidate financially if selected. The rest of the selection procedure is then carried out by the Constituency Labour Party, and the success of the union's candidate is more often than not dependent on how many delegates have been elected from union branches to the constituency. Prior to the 1974 General Election, I reported to the Executive that out of 83 union nominations to different constituencies, only two had been selected, the others being beaten mostly by candidates with a 'professional' background. This happened simply because the union branches did not take up all the places which they were entitled to at the selection conferences.

When union candidates are selected, the political officer is responsible for seeing that their legitimate expenses are paid, plus considerable financial aid to the constituency, including part of the salary of a political agent. This is of considerable help to the constituency, but, in order to protect impartiality of the constituency's choice, delegates are not informed at the selection conference which of the candidates are sponsored, so that cash does not influence their choice.

The Parliamentary Panel, including those who have been adopted for seats and those who are still trying, are invited to attend a training school annually. The union invites the leader of the Labour Party, together with Ministers (or Shadow Ministers when Labour is in opposition) who speak about their various departmental responsibilities. Harold Wilson once joked that he could not hold a Cabinet meeting during the week of the school for the Parliamentary Panel, because most of the ministers were taking part in the education programme. Such a stiff programme of selection and training ensures that the AEU-sponsored candidates are amongst the fittest for the job of Member of Parliament!

The details of these examinations and schools, and the organisation of the Panel, are of course not entirely in the hands of one person. As is usual in the AEU, final decisions are taken by a committee – in this case the political sub-committee, and the political officer is the executive officer of that sub-committee, which itself is in turn responsible to the Executive Council. The political officer acts as secretary to the sub-committee, and also to a joint meeting, held quarterly, between the AEU-sponsored MPs and the Executive Council.

Lewis Minkin, writing about the AEU political sub-committee in 'The Labour Party Conference', states categorically:

Only right-wing Executive Councillors sat on the sub-committee, and its chairman, John Boyd, was understood to be the national co-ordinator of 'The Club'.

'The Club' was the right-wing caucus in the union. It was not surprising then that the right-wing had fought so hard to keep me out of the political officer's job for eleven years. It must have been extremely galling for them to have been forced to hand over the reins to me on the defeat of Bill Cockin.

I was prepared to make the most of this opportunity, which turned out to be a double opportunity, for with the political work came the educational work. My predecessors had organised political 'schools' and courses for branch officers, and I looked forward to following in their footsteps: attending the schools, and exercising some influence over their political content, which was no more than Baxter, Conway and Cockin had done before me. Although the direction of my influence would no doubt have been different. Had I been allowed to exercise any. But suddenly the day-to-day running of the schools, having been entrusted to an AGS for years, was suddenly found to be quite within the capabilities of a member of the office staff. I was allowed only to welcome the students, then leave them in the hands of an employee in the Technical Department.

The curious thing was that when Brett, a Communist Party member, took over responsibility for educational matters in the 1969 allocation of jobs, he was allowed to revert to the practice of Baxter, Conway and Cockin: only I was the odd-man-out.

Allocation of duties was not the only thing to get under my skin. It seemed that every vestige of custom and practice was overturned in order to keep my nose to the grindstone of office administration, and away from the members.

As promised at the first EC meeting I attended, the practice of having the AGSs sitting in the Executive Council meetings was reviewed – and discontinued. But it was only one AGS that they specifically wanted to exclude, so the next review stated that only the 'senior' AGS should attend EC meetings – i.e. Bro Baxter. That was fine until the death of Baxter, when I became the senior. Then both AGSs were again excluded, until the election of Hugh Scanlon as President, when the decision was again reversed and both AGSs were summoned to attend.

The amended version of Rule 16, Clause 1 made provision for both AGSs to attend Council meetings (this had not been provided for in the Rules up to then), and at the time of drafting the amendment, I put out a statement which argued cogently for the presence of both officers in normal EC meetings. I claimed that the ten-year-old practice of having AGSs present was essential in order that they could hear any deliberations of the EC which would have a bearing on their own work, thus leading to a better understanding of the decisions which they would be required to carry out. Instances were detailed where it had been necessary for an AGS to be in full possession of EC facts (for example, when Bro Baxter took over the duties of the General Secretary while the latter was in hospital, and then I took over the duties of both General Secretary and Assistant General Secretary when Bro Baxter collapsed and was absent for fourteen weeks).

However, the will of the EC to keep me out of EC meetings predominated over the need to fulfil the proper functions of the union, and I was more or less excluded from the EC meetings until the advent of Scanlon as President. The Executive knew full well that I would not hesitate to spill the beans to members about what went on in the privacy of the Council Chamber, and that was reason enough to keep me on the other side of the door.

After the election of Carron as President in 1956, there was only one left-wing member on the Executive – the Communist, Claude Berridge. he was replaced on his retirement in 1959 by Reg Birch, founder of the Communist Party of Great Britain (Marxist-Leninist). So from his election in 1957 until the arrival of Hugh Scanlon in 1963, I was the sole representative of the Labour left-wing at Peckham Road.

Because of my non-smoking, teetotal habits, I was treated with distrust by those leaders of the working-class movement who tippled and smoked at the union's expense, and sanctioned dinners and social events where the membership's money was not spared in the struggle to provide the best of everything. They knew that I frowned on the drinking habits at Peckham Road, where a fridge full of conviviality was kept in the Executive's private sitting-room. This was for the purpose of entertaining guests, although it was sometimes said that when there was a shortage of official visitors, certain officers would invite each other instead. There was also an elitism at the General Office which ill became a trade union. There was, for example, an 'Executive lavatory' which was kept locked, keys being given to a select few, and similarly the chosen few (of whom I was one although I did not avail myself of the facilities) were admitted to the Executive bathroom, where officials could bath and brush up between engagements.

No doubt the Duke of Edinburgh was given that key when he visited Peckham Road in 1966. Certainly he was given every other kind of special treatment, including lunch in the Council Chamber. The Executive Council agreed that the two AGSs should be present on the occasion, but I decided to take one day of my annual holiday instead. The next issue of the union Journal (December 1966) featured on its cover a diagram of the structure of the union, with a broad label printed across it: 'TO BE MODERNISED'. Perhaps Conway's editorial that month was some indication of the political direction the modernisation might take. Even 'The Guardian', not noted for its republicanism, commented that the Duke

> made a hit, but how big a hit isn't apparent until you read the AEU General Secretary's own report in this month's union magazine. In six short paragraphs, the editor says 'honoured and privileged' twice, 'honoured' three more times, plus one 'very kindly agreed'.

'The Guardian' missed 'magnificent', 'great', 'first-rate', 'tireless', 'superb' (twice), 'never put a foot wrong', 'dignity and calm', and 'wisdom and restraint'. But perhaps they didn't see the bit about Harold Wilson!

The union always took up its quota of Royal Garden Party tickets, and no doubt there were enough eager hands to reach for those I turned down. But the Left was not always so scrupulous. On the occasion of the official TUC Centenary celebration, when the Queen was to be present, the AEU contingent included myself and another left-winger. I accepted the invitation because I did not see why the Queen should keep me away from such an historic occasion, but I attended dressed in an ordinary suit with a red tie. My left-wing companion, however, turned up in full evening dress, to be rewarded by Lord Carron leaning over to him and whispering confidentially, "It didn't take you long to join the Establishment, did it?"

Back at the office, a further bone of contention between the General Secretary and me was the interpretation of the function of Assistant General Secretaries. The Rules of the union were ambiguous on this point, and successive General Secretaries chose to interpret them in one way, while I read them in another light.

The difference of opinion arose because the Rules refer in some places to the 'Assistant General Secretaries', and in others to the 'General Secretary's assistants'. General Secretaries treated these phrases as identical in meaning; I maintained that they referred to two different sets of people: the 'Assistant General Secretaries' were elected officers of the union, whereas the 'General Secretary's assistants' were employed by the union to work in the General Secretary's department.

This may seem a trivial distinction, but in fact it had far-reaching repercussions.

Probably the first reference to it in writing came from Joe Scott, who had formerly been the Executive Council member for Division 7, the London area. In a letter written to me on my first being elected as Assistant General Secretary, he offered a warning:

> I saw the statement in the 'Daily Worker' this morning that you had been elected. This is very good, and please accept my congratulations and best wishes.
>
> It may not be too easy, but at least you know them!

I don't know what they will say or how they will say it when you officially meet them, but don't **you** forget that you have a somewhat unique place in Rule. Your duties are summed up in a few words in Rule 16. You are not the General Secretary's lackey, in fact an Assistant General Secretary is not anywhere in Rules a General Secretary's assistant. There is no need to get nasty about it – but don't overlook your rights....

However, I didn't set out to lecture – really just to wish you good luck in your new venture.

The most serious effect of blurring the distinction between Assistants and assistants was that of tying me to my desk to such an extent that I became known as 'the Prisoner of the Pope of Peckham', the Pope of Peckham being the Catholic President of the AEU, Bill Carron. This came about because the Rulebook calls for "the General Secretary or one of his assistants" to be present on the premises during working hours. As the General Secretary was frequently away at meetings, conferences, overseas visits or delegations of one sort or another, there were periods when he was absent for hours, days and often weeks at a time. He maintained that either I or the other AGS should be on the premises during his absences, but somehow the rule always seemed to be enforced more rigidly against me than against whichever of his colleagues happened to be the other AGS at the time.

The union's published quarterly reports made the position plain, for there was in each report a chart showing 'Attendances of EC and Officers' at Peckham Road for the quarter-year. The chart showed 'actual' attendance at Peckham Road, days spent on 'delegation' (which was official business away from the General Office for which expenses were payable), sickness and other absences. A couple of examples will illustrate my difficulties as 'the Prisoner of the Pope of Peckham':

January–March 1962				*Highest possible: 64*	
	Actual	Conference	Delegation	Sick	Total
Asst Gen Secretaries:					
Bro EA Roberts	59	–	5	–	64
Bro J Conway	5	–	5	–	10
General Secretary:					
Bro CW Hallett	40	6	17	1	64

Conway's small total attendance is due to the fact that he took up his post for the first time during this quarter, but already his delegations equal mine, and account for 50 per cent of his time. The next quarterly report shows how things were developing:

April–June 1962				*Highest possible: 59*	
	Actual	Conference	Delegation	Sick	Total
Asst Gen Secretaries:					
Bro EA Roberts	55	–	4	–	59
Bro J Conway	26	–	33	–	59
General Secretary:					
Bro CW Hallett	26	–	31	2	59

The refusals to allow me to attend meetings came not only from the EC as a whole, but sometimes from an individual member of the EC, who was entitled to prevent any other officer from encroaching on his territory. In practice, this meant preventing me from encroaching on his territory! I took the line that, as an officer elected by the members **nationally,** I was entitled to address meetings anywhere in the country without hindrance, as my electorate covered the whole country. In practice, the EC man (elected by one of the seven divisions) could veto my attendance at any meeting within his division, and that included meetings of other organisations as well as AEU meetings. The district officials within a particular area could also have their say in the matter, but this was not usually necessary, because the whole Executive Council would combine to ban me from going anyway!

The internal correspondence between the General Secretary (mouthpiece of the EC) and my office was peppered with memos about meetings which I was not permitted to attend, or – as in the following instance – had attended without permission:

> Memo from Jim Conway, asking who authorised Ernie to attend the Industrial Relations School on the 24th, 25th and 26th September 1968. [I had in fact attended in the evenings, in my own time.]

It was difficult to prevent my attendance at meetings which came outside the jurisdiction of the union, but there were two methods which the EC tried, neither of which worked. One was to refuse on the grounds that the meeting was so far away from London that I would be unable to fulfil my commitment under Rule to be at Peckham Road during working hours. I got over this one by leaving the office as soon as the bell went at the end of the day, and driving like a bat out of hell to get to my meeting in time – to Birmingham, Liverpool, Manchester, Sheffield or wherever duty called me – then driving back overnight, so I could present myself at the office bright and early the next morning. Where other officers would make a delegation of it, taking a day to travel to the meeting and a day to travel back, I flitted there and back without missing an hour's work.

Sometimes, there was not even a trumped up reason for saying no – just a flat refusal, as when I was invited to attend a week-long AEU speakers' course at Brighton, which is within easy reach of London. The EC decided that I should not attend, stating bluntly that their refusal extended to my free time, and to weekends. No reason was given, but none was necessary. Their word was law.

The EC bureaucracy was so off-putting that less tenacious individuals would have given up. The Divisional Organiser and the District Secretary had to be kept informed of any visit to be made in their area – even when it was a visit to a body other than a union branch – and non-compliance with this led to acrimonious letters of complaint from a division or district to the EC. Furthermore the General Secretary and Assistant General Secretary had to be informed of the intended absence from the office, and the EC member had to have a courtesy memo reminding him that I would be in his division at a certain time on a certain date in a certain place. Any break in this chain of information was treated like an offence punishable by death. This bureaucracy got under my skin rather more than the others', however, partly because I was never one to comply readily with bureaucratic niceties and therefore often fell foul of the rules, and partly because the offence was always treated more seriously in my case.

In persistently refusing to allow me to attend meetings, the Executive Council were making a rod for their own backs. I was a popular speaker in a good many branches where it was felt that the right-wing had a strangle-hold on the union, and from the time of my election in 1957, I began to receive scores of invitations to speak – invitations which often trod on the toes of the EC member concerned (who felt that he should have been invited himself), or on the toes of the General Secretary or the President if the meeting was of an official nature such as the presentation of an Award of Merit, which they considered should be attended by them.

So the invitations came rolling in, and as information about refusals filtered through to me, I launched a campaign in the branches which led to a fresh avalanche of invitations. The campaign took the form of a duplicated notice circulated to sympathetic branches, which was in effect a draft letter to the EC, to be used by branches when their invitation was turned down:

Our branch has requested the Assistant General Secretary, Bro EA Roberts, to speak at one of our branch meetings. Whilst Bro Roberts has agreed to do this, the Executive Council has refused to allow him to do so.

The Assistant General Secretaries were elected by members through their branches, and we have the right to hear their viewpoint on the work for which they are responsible in the union.

It is only by getting full-time officers in to the branch that we can influence them or assess their value.

We understand that Bro EA Roberts is the only full-time officer in our union who has to get approval of a properly constituted Executive Council meeting before he can attend a district or a branch meeting.

We note from the Union's Quarterly White Report that the other Assistant General Secretary is continually going round the country to branches and districts speaking and meeting the members....

Why is it that one Assistant General Secretary is allowed the freedom to go to branches and districts when invited, but the other is not permitted to do so?

Bro Roberts is the senior Assistant General Secretary and has proved himself to be a competent and loyal member of our union for 30 years. Upon examining the union's monthly and quarterly reports over the last ten years, we find that all previous Assistant General Secretaries have been permitted to perform their functions by going out to the members upon delegation by the Executive Council.

We are not satisfied with the treatment meted out to Bro Roberts, nor are we satisfied with your attitude towards the members of this branch. We elect and pay the full-time officers of our union and we insist upon the right to their services, especially when they are prepared to speak to us at our branch meetings, which are held outside normal office hours....

If the Executive Council refuse our request to permit Bro Roberts to speak to our branch, we reserve the right to take our grievance to the Final Appeal Court.

These events, building up over a period of years, naturally led to friction between the parties concerned. The 'problem' was raised time and again at EC meetings, at one of which Claude Berridge (EC member, Communist Party member, and generally sympathetic to my difficulties) made notes which he afterwards passed to me. At this meeting, Bill Cockin (at that time an EC member; he was later defeated, and then stood successfully for AGS) complained of the number of invitations received from his area for me to attend branches and other meetings. During discussion of the issue, it was declared that it was not for me, or any other official, to "race all over the country propagating and agitating". John Boyd said I was a square peg in a round hole – an unhappy administrator who should have been a national organiser. Berridge protested that I had no complaints about my job, but the members wanted me to speak, so why shouldn't I? The question hadn't arisen previously (said Berridge) because previous AGSs and the present General Secretary were not 'natural speakers'. It was eventually decided that I should appear before the EC yet again to have the limits of my duties explained to me.

The feud was still smouldering in 1969 when the officials of various unions met at the expensive Grove Tavern in Dulwich to discuss amalgamation. Jim Conway, then General Secretary, accused me (in a private conversation) of holding Executive sub-committees with only one 'chosen' member present (which would have been impossible, as there were rules laid down governing the dates of sub-committees, which had to be held on those dates, regardless of who could or could not be present); he also accused me of "going to the Co-operative Press at Manchester without his knowledge", to discuss estimates for the AEU paper, 'The Way', of which I was founder and editor. Conway threatened to 'tie' me to my desk at the office (it is difficult to imagine how he could have tied me more firmly than I already was, without actually strangling me), to prevent me from attending social functions (meaning dinners, receptions and so on, which I was inclined to avoid anyway), and to "inform full-time officers and the membership about my actions". I denied his allegations in the quiet manner which I always maintained in the face of opposition, and which proved unfailingly infuriating to those on the receiving end, who were themselves bubbling over with anger. I said that the lunch-table was not the place to discuss such issues, and suggested a private meeting in Conway's office. Conway curtly refused and I left the table – and the lunch.

I certainly did my share of stirring among the membership when I felt that the interests of the members were being trampled on. But the Executive were not averse to a little agitation on their own account! In 1964, a lobby of rank-and-file members came down to London to demonstrate outside the premises of the Engineering Employers' Federation in Tothill Street, and I 'just happened to be there' at the same time. Shortly afterwards, the General Secretary, Hallett, wrote to me, enclosing copies of letters from Speke No 2, Salford West and Bristol No 27 branches, and asking for my observations.

The Branch Secretary of Speke No 2 had written to ask why Bros Birch and I, together with the North London District Secretary, had found it necessary to attend this demonstration which was "as unnecessary as it was futile". The Secretary of Salford West wrote a letter which showed remarkable similarity to that from Speke No 2, about the same demonstration – again described as being "as unnecessary as it was futile" – and questioning the presence of the same three officials.

The identical phraseology, the identical use of underlining and capital letters, suggests even to an unsuspicious mind that the letters were composed from the same model, and it does not take much imagination to surmise where the model originated. The third letter, from Bristol No 27 branch, showed greater originality but it was still so similar as to be from the same stable without a doubt.

I replied that I had not attended any demonstration in Tothill Street on that date:

> On the afternoon of 22nd September, I visited the Industrial Safety Museum in Horseferry Road for the purpose of collecting material for 'The Way'. Tothill Street is close by and in the same direction.

> Out of interest I went along the street to see what was taking place outside the Employers' offices and in fact called in at a cafe nearby for a cup of tea.

The matter was taken no further, although the EC must have realised that I had arranged my visit to the Industrial Safety Museum to coincide with the demonstration that was taking place nearby. In fact, I took every opportunity to identify myself with such events, feeling that there was too little solidarity between the feelings and aspirations of the members and the activities of the officers they elected and paid, who generally were only too ready to condemn them for any grass-roots action which they took.

Sometimes, meetings which seemed to present no particular problem at the time, suddenly blossomed – perhaps 'exploded' would be a better word – into something big. Take the First Annual Dinner of the Shop Stewards' Committee of Wildt Mellor Bromley & Co., of Leicester, held in January 1962, at which I spoke for ten minutes on the 'Political and Economic State of the Country'. It was a private dinner, which I attended in my 'personal capacity', and probably no-one would have been any the wiser, but for the other Guest of Honour. He was Lyn Ungoed Thomas QC MP; he had recently been made a judge, and so his presence attracted some interest from the press. This resulted in a report of the dinner appearing in the 'Leicester Mercury', which headlined not the new judge, but the AEU's Assistant General Secretary, who – they said – had called for a "Fight to Get Rid of the Government" (which was interpreted as a call for a political strike). Not surprisingly, the report was seen by the local District Secretary, who complained to the Executive that he had not been notified of the visit to his area, and in so doing he drew their attention to the press statement.

I said that this was a private dinner, which I attended in my own time, at my own expense, and in my **personal capacity.** The EC accepted this explanation, and there the matter dropped.

The use of 'personal capacity' as a means of attending unauthorised meetings made the EC see red. I could not see any reason why I should not speak at a meeting in my own time, unofficially, without the EC breathing down my neck and forbidding me to go, so I used the 'personal capacity' ploy in order to attend meetings at which I was not billed as Assistant

General Secretary of the AEU, but simply as 'Ernie Roberts'. Sometimes the advertisement gave only a name; sometimes the name was followed by 'speaking in a personal capacity'.

The EC could do nothing to stop me from speaking in a personal capacity, but they always resented it. I used the argument that, although I was an official of the union, in my own time I was also an individual, and could not be tied down to what the Executive Council allowed me to do.

However, as I pointed out, other AEU officials spoke in their personal capacity without drawing any criticism from their colleagues. Bill Carron, the President, spoke as a Catholic at religious/trade union functions; John Boyd spoke as a Salvationist; Claude Berridge spoke as a Communist; I said that if he wanted to speak as a Holy Roller, or anything else for that matter, it was no business of theirs. In any case, even speaking in a personal capacity, I always stayed within the bounds of union policy, although I did not deny myself the opportunity of criticising the union leadership on occasions when that leadership had itself ignored union policy, and pointing out to the membership that their votes were responsible for the kind of leadership they got.

In trade union and left-wing political circles, I was well-known enough not to need any billing other than my name, and so the omission of my 'title' was immaterial. But sometimes the 'personal capacity' tag led to trouble because its real object was misunderstood by the organisers of the meetings at which I spoke.

Leaflets were printed for an Irish Rally to be held in Trafalgar Square in June 1959, and they referred to "Ernie Roberts, Assistant General Secretary of the AEU, speaking in a personal capacity". The CND London Regional Council distributed a circular advertising "Ernie Roberts, AEU" as chairman of the meeting. The conference called by Victory for Socialism and 'New Left Review' billed me as Assistant General Secretary of the AEU. In these and many other instances, I had made it perfectly clear that my position in the AEU must not be mentioned; in each case, the organisers had either forgotten my instruction or failed to realise its significance, thus landing me in trouble with the EC yet again.

The 'personal capacity' meeting which drew the most public attention, and which almost led to my expulsion from the Labour Party, was the 'Daily Worker' (which later became the 'Morning Star') conference scheduled for January 1960.

The conference was to have the theme 'Which way for Labour?' and I agreed early in November 1959 to be a speaker. The publicity for the meeting went out during the second week in November, and the first inkling of trouble came in an article in the 'Daily Telegraph' of November 13th, which said that the Executive Council of the AEU had written to Morgan Phillips, General Secretary of the Labour Party, protesting about my taking part in this 'proscribed' meeting. The 'Telegraph' also mentioned that Harry Knight, General Secretary of ASSET (now ASTMS), was billed to speak at the same meeting, but in fact Knight withdrew from the conference at the first sign of difficulty, and his withdrawal was announced in the 'Daily Mail' the following day.

I was surprised, to say the least, that his source of information about the EC's complaint should be a Tory newspaper rather than the AEU Executive. I was reported in the 'Daily Mail' as having said that I intended to speak at the conference in my personal capacity, not as Assistant General Secretary of the union, that I did not mean to attack the Labour Party in any way, and that in any case the conference was called by a newspaper not a political party, and "they haven't started blacklisting yet, I hope". In fact, the Labour Party did have a blacklist of publications, but the 'Daily Worker' was not on it.

The press reports, which seemed to be in every newspaper in the country from 'The Times' to the 'Dundee Courier and Advertiser', brought a flurry of condemnation on the heads of the Executive from branches and district committees in all areas. The Coventry Trades Council carried a motion "viewing with alarm the attack on the personal liberty of Ernie Roberts" and continuing:

> We are proud of the fact that Bro Roberts, who has done so much in the Labour Movement, started his TU and Labour Party work in Coventry. We demand he be given the right to express his personal point of view, which we are sure will never be detrimental to the traditions and aspirations of the Labour Movement.

The Gladstone No 2 Branch expressed "complete confidence in and support for" me. A Shop Stewards' Quarterly meeting sent in a motion of support and also wrote to me privately:

> It was noted by the District Committee that this vendetta coincides with the request for nominations for your office and accordingly you will be gratified to know that each Branch that has so far considered the question has been pleased to nominate you for a further term.

By 18th November, the press were beginning to pick up the juicy details of the conflict, although I did not know what the AEU Executive had written to the Labour Party, or what the Labour Party's attitude was. 'The Guardian' gave a very detailed account of the joint meeting between the AEU Executive Council and the AEU Parliamentary Group – a quarterly event – at which both Carron and EC member Bill Tallon had attacked personal-capacity speaking:

> Tallon's lash also extended to those union members who excused their attendance at unofficial gatherings by saying that they were there 'solely in a personal capacity', and yet made certain that the audience knew they belonged to the AEU.

'The Guardian' continued with a report of Carron's speech and then commented:

> Neither leader mentioned any names, but a certain tension was engendered by the presence at the meeting of Mr Ernie Roberts, an AEU national officer who was recently the subject of a letter to the Labour Party.

At last, on 25th November, the Labour Party wrote to me that the National Executive had reached a decision about the 'Daily Worker' conference: that participation in the conference would be, in its opinion, incompatible with membership of the Labour Party. The letter concluded by asking for my comments on this decision.

This was the very first **official** intimation of dissatisfaction, although the subject had been bandied about by the press, national and local, almost every day for a fortnight. My reaction was to write to the Executive of the union, saying that I wished to see a copy of their letter to the Labour Party, "in order that I may know the matters raised about me by the Executive Council", which would put me in a better position to answer the party's letter to me. It was not until 14th December that the EC officially refused to allow me to see a copy of the letter that had gone to Transport House, and by this time Transport House was clamouring for an answer from me.

In the meantime, the newspapers were keeping up the pressure: "Labour Party Sees Red" was the 'Daily Mail's' headline for an account of a meeting of the Labour Party Organisation Sub-Committee, chaired by Harold Wilson, at which the 'Daily Worker' conference was said to be "incompatible with membership of the Labour Party". The 'Daily Express' came up with an enormous headline "TUC Slams the Reds". A large proportion of the article was about my association with the 'Daily Worker' conference.

The 'Coventry Evening Telegraph' gave me a fair chance to state my case – naturally enough, because I was an ex-Coventry councillor, and well-known enough to be 'news'. Their article quoted me extensively:

"I think it ought to be said whether this newspaper (the 'Daily Worker') is a proscribed organisation and whether its activities have to be proscribed," he said.

If one newspaper was proscribed because it was anti-Labour then others would have to be proscribed for the same reason – and that would mean that Labour MPs and others would have to stop writing for them.

"I suppose one must say that the 'News Chronicle' was anti-Labour, and we have leading members of the Party writing in that," he declared.

On the other hand, he said, the Parliamentary Labour Party had only just decided to relax standing orders to give more freedom to members. "If this gag is being loosened I should have thought that leading trade unionists and members of the Labour Party were going to be given a similar amount of elbow room and freedom of expression."

When I asked if he still intended to go to the 'Daily Worker' conference, Mr Roberts said he could not give a straight 'yes' or 'no' at this stage.

"I did not lightly agree to speak there and I cannot, at first shout, throw up my hands and withdraw. I must at least look into the question," he said.

"What I say is this: as a loyal member of the Labour Party, if the Party proscribes a body then I am clearly prepared to abide by that decision. If they proscribe an organisation, then I do not associate myself with that organisation. The Communist Party is proscribed, and that is clear enough. But the 'Daily Worker' is not on the list of proscribed organisations – and they conduct all kinds of activities, bazaars, meetings, demonstrations and so on. The list of proscribed organisations is drawn up at the party conference – it is not drawn up by any committee."

The reference to other Party members writing for anti-Labour publications was picked up in other papers, which quoted chapter and verse:

Harold Wilson had written in 'The Star' (A London evening paper), Nye Bevan was about to write on "Labour's Way Ahead" for the 'News of the World', and Bill Carron had contributed to 'The Times Review of Industry'.

While all this press comment and private correspondence was going on, I had to consider carefully how to reply to the Labour Party NEC's letter of 25th November. Their letter had asked for my comments; I answered by asking some very pertinent questions, which in summary were:

1 Are all conferences of the 'Daily Worker' proscribed by the Party?

2 Is there a list of proscribed newspapers?

3 Which Annual Conference gave the NEC of the Labour Party the right to declare such events as "incompatible with membership of the Labour Party?

4 Is a Labour Party member permitted to write for the 'Daily Worker'?

5 Why cannot some freedom be accorded to members to put the Party's viewpoint in any places where it would do good?

I concluded with a statement that, should I be threatened with expulsion as a penalty for attending the conference, then I would certainly not attend. The Party's answer came quickly and decisively:

1 The Party decided that attendance at this particular conference was proscribed.

2 Two newspapers were on the 'proscribed' list: 'Socialist Outlook' and 'The Newsletter'.

3 The 1934 Annual Conference.

4 What members write in the press about the Labour Party was a matter of concern to the National Executive Committee, although the NEC had not stated that members should not write for the 'Daily Worker'.

5 The NEC believed that participation in the 'Daily Worker' conference would not be in the interests of the Labour Party.

The newspapers were unwilling to let the matter drop – as they invariably are when it comes to any matter of internal dissent in the Labour Party – and when news came through that a second conference had been banned, they seized on it joyfully.

The 'Daily Worker' report of 31st December 1959 was typical of press accounts of this latest development, saying that the AEU Executive had written to me asking why I had agreed to speak at a conference called jointly by Victory for Socialism and 'New Left Review'. They also said that I had declared my determination to attend this latest conference, even though the ban on the 'Daily Worker' conference still stood.

Again the 'Coventry Evening Telegraph' came out top of the poll for fair comment, giving a full account of my point of view as well as the Labour Party's:

"I still think it is wrong that they should stop members of the Party from attending a conference where they would be free to express a point of view which would be in accord with Labour Party policy," he said.

"I think they would be right if they took action against someone who went to the conference and spoke in complete conflict with Party policy. I do not want to sever my connection with the Labour Party because I believe that, through the Party, the trade union movement and the working people of this country can establish a better and more just order of society...

"It has always been my opinion that the Labour Movement does not exist to give unquestioning or uncritical support to leaders, but rather to give unflinching support to the principles of the Movement."

So I did not speak at the 'Daily Worker' conference in 1960. But I took full advantage of the leeway offered to me in the Labour Party's answer to my letter, and contributed an article to the 'Daily Worker' a few days before the conference took place.

I also accepted the 'Daily Worker's invitation twelve months later to attend their 1961 conference, thus precipitating what was virtually a carbon copy of the 1960 row with the Labour Party.

The Labour Party's continued hostility was curious in view of the fact that the 1961 conference was specifically called in **support** of the Labour Party's decision on nuclear disarmament at its 1960 Scarborough Conference. And, as I pointed out, many Labour Party members, including MPs, were loudly proclaiming their **dis**agreement with the Conference decision in the Tory press, but the NEC was not making any move to enforce against these dissenters the 1928 Conference decision that "affiliation to the Labour Party implies general loyalty to the decisions of the Labour Party Conference."

In spite of the strong arguments in his favour, I was again obliged to withdraw from the 'Daily Worker' conference, under threat of forfeiting my Party membership.

Bill Carron, on the other hand, was always on good terms with the Labour Party leadership, even when he had put himself in bad odour with the AEU in order to remain so. As President, he led the union's delegation at Party Conference. And as President, he reserved to himself the right to cast the union's card vote as he wished. What he wished was generally in line with the Party leadership, except on the few occasions when grass-roots pressure was so great that even he could not ignore it.

Carron was a strong Catholic, and in addition to his knighthood and his peerage, achieved some religious honours as well, notably the Papal Order of the Knights of St Gregory. His belief in infallibility extended into his political career: to him, all (right-wing!) leaders were infallible, and should expect and receive total backing from their electorate, who had a duty to support those they elected, for good or ill.

I had attempted to clip the wings of previous presidents to a certain extent by establishing, in the early 1950s, the procedure of passing a 'pad' round the delegation before a card vote, so that it could be seen in black and white exactly what support there was for the motion among the delegates. Carron had little respect for the pad. Lewis Minkin writes, in 'The Labour Party Conference':

> However, though the Secretary carried the pad it was the President's decision when to pass it round. The scene in the hall therefore often went something like this:
>
> **Conference Chairman:** 'Card Vote!'
>
> Low hubbub of noise in the delegation and throughout the hall.
>
> **An AEU delegate** three rows behind Carron: 'Pad, Bill.'
>
> Carron appears to be deaf.
>
> **AEU delegate** again: 'The pad, Bill. Can we have the pad?'
>
> No response. The delegate – a left-wing opponent of Carron – pushes his way through several jutting kneecaps and eventually bends over Carron's shoulder.
>
> **The Delegate:** 'Which way are we voting, Bill?'
>
> **Carron,** smiling pleasantly: 'For the platform.'

Delegate, not so pleasantly: 'Why?' He shouts his reasons why the vote should go the other way and refers to the National Committee's decisions.

Carron: 'We are voting for the platform.'

Delegate, exasperated: 'Why?'

Carron: 'Because Mr Gaitskell asked us to' (or 'Because it's National Committee policy' if in democratic mood, or 'Because I say so' if in autocratic mood). Loud hubbub from the delegates around, listening. Angry words are exchanged. A crutch is brandished. A delegate runs to the platform.

Delegate: 'Point of order, Mr Chairman.'

Conference Chairman: No points of order during a card vote!'

Delegate mounting the rostrum: 'I want to protest that the AEU vote is being cast without any consultation of the delegation.'

Conference Chairman: 'All right, brother. You've made your point. How the vote is cast is up to your union. It's got nothing to do with us.'

The delegate returns to the delegation glaring at Carron. The delegation subsides into fierce muttering. Carron keeps his faint cherubic smile.

In this composite version of events, the delegate with the crutch was Norman Dinning, who declared that 'Carron's Law' had come into prominence when one of the delegates had discovered a picture postcard showing an irate chairman in a trade union meeting, saying "When I want your opinion, I'll give it to you" which so reflected the delegates' opinions about Carron that they bought up all the available supplies of the postcard.

The reality of Carron's Law was not so funny. Delegates saw their union's vote cast year after year in ways which could not be justified by union policy. They believed that votes should be cast in accordance with the policy laid down by National Committee, but that it was the function of the delegation to decide in cases where there was no National Committee decision, or where the decision was unclear in terms of the actual motion under discussion. An example of the latter occurred when the pad was sent round before a vote on the abolition of National Service. The result on the pad was 20 for the motion, 6 against. Carron voted **against.** He likewise went against the delegation on public ownership, defence, prices and incomes policy.... time after time, the three quarters of a million or so union votes were cast for 'the platform' and against National Committee or delegation policy.

119

In the matter of electing the Party Treasurer, the flouting of the delegation's wishes was so blatant that some AEU members took the case to the Final Appeal Court. The appeal was upheld: the delegation should decide how the vote for the Treasurership should be cast. Nevertheless, the following year the card vote was again cast without reference to the delegation. Again, the Final Appeal Court upheld the delegates' rights. But there was no way of enforcing the decision: Carron carried the card! Minkin points out that, when it came to card votes,

> occasional deviations could take place in the understanding that few union members would ever have direct knowledge of how the union voted at Party Conference; delegation reports through the Journal rarely mentioned the voting record of the union.

That was why Carron rapped the knuckles of those delegates who issued their own written report, at their own expense, to the members who elected them as delegates. He said that the official report in the Journal "should suffice." The report in the Journal was made suitably harmless before publication, as when I was elected by the delegation in 1956 to write the union's report on the TUC Annual Congress, which Carron (newly elected) refused to publish until it had been purged of all references to the differences of opinion about how votes had been cast, which, he said, could not reflect the opinions of the delegation as a whole.

But while he could censor what went into the Journal, he had no control over the private reports which I and other delegates issued to their electors. It was not in Carron's interests that members should read such comments as that written by Lance Lake, delegate from No 9 Division, after the 1956 vote on the Treasurership:

> After a long debate on these lines, Bro Carron.... proposed to close the discussion without taking a vote.... The union's vote would go to Bro Pannell, without regard to the views expressed. This announcement produced angry protests from delegates. Later 25 out of the 26 elected delegates signed a written protest to Executive Council against this decision.

The question that springs to mind is: why have a delegation at all? It would be simpler and much cheaper to give the President the card to do with as he will, and leave the delegates at home.

The relevant Rule in the AEU Rulebook read:

> The Executive Council shall, previous to any National Meeting of the British Trade Union Congress or Labour Party, call together the officials and delegates appointed to represent the Union at the meeting named.

Carron argued, as his predecessors had done, that this Rule only called for the delegation to meet. It did not give them any rights. Again, why have a delegation?

In 1954, the Final Appeal Court, whose decision is binding on all members, took the same view, upholding the right of delegates to decide how the vote should be cast for the Party Treasurer. The following year, Leeds District Committee went to the Final Appeal Court in very specific terms, and their appeal was also upheld:

> .... to place the question of delegates' voting rights before recalled Rules Revision Committee, to re-word Rule to make unmistakable full voting rights to Labour Party and TUC delegations.

Nevertheless, when the Rule was revised, it merely required that a delegates' meeting be called to 'inform' delegates of National Committee policy, and to 'discuss' the Agenda. The Final Appeal Court decision had been ignored.

In December 1956, a year after the successful Leeds District Committee appeal, a long article in the Journal was devoted to the matter of delegates' voting rights at Party Conference. The gist of the article was: delegates had **no** voting rights at Conference, even on issues where there was no National Committee mandate.

The dictatorship of Carron's Law was much valued by the Labour Party leadership, as he could always be relied upon to squash the opposition and deliver the 'right' vote. He took a similar line in wage negotiations; by settling for what the employers wanted, instead of what the members demanded, Carron was literally worth his weight in gold to the engineering bosses!

The Left regarded Carron's behaviour as undemocratic, but so long as he was the elected President of the union, with elected representatives such as Tallon, Boyd and Conway to back him, nothing could be done to combat the activities of the right-wing, except to publicise their activities as widely as possible and to promote alternative candidates with left-wing policies.

In order to do this, I founded 'Voice of the Unions' and its offshoots. The 'Voice' papers – originally run from my home – were used to organise the Left in much the same way as the Right had long been organised.

The paper and its supporters came under immediate attack. Meetings were infiltrated by undercover right-wingers, and the proceedings reported almost word-for-word in 'IRIS News', a rival right-wing publication. But not enough people saw 'IRIS News'; Carron wanted to reach a wider audience.

In July 1966, he took over the front cover of the AEU Journal with a bold headline: "MEMBERS – BE VIGILANT!" Beneath it was a denunciation of a 'Voice' meeting held in Birmingham:

> Members who are proud and jealous of our Union's democracy, of our Union's autonomy and of our Union's integrity, will be offended and repelled at the purpose of the meeting and the views and policies expressed.

What was the purpose of the meeting? According to the two-page report in the Journal, it was "an extremist bid to take control of the Amalgamated Engineering Union". The "views and policies" reported in the Journal amounted to the promotion of Left candidates against right-wing sitting tenants, in order to bring about changes in the union's policy in the interests of the members.

My share of the meeting was the only paragraph to be picked out in bold type. I had "strongly attacked Jim Conway, who he alleged was attacking union democracy." I had said that I would support a lobby of Parliament if my union duties permitted it. I had said that the role of the 'Engineering Voice' was to organise left-wing support, to provide education about its policies, and to act as a leader. One statement I made was apparently so appalling that it was picked out in inverted commas for special attention:

> He said that "the grass roots of the union was in the branch" and that this was where the real power was to be found.

The only clear points to emerge from the 'Be Vigilant!' episode were that the Left was organising, and the Right were unhappy about it. They were particularly unhappy about the number of CP members who were involved, even though the 'Voice' papers from the outset were Broad Left in concept, and have always been run by Labour Party members.

Carron's splash in the Journal succeeded in its aim: it gave the impression that a vicious and unscrupulous Left, pulled along in the wake of the Communist Party, was plotting against an innocent right-wing to bring about the downfall of democracy.

The Journal naturally failed to point out that the tactics being used by the Left (which was largely composed of Labour Party members) were copied from the methods already established on the Right. The right-wing newsheet, 'IRIS News', was doing the same thing for the Right as 'Voice' was now attempting to do on the Left: it rallied support around its own candidates, and 'exposed' the opposition. 'Voice', however, was much more open than 'IRIS News'. The 'Voice' papers always carried a list of sponsors, the names of the editorial staff, details of who supported it financially, and signed articles. 'IRIS News' was less forthcoming, carrying no names of organisers or staff, no sources of income, and virtually no signed articles. It was – and is still – a very professional-looking job, calling itself "a review of trade union services", but who paid for it and who sponsored it were mysteries. Some said the employers financed it; others claimed that the CIA had a finger in the pie. In the end, it was the 'Daily Telegraph' which revealed its true connections.

About the time of the 'Be Vigilant!' uproar, I, attending a full-time officers' conference, stumbled on some information which interested me. I found that a hall had been booked in the name of the General Secretary (at that time Cecil Hallett) for a union meeting, but that I had not been invited. As a full-time officer, I was entitled to attend all the official meetings and functions which took place during the conference; I therefore concluded that this was to be a right-wing caucus meeting, and accordingly stationed myself outside the entrance as members began to arrive. With a notebook and pencil in my hands, I blandly greeted each new arrival and jotted down his name:

Good evening, Bro Hallett.

Good evening, Bro Carron.

Good evening, Bro Tallon.... Bro Hanley.... Bro Cockin....

As a member of the union, I felt I would like to know what went on in this private meeting and so, as the last of the select bunch of invited

123

members went in, I tagged on at the end of the line; only to be told, "This meeting is not for you." Of course, the Left held its caucus meetings, too, but they never employed 'bouncers'.

In a '24 Hours' programme on BBC television on 1st July 1966, in which Scanlon and Boyd were interviewed by Cliff Michelmore, the interviewer pointed out briefly at the start of the programme that unconstitutional meetings had been held secretly by the right-wing, addressed by John Boyd, but this point was never developed, and the bulk of the interview was about gatherings of 'left-wing extremists'. When Scanlon returned at a later stage to the secret meetings which Boyd had spoken at, Boyd shamelessly reported that it was "quite regular for **right-minded** people within an organisation to gather together." A remark which is reminiscent of a quotation from an eighteenth-century bishop, William Warburton:

Orthodoxy is my doxy; heterodoxy is another man's doxy.

I often quoted this in situations of political intolerance, but unfortunately the full force of it was often misunderstood!

In 'Comparative Union Democracy' by Edelstein and Warner, Boyd admitted in an interview that "it was no secret that he was the uncrowned head of the anti-Left alliance in the union", although "his organisation within the union was essentially informal: it had no formal office-holders and no **formal** meetings...."

Nor was it any secret that meetings of the right-wing, formal or not, were frequently held, and that the history of them is a long one. The Right had organised itself into 'The Club', which had branches at District and Divisional level, and which met regularly in much the same way as the Left. I was too well-known to be allowed by mistake into any right-wing caucus meetings, but some of my friends were not, and they reported back on the proceedings just as Carron's friends reported back to him. Such a meeting was held on 17th March 1951, and will serve as a typical example of The Club's operations. The meeting was attended by about twenty people, including a Moral Rearmament delegate and others who were not AEU members. The principal figure was Cecil Hallett, the AEU General Secretary. The meeting opened with a discussion about money. The Left always put their hands into their own pockets to pay for their activities, but this was apparently not good enough for the Right, as the secret report of the meeting states:

> The question of expenses was raised to pay for this meeting and others in the future. Rutherford said that we come under Rule 46 Political Fund and all our financial obligations can come from that and asked Hallett to support it.
>
> Hallett shook his head in dissent and urged that we should go very careful about what we are doing because the other side could get hold of this....

It is interesting to note that the objection to this suggestion of gross misapplication of the political fund is not that it is illegal, but that the Left might get to hear about it. One of Carron's objections against 'Voice' was that it amounted to "an organisation within an organisation" and as such was unconstitutional, although he never objected to the right-wing caucus, which had organised in this way for years.

It is a notable feature of the Left/Right conflict, whether in the unions or in the Labour Party, that the Left fights on principles, whereas the Right indulges in name-calling. It is apparently sufficient to call somebody a 'Communist' or a 'Trotskyist' or a 'fellow-traveller', without actually having to enter into the realm of policies. When they do approach policy, the Right are apt to make themselves look ridiculous, as when 'IRIS News' took up the cudgels on behalf of Jim Conway in the election for General Secretary in 1972. Conway's main rival, they said, would be Mr EA Roberts, who "will be supported by the Communist Group within the union". After quoting extensively and approvingly from Conway's election address, they turn to the attack made by me on Conway's role as editor of the Journal, saying only that "the minor points made carry very little weight." The 'minor points' were in fact quotations of specific instances where Conway had used the Journal to promote the Tory Industrial Relations Act, by handing over the Journal's lead article to Robert Carr, a Tory Minister, and by supporting Carr in his own editorial, in opposition to union policy. The very worst quote they can find from my election address is:

> As General Secretary, I would make the Journal and administrative machinery of the Union serve only the interests of our members and the policies decided by National Committee.

This paragraph is printed in 'IRIS News' without comment. Indeed, one wonders what they could have found to say against it!

Chapter 4

There are some common rules as to the expediency of compromise and conformity, but their application is a matter of endless variety and widest elasticity.
John Viscount Morley

1   Election fights
2   Postal ballots
3   Workers' rights
4   Witch Hunt in the union
6   Suspension from union office

The Left/Right struggle was an ever-present feature of union activity, but never so much accentuated as at the time of an election. To an active member, elections become a way of life. In the twenty-six years from my first attempt to be elected as a national officer in 1947 to my last election in 1972, I was involved in fourteen elections, nearly all involving two ballots and lasting for about eight months each. In addition, I was nominated twice for President and once for EC Division 4, but declined to stand.

I have always maintained that the election of officers and other representatives is the cornerstone of the union's democracy, and I fought for this point of view even in the teeth of Harold Wilson who, whilst Prime Minister, maintained that the AEU Rulebook was 'archaic' and should be consigned to the dustbin – an opinion in which he was strongly supported by Jim Conway, then the General Secretary.

Whether democratic or archaic, ballots were subject to constant interference both internally and externally, but whilst gross interference from the Right was tolerated and even encouraged, even minimal interference from the Left was denounced, often in the press.

The Left had no resources for large-scale interference, even if it had the inclination. It had no say in the union's journal, little money to spend, no assistance from the national press – in fact it lacked all the instruments which the Right used to full advantage at election-time.

Both Right and Left circulated duplicated sheets – against union rules – encouraging members to vote for certain candidates. The Left used 'Engineering Voice' to promote its protegés, and the Right used 'IRIS News'. However, the only **official** channel of communication between candidates and electorate were the election addresses which were distributed in the form of a booklet to the branches. The coverage however was inadequate, as branches received only one copy for every ten members, and thus even many of the active members never saw one, let alone the armchair trade unionists, who were entitled to vote, although they never attended the branch to find out who was who. A member, writing to me during the 1947 election for Assistant General Secretary, put it in a nutshell:

> Let me at this stage congratulate you on your election address as I believe you will get results from it. Unfortunately not too many read it.

In the 1947 election, eighteen candidates contested the post, and I got into the second ballot against AJ Caddick, the eventual winner. In the following year's election I was less fortunate, coming sixth in a field of forty-five candidates, which included some distinguished competitors – two who eventually became Assistant General Secretaries (Walter Baxter and Bill Cockin), one who founded his own political party in addition to being an EC member (Reg Birch), two future General Secretaries (Cecil Hallett and John Boyd) and an MP who later went into the Lords (Charles Pannell).

My election addresses were mainly policy documents, and indicate the change in emphasis over the years as new issues superseded old ones, although some topics were hardy annuals, like prices and profits, equal pay, the right to work, and peace. Only once did I lapse into self-pity, when in the 1948 AGS election I made an unfortunate personal appeal about my victimisation and twelve-month period of unemployment.

Once I indulged in a passage of purple prose, hardly relevant to the election, but an accurate reflection of the way I have lived my own life:

The philosophy I like is here in these words: 'The thing one prizes most is life. Life comes to us but once and it should be possible to live one's life in such a way that, looking back, one feels no regret for years lived pointlessly, no shame for a petty, worthless past – so that as one died, one could say: all my life and all my strength have been given to the most beautiful thing in the world – the struggle for the freedom of mankind.'

Less lyrical, but more typical of my usual style, was the 1960 effort, in which I pointed out that the volume of output in the engineering industry had increased by 75 per cent between 1946 and 1959, and declared profits were up by 300 per cent, yet the national minimum wage-rate for engineers, allowing for inflation, was only 3 per cent to 5 per cent higher. I went on to say that as much production was lost in one **week** of unemployment as in one **year** of strikes. Then:

> The Tory press interferes in union elections. On behalf of the employers they try to tell us who are the most suitable persons to elect – we should reject their interference and sponsorship.
>
> The Millionaire Press interferes in the Labour Party, giving spurious advice on the changes we ought to make in our Party policy in order to win elections, as if **they** want us to win power!
>
> We must fight to safeguard Clause 4 of the Party Constitution, our fundamental socialist aim.

The more things change, the more they remain the same!

The election addresses of all candidates were carefully scrutinised by the Executive before going into print, and quite often candidates were asked to reword certain parts of what they had written. This happened to me in the 1953 election, when the Executive wrote to me to say that the part of my address which read

> Wages can be increased out of the fabulous profits still being made in engineering (look at Mr Docker!).

might rightly be construed as offensive by Mr Docker, who could take legal action against the union. The parenthesis was taken out of the printed version.

A more serious instance occurred in 1964, when reports appeared in the 'Sunday Telegraph', 'Daily Telegraph' and 'Daily Express' that the ballot for General Secretary had been delayed because I had been asked to 're-write' my election address. According to the 'Telegraph', this was because of a "personal attack on Mr Jim Conway"; according to the 'Express', I had wrongly claimed credit for certain technological innovations at the General Office.

The three newspapers concerned, under legal pressure, printed retractions of their allegations, but a retraction never carries the weight of the original statement.

So strictly were the rules applied on canvassing that the procedure of 'election-tying' led to some absurdities. Rule said (at that time) that **only** election addresses were permitted as canvassing material. This meant that all references to the names of individuals concerned in elections had to be omitted from any published documents. For a period of up to eight months, therefore, candidates to all intents and purposes did not exist.

As editor of 'The Way' I wrote "by the Editor" against my work when I was election-tied, instead of the usual "by Ernie Roberts". On one disastrous occasion, in March 1972, the printers in their usual fashion wrote my name over the front-page editorial, and by an unfortunate coincidence it was on this occasion that the advance copy sent to me for checking was delayed in transit, and I did not notice the slip until it was too late: the printer, believing silence to imply approval, had printed 90,000 copies and many of them had already been dispatched to branches all over the country. Seeing a strong possibility of my being disqualified from the election which was then in progress, I urgently recalled all the copies and, with Executive approval, arranged for a corrected reprint to be made.

Occasionally, election-tying produced some amusing results. I had been with a union delegation to Finland, and on our return a photograph of the delegation with their hosts appeared in the Journal. Conway could hardly refuse to publish the picture, neither could he remove me from the middle of it. However, the "delegates from left to right" caption ignored my presence completely, and Conway sent me a memo explaining that this was because I was election-tied. 'Tribune', mischievously quoting the story, wondered whether my name would appear in the report of the visit which was scheduled for the next Journal. The report never appeared.

The Executive could not prevent members from issuing duplicated matter on behalf of their chosen candidates (or against the opposition) because such matter was generally anonymous, but they did instruct branches to ignore such material, and on no account to read it out at branch meetings. If the perpetrators were identified, they were occasionally fined for infringement of Rule 2 Clause 10 on additional matter, although there were cases where the Executive admitted that certain named members had infringed the Rule, yet action was not taken against them.

'Voice' printed broadsheets during elections, but as these were put out by a newspaper rather than by any individuals, nobody could be taken to task for them. The 'Voice' broadsheets always carried a printer's imprint and a contacting address, as required by law, but various printed leaflets promoting right-wing candidates (of the 'Vote to save the AEU from the Communists' variety) came from sources which refused to identify themselves.

Occasionally, quite blatant notices were posted up in factories, signed by right-wing union officers, such as the one which read:

For the information of the members in your establishment, the candidates we are supporting are:

Gen Sec   Jim Conway

Reg Officer   Gavin Laird

Ass Div Org   Bill McWilliam

This was a duplicated notice sent out under the name of an elected right-wing official of the union, but no action was taken against him. Such notices were not necessarily sent out with the connivance of the candidates, but their very existence put the future of the elections at risk. Most of the 'additional' matter put about at election time was anonymous, and much of it emanated from the right-wing. As usual, it attacked personalities, not policies.

The collection of anti-Roberts material is at once entertaining and disgusting; entertaining in its imaginative content, disgusting in that any union member could stoop so low in an effort to prevent the election of a candidate. Much of it is the usual "well-known for his support of Communist fronts and Communist policies" material, with the occasional original twist:

He has recently attended the 20th anniversary celebrations.... organised by the Hungarian Embassy in London. On the other hand, he has been observed having lunch with a leading Tory agent.

The document which went to the greatest lengths to ensure that I was not elected was distributed during the 1972 ballot for General Secretary. It amounted to four foolscap pages, with another full-page covering letter. To give the authors their due, for once they tried to attack on policy, though with very narrow unconvincing arguments.

You could even begin to feel sorry for people who do not know why the Tories should not be allowed to use union magazines in addition to the unlimited resources of the national press. The authors continue:

Bro Ernie should recall the dialectical materialism that he was taught when a Coventry Communist Party member. It was about the time he gained a local notoriety.... by accosting the late King George VI when he visited Coventry. As the King walked by his machine, Bro Ernie stepped in front of him, saying, "Excuse me, King! When are you going to open up the second front?"

Also:

Concern for the 1,250,000 unemployed is not Bro Ernie's monopoly. Anyway, he is well-known in our union's circles for the very few hours he is in the office.

Perhaps the writers had not seen the official delegation absences figures for the Peckham Road officers, of which the examples on page 106 are typical.

My concern for old-age pensions is spurious, they claimed, because after my retirement "Bro Ernie will be succoured by pro-Moscow or pro-Peking embassies." As a final shot, they comment that the 85,000 copies of 'The Way', edited by me, were wasted:

Who bothers to read it? Unlike Jim's Journal, it is unquoted in either the press or other media.

Who bothered to read it? The Executive, with a view to axing this quarterly newspaper, sent out a questionnaire to branches on the matter – and obtained the best response that they had had to any questionnaire for years, the overwhelming majority of the replies being favourable to 'The Way'. The paper was not axed, whereas there was a general complaint in the union that parcels of Jim's Journal were deposited in branches, never opened, finally to be thrown away. Moreover, nobody who read the

Journal could be surprised that it was quoted with approval in the Tory press.

Not content with four pages of slanderous attacks, the 'Three Branch Secretaries' responsible prefaced them with a letter which is worth quoting in full. The bulk of the attack managed to maintain some semblance of being reasoned and objective; the covering letter abandoned all pretence of decency and truth, and plumbed the depths of vilification:

Read the attached comments on Bro Ernie's election address, take a trip down to Bro Ernie's flat, press the bell and listen to the quick shuffle of Bro Ernie's Chinese slippers coming towards the door.

Slowly it will open and, with an attempt at oriental dignity, the 59-year-old, young-looking features of Bro Ernie, with its weak chin and even weaker mouth, will peep round the door. His somewhat embarrassing smile, and the nervous pulling of his pig-tail wig will make you almost feel sorry that you've brought him away from his meal of 'flied lice'.

Follow him into his Chinese-decorated flat, note his plastic jade and realise that our 'Walter Mitty' official shuffling in front of you, each hand disappearing up the opposite sleeve of his embroidered mandarin's smock, is one of our members who is offering to take on the responsibility of being able to lead this great union. Not even the Communists, Trotskyists, Maoists, or even the milkman, are fooled. Bro Ernie is wanted because he is the Chinese puppet that he has always been since his first trip to Peking in 1965.

Whether he wins this election or not, he will spend little of his time doing the job he has been elected to do, the only difference being, and it's a most important difference, is that as General Secretary he can commit our union to all manner of left-wing extremist activities – and find the cash to sponsor them as well.

Let's leave Bro Ernie to his fantasies, Chinese or otherwise, and ensure our union begins to get back on the road that once made it proud to belong to.

All correspondence concerning candidates was against Union Rule, but that which emanating from the right-wing always seemed to escape censure. The same full-time official who distributed notices in support of right-wing candidates knew this full well when he sent out the following letter, signed by him 'in a personal capacity':

PRIVATE. DO NOT CIRCULATE.

Dear Brother,

I wish to take this opportunity of thanking you for your efforts during the recent Union elections.

> Please convey these thanks to your colleagues at Branch and Factory level.
>
> Also please ensure that all previous letters and notices are destroyed.

Yet the Executive persisted in maintaining the public fiction that only the left-wing was involved in illegal electioneering. Unofficial meetings, whether connected with elections or not, were also outlawed, along with written material, and such meetings held by the Left and detected by the Right could have serious consequences, although those held by the Right went unchallenged.

I was a national officer, frequently contesting elections either to retain my own office or attempting to be elected as General Secretary, and I was prevented from making myself known to the members by the deliberate instructions placed in my way by the Executive. Yet my chief opponent was free to make visits to branches up and down the country and did so with the Executive's blessing. I was therefore obliged to go undercover, otherwise I would have had no chance at all to meet the electorate; and going undercover could easily mean using my annual holidays to make whistle-stop tours of places I would not normally be able to visit.

Right-wing candidates often won important national elections because the press set out to destroy the efforts of the Left whilst not necessarily campaigning for the right-wing candidates. As a result of this interference, I was often defeated, but in the many elections when there was no interference, I received a majority.

Although canvassing was illegal, plenty of it went on. It happened on a massive scale, unchecked by the Executive, in the form of newspaper articles which reached thousands of readers, including large numbers of AEU members. May of the articles were ostensibly 'objective' reports about forthcoming elections, but when the language of the reports is analysed, it constitutes no more nor less than interference in the elections, in degrees varying from subtlety to sledge-hammering. Sometimes only a right-wing candidate was mentioned. Reports which mentioned other candidates always included 'labels' – some fairly mild (e.g. "is expected to receive left-wing support"), others virulent (e.g. "whose candidature is being vigorously championed by the Communists and their supporters"). Always 'Communist' is used as a dirty word, without any attempt at explaining why. In covering the elections of General Secretary, 'The Sun' refers to Conway as 'anti-Communist' and me as 'Communist-supported'; 'The Times' of 6th June 1972 covered itself more carefully, but the result was the same:

> Mr Roberts is considered farther to the Left of the Party than Mr Conway, and has, inaccurately, at times been branded a Communist.

Mud, however carefully thrown, sticks, and a description at the end of 'The Times' article in which I appear as "a far more shadowy figure than the nationally-known Mr Conway" could not have helped my electoral image.

Another example of mud-slinging came in the 'Sheffield Star' – always violently against me – on 1st May 1964:

> Mr Roberts, who is thought to represent the extreme Left, was suspended by the union in 1961 for an alleged infringement of election rules.

I had been suspended. But I had not committed **any** breach of rules, and was subsequently reinstated in my post by the Executive. So why mention the event three years later, if not to deter members from voting for me by implying that my electoral activities had been dishonest? The article in which this appeared was the subject of legal action by me, since it claimed that I had spoken at a union meeting in Sheffield (which would have been 'illegal') whereas in fact I only addressed a Trades Council meeting (which was 'legal').

Occasionally the press so fell over themselves to label candidates that they made unfortunate mistakes, as when the 'Evening Standard' of 11th August 1964 commented that both Conway and I were "members of the Labour Party, but Mr Conway receives left-wing support." The following week, the 'Standard' wore sackcloth and ashes, referring to "48-year-old right-winger Mr James Conway, who certainly does **not** receive left-wing support."

When the press cannot find anything bad enough to say, they will not flinch from publishing lies. The 'South London Advertiser' of 12th June 1964 contained a long article entitled "Red Exposure", which claimed that:

> MR ERNEST ROBERTS.... is a known Communist, now running for the post of AEU General Secretary.

The 'Financial Times' in an article on "How the party draws its Strength", on 8th March 1972, was more careful in its wording; nevertheless, from this small paragraph buried in a half-page article on the Communist party, who but the most discerning reader would guess that I had been a member of the Labour Party for thirty years?

> Wright, Dixon and Birch, with Ernie Roberts and Party member Ken Brett as Assistant General Secretaries, with party members Ambrose, Foster and Walmsley occupying three out of the seven posts of national organiser, hold the union firmly behind Scanlon. Jim Conway, the moderate general secretary, is now fighting to retain his post against Ernest Roberts.

'Moderate' was, and still is, a favourite euphemism for right-wing, as in the headline "Moderate men win in the AEU". The right-wing beat the Left hands down when it came to favourable comment in the press. The Left had their own little news-sheets, but these were a flea-bite compared with even a local paper. On only one occasion did I receive even a neutral write-up, and that was in the 'Bath and Wiltshire Evening Chronicle' of 14th June 1972. The journalist wrote:

> His background is straightforward for a trade union officer. But the panellists of the old telly-game, 'What's my Line?' would probably be fooled by his appearance. he is small and dapper. In his fashionable grey suit and mauve shirt he could have walked straight off the pages of a colour supplement. He looks younger than his years....

> 'The Times' recently published a lengthy attack on left-wing trade unionists in general. Mr Roberts was one of the 'dangerous' men named. I find it hard to imagine him as 'frightening'. But then, I have always found witch-hunters far more terrifying than the witches they seek to unearth.

Not unfavourable. Until the sub-editor got hold of it, and headlined the article "The dapper little union man has a label: Dangerous".

So much for 'objective' reporting. Quite often, however, the media made no pretence of being objective. They reprinted the anti-Left 'IRIS News' election material word for word, with a few choice phrases thrown in as an encouragement to their readers, as in the 'Scunthorpe and Frodingham Star' of 12th June 1964:

> The 3,200 members of the AEU in Scunthorpe should take notice of the plea in the union magazine 'IRIS News....

With the headline "Call to AEU members", this 'reds under the bed' article implies that 'IRIS News' is an official organ of the union, of which members **should** take note.

'Reds under the bed' was the line commonly taken by newspapers when publishing their long articles on the union which, by some coincidence, always managed to appear at the start of an important election. In an engineering city like Coventry, probably the majority of readers of the 'Coventry Evening Telegraph' would be engineers or their families, so an article such as "AEU ripe for the Communists", which appeared on 14th May 1956, would reach an audience far wider than the official election addresses of candidates:

> All the Communists vote, of course and they could win enormous industrial power because 750,000 good democrats preferred their TV sets to picking up and filling in a few forms.

One of the candidates mentioned in this long article came in for special praise:

> As a champion of causes in many fields – equal pay for women is his present preoccupation – this smiling Cockney is immensely popular. He is known as a brilliant negotiator and it is a well-earned reputation.

Who was this man? He was Joe Scott, a Communist Party member, and the article states categorically that members should **not** vote for him, despite his obvious qualifications for the job. This kind of contradiction was not an isolated example. Bob Wright suffered the same way as a candidate in 1975, when all the press united to attack him as a "left-wing sitting member with Communist backing" (forgetting to mention that he had been a loyal member of the Labour Party all his political life), and only **after** the election did the 'Financial Times' point out (on 19th November 1975) that in terms of competence, Wright was the man for the job:

> With one or two notable exceptions, Mr Wright's colleagues on the Executive Council do not match his soundness and ability: some of them frequently amaze the employers and MPs with whom they deal and have sometimes been regarded as an embarrassment by their counterparts in other unions.

Bob Wright lost the election, and his seat on the Executive Council.

It was not unusual for elections to be regarded as personal victories or defeats. The article "Reform of cloth cap revolt?" ('The Times', 16th May 1967) in which Conway represented "reform" and I the "cloth cap revolt", was supported by a large close-up of Conway with the caption: "Jim

Conway: his destiny in the balance." What about the destinies of the AEU's million-plus members?

When John Boyd was elected as General Secretary in 1975, he was much aggrieved when 'his' place on the TUC General Council went to another member of the AEU Executive (the post is traditionally held by an EC member), and he claimed that the vote which displaced him was undemocratic. The 'Daily Mail', hardly noted for its general sympathy towards trade unions, printed a half-page article about Boyd which was countered by a reader's letter, on 6th August 1975), which made some very relevant points about trade union leaders:

> The dire consequences to Mr Boyd's career prospects were hardly the most important consideration. Having been the President of the Confederation, Chairman of the Labour Party **and** President of the TUC might have been good for My Boyd's personal glory, but not necessarily for the trade union movement. Much more important than personal aggrandisement is that the elected member of the General Council should be relied upon to promote the union's policy within the TUC. Mr Boyd is not in a position to do this with conviction, since he is strongly in favour of the incomes policy (his union is not) and has held similarly out-of-step views on the Common Market and other matters.

The 'Mail' was only too eager to print a long piece about John Boyd (who later became Sir John Boyd), since a lot of their policies coincided, but at least their article was published after the election was over. Bro Carron (who later became Lord Carron) also went to press in the 'Evening Standard' of 27th February 1959, but this case was taken to the Final Appeal Court, as being an article "that would influence an election in the union, which was at the time in progress." The Executive argued that the responsibility for publishing an article made no reference to the Presidential election, nor did Carron distribute the article to branches or members. Nevertheless, Carron need not have written the article, which certainly found its way into the homes of thousands of AEU members at a time when its author was up for election.

No action was taken against Carron, nor against Bill Tallon for his interference in the ballots for General Secretary and President in 1964. Although not a candidate himself, he was barred by Rule from making a statement to the press about elections. Yet the statement he made was printed prominently in national and local papers under such headlines as "Vote to beat Red Menace". However, when the Left protested, and called for disciplinary action to be taken against him, this only resulted in the press using the protest as an occasion to repeat Tallon's remarks!

Woodrow Wyatt must undoubtedly take the prize for blatant interference. In the 'Sunday Mirror' of 12th October 1975, he reminded union members that their ballot papers had to be returned by 23rd October, and told them that the 'common-sense' candidates to vote for were Gavin Laird, Terry Duffy and twelve other named men. Most candidates on his list were 'unknown' names standing for local office. Certainly they could be of no interest to anybody other than an AEU member with a postal ballot paper in front of him. Wyatt concluded:

> If any AEU members not certain about the rest of the list write to me through the 'Sunday Mirror', I will try to help.

Wyatt has been a consistent ally of the right-wing for many years. Even in 1956, I was writing in the Coventry Evening Telegraph's correspondence column:

> Our union's rules forbid any member even to write to another soliciting support in an election, yet you (i.e. the Telegraph), Woodrow Wyatt, and a group of right-wing individuals under the guise of 'IRIS News' are doing your best to foist individuals whom you favour upon our members. You and they are advertising certain persons in the press in order to give them an advantage over other candidates....
>
> It is very significant when the anti-Labour and anti-trade union press tries to advise us for our own good as to who our leaders should be. Your support is no recommendation.

Press interference drove a coach and horses through the strict rules on election canvassing within the union, but since 99½ per cent of the promotion was in favour of the right-wing (the other ½ per cent being the 'Morning Star'!), no action was taken to curb it.

Electioneering did not only take place during elections. It was to a candidate's advantage to keep his name to the forefront of union affairs at all times, and nobody was in a better position to do this than the General Secretary, through the union Journal. Jim Conway, while General Secretary, used the journal for promotional purposes to such an extent that it came to be known, even among the right-wingers, as 'Jim's Journal'. Even when the union was at loggerheads with the Labour Government, pages of the journal were given over to a defence of policies which the AEU had rejected, as in the June 1967 issue, in which Labour Minister Fred Lee "hits out at those who by voting against prices and incomes policy opted out of the economic problems which face the nation." This was printed **after** the union's decision to oppose prices and incomes policy. Other issues featured front covers and lead articles by Roy Jenkins (writing **for** the Common Market; the union was against entry), Harold Wilson (on Labour Unity, when the National Committee had decisively rejected his economic plans), Roy Jenkins again (pro prices and incomes policy), Jim Callaghan (against strikes), and the crowning glory: Barbara Castle, perpetrator of 'In Place of Strife', denouncing the Tory version of industrial relations legislation, in company with Robert Carr, the Tory Minister, writing in support of his Industrial Relations Bill, which was modelled on Mrs Castle's own efforts.

These articles were rarely matched by contributions from the left of the Party. And Jim made such complimentary remarks about his choice of contributors that readers might easily have thought that he had half an eye on the Honours List. 'Voice of the Unions' in March 1967 made an analysis of the 1966 Journals, and threw out comments about Jim's sycophancy, but their chief complaint was the use made of the Journal to bolster his own image.

Noting that references to me and EC members were "almost non-existent", continuing: with the comment "that the General Secretary is bound to feature in his Union's Journal – but members will form their own opinions as to whether he needs to publish his own photo and opinions on an average, nearly **three times in every issue."**

The General Secretary's name and photograph disappeared while he was election-tied, but that did not stop his name appearing on every sheet of Union paper. Every previous holder of the office had been content with 'General Secretary' alone to appear, as the title of the Chief Officer of the Union, and as if that were not enough, large amounts of free publicity were distributed, which were advertising the Union, but which happened incidentally to have the name Jim Conway in a prominent position. Half a million biros and books of matches were distributed free among the membership with many thousands of rulers, bookmarks, beermats, all bearing the name of 'lucky Jim'. His name appeared twice on every election address – on the cover and on the flyleaf. When a million copies of a Union newspaper were produced, his photograph appeared in a key position alongside an article by him, even though he was election-tied. At a full-time officers' conference one year, each of the FTOs (about 150 of them) was presented with an attractive coloured box containing five cigarettes, a book of matches and a Havana cigar. The presentation card inside came "With the Compliments of the President, General Secretary and The Executive Council", but the padded lid bore only two names – the name of the union, and "J Conway, General Secretary". All this was of course paid for by the members through their contributions.

After the 1972 election, I wrote to the Executive, complaining about Conway's misuse of his position during the election, naming specifically his prominent place in the 'AUEW Herald', and the advertisements bearing his name and photograph which had appeared in 'Tribune', 'Labour Weekly' and the 'Morning Star' on 1st May. Scanlon defended Conway in his reply to my letter, but Conway issued a memo only two weeks later, saying that the Executive Council had agreed that names of officers should not appear on advertisements for the union in future, nor on union publications.

Finally when all the canvassing – legal and illegal – had been done, it was up to the members to cast their votes. The method of doing this under the old branch-ballot system was so secure that large-scale ballot-rigging would have been an impossibility. Certain irregularities did occur, and these cases were brought before the Executive Council, who judged whether or not the votes from the branch which had been complained about should be invalidated. The complaints were presented to the EC anonymously, so that the EC members had no idea whether the result had gone Left or Right.

Many of the complaints were on technicalities of Rule – whether or not the tellers had been changed in the course of the evening, whether the ballot had been held on the right date, or at the normal meeting place – all of which may affect the voting rights of members in the branch. Of course, only branches about which a complaint was lodged were investigated, but when the results were published in the Half-yearly Report, some very odd figures came to light which were not queried.

Two instances are worth recording as examples, both involving branches in Scotland. In one case, two left-wing branch officers were sentenced to terms of imprisonment for falsifying a ballot. On another occasion, when I was sent to investigate personally, a right-wing officer had altered the voting returns by putting a '1' in front of the voting figures and adding a hundred names to the sheet of voters' signatures. The hundred names had all been added in the same handwriting. The Executive decided not to pursue the matter, and the case was dropped.

Election-times were thus a particularly sensitive period, and a time for keeping well out of trouble. The AEU Rulebook makes sure that the union is in a constant state of electioneering. The Rules provide that an elected officer must stand for re-election after three years of office, and thereafter at five-yearly intervals. I was elected in 1957, and was therefore up for re-election in November 1960. This resulted in a win for me: my 1957 majority had been 5,000; my 1960 majority was over 11,000. The Executive Council appeared to be lumbered with me for another five years. Or were they?

For a few weeks in 1961, it looked as if they might not have to put up with me for the remainder of my term of office. The following summary of what happened in those few weeks is not in dispute. Both parties agreed on the basic facts. But the interpretations of those facts, and their implications, led to a case in the High Court before Mr Justice Russell.

During the series of elections immediately following my own re-election in 1960, a good trade unionist named John Foster, who was a Communist, was a candidate in an election for National Organiser. He asked me for my support, and I agreed to allow my name to appear on postcards which were used as canvassing material during the election. Two other officers, Claude Berridge (an Executive Councilman) and Les Ambrose (a National Organiser), also had their signatures on the same cards.

The election for National Organiser was due to be completed on 14th June 1961, but on 30th May something happened which threw the whole procedure out of gear. I was called into an Executive meeting on that day (the 'senior' Assistant General Secretary, Walter Baxter, had died only a month before, and I was temporarily taking his place), and one of the items on the agenda was a batch of complaints from branches that they had received postcards in connection with the Foster election, and that these had been signed by Berridge, Ambrose and me. I was asked to leave the Council Chamber while the Executive (including Berridge, one of the other signatories) discussed the matter. When I returned, the President declared that I had been in breach of Rule in signing the cards, since I was the Returning Officer in the election for National Organiser. I defended myself by saying that I had **not** been the Returning Officer in this election, and in any case there was nothing in the Rulebook to prevent any officer, from the President downwards, from doing what I had done. Again I was asked to leave the room, and the Executive deliberated further. The next time I was recalled, the President – Bill Carron – said that this was the most serious thing that had happened in the union for a considerable number of years, and that I was suspended from office forthwith. In answer to a request from me, he said that he would provide a written account of precisely what I was supposed to have done to merit suspension, but that written statement never arrived.

So, at 3.30 in the afternoon, I – an elected officer of a supposedly democratic union – walked out of the office at Peckham Road without a job. It was the end of May. As an AEU member, I had the right to appeal against my suspension at the Final Appeal Court, but the Final Appeal Court did not sit until October, and that meant nearly five months' waiting, without wages.

There was only one course of action open to me – to go to law. I took up the matter immediately, and was advised that I should take out injunctions to restrain the Executive Council from suspending me, and to restrain them from declaring the ballot for National Organiser void.

The first hearing in the High Court of Justice, Chancery Division, with John Platts-Mills QC appearing for me, took place on 2nd June, only three days after the suspension. The judge refused the injunctions, and put back the hearing until the following Tuesday, when the defendants would be able to submit their evidence. The judge commented that "Mr Roberts was not going to be destroyed in body, soul or position over the weekend."

But he had reckoned without the Executive Council. Over that weekend, they issued instructions to all branches to destroy the ballot papers in the election for National Organiser, at a cost of thousands of pounds to the union (the ballot was within two weeks of completion, after six months of work between calling nominations and the final voting date). The news of my suspension had already been in the press; the instruction to destroy all the ballot papers only served to reinforce the suggestion that I had done something so reprehensible that the whole ballot had to be scrapped. Yet even the right-wing 'IRIS News' had to admit that, even if I had been Returning Officer, which I contended that I was not, I had never carried out any of the duties of Returning Officer in this election.

One thing that I did get out of the Friday hearing was the right to go back to my office at Peckham Road and remove papers which may be of use in the case. I returned to Peckham by car immediately after the hearing, only to find that news of my visit had preceded me – the office manager was waiting for me in my office, and remained there while I sorted through my papers. Shortly afterwards, Carron and Hallett got back from court and made their way straight to my office, where they stood in a corner of the room, hands behind their backs, watching until I finished collecting my papers; and then they watched me off the premises.

The next hearing, on 6th June, also resulted in a refusal by the judge to grant interim injunctions, on the grounds that the Defendants had not produced any evidence. By that time, the Defendants had in any case pre-empted the injunction attempting to restrain them from declaring the ballot void; there remained only the two injunctions to allow me to continue my work as Assistant General Secretary. The next hearing was on 9th June, and this time the Defendants produced sworn affidavits, claiming among other things that the union had received 82 letters of complaint about my activities in the election, from different branches all over the country.

There was another adjournment, this time until 12th June. At this hearing, the judge professed himself to be 'astonished'. The cause of his astonishment lay in the fact that Sir Frank Soskice QC announced that my wages were not being withheld from me. I could have collected them at any time from Peckham Road, and they were at present in court, ready to hand over to me. The judge said:

> If I were told I was suspended from my job, I would assume I was not getting paid during the suspension. One of the grounds for Mr Roberts' ex-parte application was that he had up to the time of the application lost only one week, but if I did not grant him relief he would lose more wages. I am astonished that I have not been disillusioned before this stage.

The paying of the wages marked what was virtually the end of the hearings in court. On the following day, the injunction was refused on the grounds that there was now no urgency in the case: the ballot had already been declared void, and that could not be remedied; the Plaintiff was to get his wages during the period of the suspension, and was therefore suffering no hardship. The rights and wrongs of the suspension, said the judge, could better be argued when the case came up for trial. But for various reasons, that trial never took place.

It was now 13th June, and I was still suspended from my job. My first inclination was to proceed with the trial, as I was sure I had a very strong case. In fact, throughout the hearings which had already taken place, it seemed that the judge was hinting strongly to the Defendants that they were on a losing wicket. By this time they had put in their defence, and my own affidavits made mincemeat of their case.

The union stated their grounds of complaint against me as being:

> namely that the Plaintiff had allowed his name to be circulated in order to promote the return of a particular candidate in an election, in which he was the Returning Officer, or discharging the functions of Returning Officer.

The fact that I had allowed my name to be circulated in support of John Foster was not in itself a breach of Rule. In court, I produced a sheaf of election addresses to demonstrate that officers at all levels from the President downwards had done precisely the same thing by appending their names to the election statements of certain candidates. Nor was the manner in which my name was circulated a breach of Rule, because a new clause – Rule 2, Clause 10 – had been inserted to cover "additional matter". This had been done by the Rules Revision Committee in 1960. Prior to that date, no "additional matter" had been permissible, but the new clause permitted additional canvassing material (i.e. additional to the printed election address) **providing that it was handwritten.** The cards with my name on, although they had not been written by me personally, were handwritten, and therefore did not contravene this Rule.

The real bone of contention was whether or not I had been "the Returning Officer or discharging the functions of Returning Officer" in Foster's election. The Executive used Rule 2, Clause 7, to show that the Assistant General Secretary **was** the Returning Officer:

> Elections for all General Officers.... shall be conducted by the General Secretary or the Assistant General Secretaries except election to their own particular office, which shall be conducted by one of the others, but all such elections shall be subject to the General Control of the Executive Council. Any questions which may arise in the course of such elections shall be referred by the Returning Officer for that election to the Executive Council for their decision.

The Executive were claiming (although they had never done so before) that, in the absence of the General Secretary, the mantle of Returning Officer fell upon the Assistant General Secretary. This meant that, in normal circumstances, Walter Baxter, the 'senior' Assistant General Secretary, would have assumed the role when Hallett was absent. But Baxter had died during April. The Executive maintained, therefore, that at any time since Baxter's death, I **could** have been called to be Returning Officer, and during the period between 22nd April and 14th May when the General Secretary had been absent from the office, I had **actually** been the Returning Officer. They did not claim, however, that I had carried out any of a Returning Officer's functions, or attempted to interfere with the ballot in any way.

I maintained firmly that I had **never** been the Returning Officer in this election. To begin with, the department concerned with the conduct of ballots was the only office department which had not been delegated as the responsibility of either of the Assistant General Secretaries. Furthermore, the only election which was accepted as the province of either of the AGSs was the election of the General Secretary himself, since this was the only one which he himself could not conduct. And, most important of all, in the absence of the General Secretary, neither of the AGSs automatically assumed responsibility for his functions, and they would have been promptly called to order if they had. As I pointed out in my affidavit, the General Secretary had the job of hiring and firing office staff, and of editing the AEU Journal; but there would have been all hell let loose if I had sacked the office manager or re-written the Journal editorial while Hallett was away from the office! While the General Secretary was absent, an AGS might be called upon to make certain day-to-day decisions about office organisation, but he would never be expected to usurp major functions of the General Secretary.

I was also attempting to prove that, even if I had been Returning Officer, I would have had no opportunity to influence the result or interfere with the ballot in any way; in fact, the function of Returning Officer under the AEU Rules is a purely mechanical one – that of reporting the result to the Executive Council.

Other union representatives could have had a much more direct influence on the election, had they wished: I produced evidence to show that members of the Executive Council, branch tellers, branch presidents and secretaries (all of whom had responsibility directly for conducting ballots) had allowed their names to be used in support of certain candidates. In the case of Executive members, this could have proved far more serious than in my case, since Rule declared that any query on the ballot must be brought before the Executive for a decision to be made – the Returning Officer was never responsible for making such decisions.

The Executive Council had in the past (I claimed) taken decisions which may have had a bearing on the outcome of the ballot, yet no action was taken against them for so doing, even when they were in direct contravention of Rule. In support of this claim, I quoted a specific instance which occurred during the ballot for an Executive position, in which Bill Cockin was defending his seat on the Council against Hugh Scanlon. Quoting Rule 15, Clause 4, which stated that the General Secretary should have charge of all election addresses in ballots for Executive Councilmen, and "should in no case place advance copies in the hands of any member or members of the Executive Council", I say:

> Mr Hallett on a date earlier in May produced Mr Scanlon's election address to the Council in my presence and copies were supplied to members. The Council then

debated its terms and then deleted certain parts critical of the Council and of Mr Cockin. Mr Cockin, an Executive Councilman and one of Scanlon's opponents, argued and voted for the deletion.

It is not too difficult to see why I was an unwelcome visitor in Executive Council meetings! On this occasion, I was present only because the death of Walter Baxter had left the AGS's chair vacant.

The point was clear: an EC member could carry a lot more weight in an election than an AGS, or the Returning Officer. It was curious that during the Executive's deliberations on my alleged misconduct in signing cards on behalf of Foster, Claude Berridge – another of the signatories – should have sat in the meeting throughout, and yet escaped censure for his part in the incident, even though Rule makes the Executive Council **directly** responsible for the conduct of all elections.

The Executive, in defence of their decision to suspend me, declared that they had received eighty-two letters of complaint against my action in signing postcards on behalf of Foster while being a Returning Officer. In later evidence, it emerged that this was not quite true. Only five of the letters had been of this nature. The remainder were in fact the result of a misunderstanding. In previous years, the Rule on conduct of elections had admitted only the election address as canvassing material. The new Rule, introduced in 1960, permitted handwritten but not printed or duplicated matter in addition to the election address. Seventy-seven of the eight-two letters were submitted by branches which were ignorant of the change in Rule; they complained, not that I had been Returning Officer, but that I had signed "additional matter" which they were not aware was now permitted under Rule.

The Defendants in their written statement admitted that the postcards were not in breach of Rule 2 Clause 10, and therefore all but five of the letters were totally irrelevant. (And since it would never have occurred spontaneously to any branch that I might have been the Returning Officer in the Foster election, the question arises: who or what prompted the writing of those five letters in the first place?) Whatever their origin, the remaining five letters – which had no basis in fact, since I was not the Returning Officer – were blown up out of all proportion to their significance, and used as a reason for scrapping an expensive ballot, and dragging my name through the mud.

The final point of contention between the two sides was the suspension itself. The Rulebook nowhere gives the Executive the right to suspend any officer for any reason. It gives the right of expulsion. But this was not what they had intended, and in any case under Rule notice must be given of expulsion, and I had been given no notice whatsoever. The Executive maintained that the rule on expulsion also included the right to suspend. And, should the court decide that it didn't, they covered themselves by invoking the 'Silent Rule'. This covered a multitude of sins, stating:

> The Executive Council, in the event of any question arising in which the rules are silent, shall have an original jurisdiction to give a decision, which shall be published in the monthly Journal following, stating the particulars of the question and the decision thereon with reasons; but in no case shall they alter the established rules of the union. (Rule 15, Clause 17)

It was my argument that I had broken no rule, and therefore deserved no punishment. But even if I could be proved to have contravened some rule, the Rulebook only gave the Executive the right to expel. The Rulebook was not silent on the issue of wrongdoing – it explicitly recommended expulsion. Therefore, the Executive had no right to invent a rule of their own in order to suspend me.

These then were the arguments in the case. But it was destined never to come to trial. As usual, it was "one law for the rich, another for the poor", and I, being 'the poor', could not afford to continue. I had already run up legal costs amounting to nearly £1,000, which was a year's wages. My fear was that, if the case came to trial it may be decided that, although I had right on my side, I should nevertheless bear my own costs. By that time, the costs could amount to tens of thousands of pounds.

As soon as my suspension became public information, I began to receive letters of sympathy from individuals, branches, districts and organisations throughout the country. Of the scores of messages, the following are typical: first, a letter from the London Region Campaign for Nuclear Disarmament:

> While it is obviously impossible for us to comment too much on matters which lie between you and the union, and which are in any case sub judice, we all feel

that you have been the victim of your outspoken and courageous views, and most sincerely hope that matters will be brought to a satisfactory conclusion for you.

The next letter was from friends in the labour movement:

We were horrified by the news in this morning's 'Daily Herald'. Horrified, not so much for your own situation, as we are convinced that support for you at grass-roots level is both strong and sure (and what more valuable support could any trade union leader wish?), but horrified that the Executive of the AEU could act in so contrived a manner to a brother member, nominated and elected by the thousands of workers who are, after all, their employers....

Anyone who has had the honour to work with you in so many causes dear to the labour movement as a whole, can have nothing but respect for your courage and honesty.

With letters of support (there were none of condemnation), came offers of financial assistance. Having ascertained that there was no legal barrier to my accepting such help towards the expenses of my case, I took up the offer of a friend to act as Treasurer of the fund, and collection sheets were issued on which sixpences and shillings and halfcrowns were entered as donations by well-wishers. I undertook to donate any surplus to an agreed cause, but in fact the collection fell many hundreds short of the legal fees, and I made up the remainder myself, paying piecemeal over a long period of time.

The problem of money was a strong influence in my decision to drop the case. Nevertheless, I would have been obliged to continue it, but for a decision of the Executive Council early in July, when they agreed to reinstate me in my post as Assistant General Secretary. I accepted reinstatement (even though some of my former duties were taken away from me), so the prime reason for proceeding with the case was removed. The final agreement between the parties was that a Declaration of Discontinuance should be filed, each side being responsible for its own costs.

There was an interesting sequel to this tale in the 1972 elections. This was the first series of elections to be held under the postal ballot system, and the Returning Officer was therefore much elevated in importance, since the whole ballot was conducted from Peckham Road, and all the votes were returned and counted there. The ballot for General Secretary opened in January 1972, when nominations were called for. 'Acceptance of

149

nomination' forms were issued by the General Secretary, to be returned to him with the candidates' election addresses, although he had already declared his intention of standing in the election himself, and it was against Rule for any candidate to have sight of another candidate's election address prior to publication. It was not until 7th March that Bro Hugh Scanlon, the union's President, was appointed Returning Officer, in contravention of Rule 2 Clause 7, under which Ken Brett, the Assistant General Secretary, should have had that responsibility. When tackled with this, the Executive replied that it was not known whether Brett would himself be a candidate for General Secretary; however, acceptance of nomination had to be submitted by 3rd March, and Scanlon was not appointed Returning Officer until 7th March, by which time it was clear that Brett was not a candidate. Brett appealed against the Executive's decision, but the appeal was dismissed by the 1972 Final Appeal Court by seven votes to four.

Later in the year, mindful of the 1961 decision, when I had been accused of being Returning Officer without my knowledge, I wrote to the Executive, asking them to take a decision as to who should be the Returning Officer in the other ballots, in the absence of the General Secretary. There was no reply to the memorandum, but the following took place in the next Executive meeting, when all seven EC members were present, the President having a casting vote:

It was agreed by 5 votes to 2 that an Assistant General Secretary should be Returning Officer in the absence of the General Secretary.

On the motion that I be Returning Officer in the absence of J Conway, the voting was 3–3, with one abstention.

On the motion that Ken Brett be Returning Officer in the absence of J Conway, the voting was 3–3, with one abstention.

The President did not give a casting vote, and insisted on all the Executive voting.

It was then moved that the previous decision taken be declared void, and it was agreed by 5 votes to 2 that the President should act as General Secretary while the latter was absent, and should therefore be Returning Officer in all ballots.

This, in spite of the clarity of the Rulebook, which insisted that the Returning Officer in all ballots should be either the General Secretary or one of the Assistant General Secretaries.

Life in the General Office at Peckham Road was no bed of roses. It was more like a daily walk, barefoot, over broken glass. Time after time, I found myself fighting a lone battle. But the fight was not one of man against men: it was the fight of Left against Right.

The key issue around which the struggle centred was the union's Rulebook. The right-wing was anxious to 'modernise' the rules or – on the suggestion of Harold Wilson – to consign the 'archaic' Rulebook to the dustbin and start afresh. The Left, believing that strict application of Rule was the only defence of the union's democracy, fought to keep the Rulebook intact. The right-wing argument that the rules were too oldfashioned to suit the changing circumstances of a modern union was untenable, disregarding entirely that every five years the Rules Revision Committee debated and voted on the rule-changes proposed by the membership, and so in one sense the Rulebook was never more than five years old.

One of the archaic practices condemned by the Right was that of electing union officers through branch ballots, and it was in this field that a major change was made in 1970, when the old system of balloting was scrapped in favour of postal ballots. The new system was to apply to 'general officers' only – the officers at District and Branch level continued to be elected in the old way. The acceptance of the principle of postal ballots was by no means enthusiastic. The 1970 Rules Revision Committee voted by 26 votes to 25, with one abstention, to change the rules, and the close result meant that the Committee was recalled in November 1971 to reconsider the matter. There was so much grass-roots pressure on the Committee to reverse its original decision that it was half-expected that postal ballots would never materialise, and therefore no preparations were in hand for the operation of the March 1972 series of elections under the new system. But the Rules Revision Committee again voted in favour of postal ballots, this time by 27 votes to 25, and the Executive was left with four months to get the system working.

Comparing branch ballots with the postal ballot system as it was to be operated from Peckham Road, the deficiencies in the new system were glaringly obvious. My own analysis at the time picked out half a dozen defects which rendered the whole system open to abuse. For one thing, there was virtually no scrutiny of the count (branch ballots had provided for two tellers to be present throughout the ballot in each of the two and a half thousand branches). In the branch, each voter had his credentials checked, and had to sign his name on a recording list before casting his vote; the postal ballot provided no means of checking that all those who received ballot papers were eligible to vote, and there was no proof that the ballot paper had been completed by the member to whom it had been sent.

In the branches, the two tellers, the Branch President and the Branch Secretary had to sign the voting returns, and the results were read out to the Branch and written into the minutes on the same night. In the event of any query, a branch vote could if necessary be invalidated without affecting the rest of the ballot, whereas this would be impossible under the new system: the postal ballot was organised so that ballot papers were sent out from and returned to the Peckham Road office, where they were counted en masse, and one final result published. Furthermore, the branches retained all ballot papers for three months after branch balloting, in case any query should arise, and the results of each branch were published in an official report, so it was possible to check that the figures read out to the branch on voting night were the same as those sent to the General Office. Under the postal system, although ballot papers would be returned to Peckham and retained there, there would be no means of knowing that all the papers were genuine votes of bona fide members.

Finally, when members attended branch meetings in order to vote, they had access to information about candidates prior to voting. In the postal ballot, members did not need to go to the branch (where the election addresses were sent) and most voters therefore had no access to official electioneering material – although a good number would have seen the promotions of various candidates in the national and local newspapers. Even 'IRIS News', which was strongly in favour of postal ballots, conceded that the limited distribution of election addresses was a mistake, and suggested sending them out with the ballot papers to all registered voters. After the first series of elections was over, 'IRIS News' put out a booklet in praise of postal ballots, in which the 'advantages' of the system were listed. These 'advantages' were that:

every member registered to vote would receive a direct communication from the union – perhaps his **only** contact with the union. (Problem: in 1972, nearly half a million members were not registered to vote and were therefore disenfranchised. In the branch ballot, any paid-up member could vote.)

members could choose to vote or not, whereas in certain circumstances they might be disenfranchised in a branch ballot. (My objection was where branches had not bothered to elect officers whose responsibility was to conduct ballots, the membership would be disenfranchised even in a postal ballot, since it was the Branch Secretary's duty to provide information about members for the electoral roll; where members were not interested enough to know that an election was taking place, their disenfranchisement was their own responsibility, and these members would probably not get a postal vote anyway, because they would not have provided the Branch Secretary with up-to-date information for the Electoral Roll.)

members receiving ballot papers would "try to inform" themselves about the ballot (How? Election addresses were sent to branches. The only other written information was through the 'establishment' press.)

a higher percentage vote would be good for solidarity and unity. (My objection to the figures quoted – 25–30 per cent for postal ballots and 2–3 per cent for branch ballots – were in the first case too high, and in the second case too low. The true figures were much closer together, and the benefit of a few extra percentage points is arguably far less important than the enforced disenfranchisement of hundreds and thousands of members.)

Quite apart from the mechanics of operating the new system, there was also concern about the cost. The previous branch ballot method involved printing and distributing ballot papers and election addresses to branches, and the cost of postage. The counting was done by elected officers in the branches. The only 'payment' was 30p to each of the two tellers (plus an extra 7½p if the ballot ran on outside normal meeting-hours). There would be a minimal amount of work in the General Office, in the collation of results.

When postal ballots were introduced, in addition to the printing costs and postage of ballot papers to each registered member, all the work of counting had to be done by full-time paid staff, which added enormously to the cost of elections. The counting itself took months; to quote a figure from 'IRIS News', even the opening of envelopes in the second series of elections in 1972 accounted for 1500 man-hours of work, and that was followed by weeks of sorting and counting papers. The result was that, although the General Office published figures to show that the cost **per vote** could be shown to be less than under branch ballots, the extra expense of postal balloting meant that it cost considerably more to elect an officer than it did to pay his wages for his term of office.

Even leaving the cost out of consideration – for who can put a price on democracy? – the other disadvantages of the postal system far outweighed the alleged advantage of a higher percentage poll. The first difficulty was the compilation of an electoral register of nearly a million and a quarter members. This required the co-operation of branch secretaries in providing the names and addresses of all their paid-up membership, which in turn needed the co-operation of individual members in giving the necessary details to the branch secretaries. Inevitably there were problems: people whose membership had lapsed were included on the register, members changed addresses without passing on the information to the branch; some branches failed to register any of their members, through laziness or lack of organisation; some branches submitted registration cards which were not included on the register; the register was closed in February 1972, but the elections did not take place until May, so even more members lost a vote; some 20,000 envelopes were returned by the Post Office as 'undeliverable' in the first ballot, and the second ballot figure was even higher; and, to cap it all, Head Office afterwards sent out a circular to branches stating that the computer agency used in the compilation of the register had not provided "a fully accurate service".

It is in this context that the exaggerated claims about the increased numbers of members voting must be seen. Of course it is important to have as many members as possible participating in election. But it cannot be ignored that a large proportion of the membership had no vote at all in the 1972 election, often through no fault of their own. When postal ballots first started, voting figures of 40–50 per cent were claimed in ballots for national officers, compared with about 10 per cent under the branch ballot system. Such figures were bandied about so freely that few people thought of asking "40 per cent of what?"

The electoral roll in the first elections comprised about 730,000 names, out of a total membership approaching 1,250,000. That is, 520,000 members had no vote, either because their names had not been submitted for registration, or the registration cards had arrived too late for inclusion on the electoral roll. The ballot for General Secretary polled a total of 286,530 votes, which is a 39.97 per cent poll. That is, 39.97 per cent **of the electoral roll.** But the electoral roll was only 60 per cent of the total membership, therefore the votes cast, as a percentage of the total membership, represented not 39.97 per cent but 23 per cent. 23 per cent is significantly higher than the 10 per cent which might have been expected under the branch ballot system, but undoubtedly quite a few percentage points were gained by the fact that this was the first election of its kind, and was therefore accompanied by all the ballyhoo of extra media coverage.

Looking at some of the 1981 results, after the system had been operating for nine years, the overall picture is not so rosy. The first ballot for General Secretary in 1981 produced a total vote equivalent to 17.7 per cent of the membership (according to figures in the Journal); that is, 82 members out of a hundred still do not vote. Because of change of address, lax branch secretaries, hiccups in the postal service etc., many thousands of members who actually **want** to vote are denied the opportunity to do so; this seems a high price to pay for the advantage of an extra 7 or 8 per cent of votes. It is also significant that, as the electoral roll has become more complete over the years, the proportion of its members actually voting has declined: from 39.9 per cent of the electoral roll in the 1972 General Secretary's ballot to 22.6 per cent in the 1981 series.

In 1972, I was a candidate in the ballot for General Secretary, along with my old adversary Jim Conway, and eight other candidates, including that rarity in AEU elections, a woman candidate. She was Sister Nora Bance, who featured largely in the complaints which arose after the election was over. The first ballot, which under Rule should have taken place in March, started in May. On 22nd May, I submitted a memo to the Returning Officer, Hugh Scanlon, asking for certain information, including two vital questions:

1   Will all candidates be informed.... of the number and names of all those branches whose members were refused permission to be placed on the electoral roll?

2 Will candidates have the right to scrutinise at any stage of the ballot?

Scanlon declined to answer the memo, later giving as his reason that a reply to these points would give me an unfair advantage over the other candidates, though it is difficult to see how this could have been so, since other candidates could **and did** write to the Returning Officer with similar queries of their own at this period.

Biding my time, I waited until the ballot was complete before writing to Scanlon again, this time putting my letter through the official channels – that is, via my own branch, Coventry Central. My letter drew attention to some very pertinent points: all the arrangements for rooms, staff, mailing, etc in the General Secretary's ballot were officially under the control of the General Secretary; the scrutiny of ballots had been virtually non-existent, and the candidates themselves had no right of scrutiny; members had not discovered that they had no vote until **after** the election, because the electoral roll was not made available to branches for checking; many members had received their ballot papers too late to vote; and there had been many other complaints about the conduct of the ballot, many members claiming that their complaints had not been placed before the Executive Council prior to the result being declared.

The reply from Scanlon, the Returning Officer, was hardly satisfactory. Some of my points were considered to be not specific to the General Secretary's election, and he therefore declined to answer them. The Executive had, it was said, taken all reasonable steps to ensure that those entitled to ballot papers had received them. The information I had asked for about the conduct of the election could not be supplied to me, as these were matters for which the Executive was totally responsible; although a glance at the information I had requested shows that it should have been available to every candidate – every voter, even! I had asked:

the numbers of members on the electoral roll in both the first and second ballots;

the numbers of ballot papers printed in each ballot, who fixed the numbers, who checked the delivery, and what happened to the surplus;

how many pre-paid envelopes were printed, and what happened to those which were not sent out?;

what happened to all the returned ballot papers and envelopes which the post office was unable to deliver?;

what proof there is that only those members who were entitled to vote actually voted?;

how the Executive Council decided that all votes were valid, and who examined any invalidated papers?;

what steps were taken to ensure the security of blank ballot papers and envelopes while they were being kept at the General Office?;

who was Returning Officer in the ballots when Bro Scanlon and Bro Conway were absent from the office?

The complacency of the Executive and the Returning Officer was matched by that of the 'IRIS News' booklet, which claimed that the members' complaints were 'alarmist' – 'human error' and 'mechanical error' accounted for the various things that had gone wrong. They stated calmly that if the wrong code number was fed into the computer, then the wrong ballot papers would be dispatched to that particular area; this was not only understandable, but acceptable. It was anything but acceptable to individual members and whole branches who had been prevented from taking part in the election, and the complaints flooded into the General Office.

One of the complainants was Ron Halverson, a candidate for the position of Divisional Organiser 21. He accumulated a mass of information which was typical of that submitted to Head Office from branches and districts all over the country. He sent in the names of 136 members who were on the electoral roll but had received no ballot papers, 212 members who had received their ballot papers on or after the closing date of the election, 28 members who had not received all the ballot papers for elections in which they were entitled to vote, 3 members who had received two sets of papers each, and an allegation from Hatfield 6 Branch Secretary that members had received ballot papers for elections taking place in a different part of the country. In all, Halverson's report detailed complaints from 41 branches and district committees in the Hertfordshire/East Anglia area. These were, of course, complaints from members who were interested enough to complain – there must have been many, many more who did not know or care that they had been disenfranchised.

As these cases were repeated all over Britain, the scale of the problem was much larger than 'IRIS News' was prepared to admit. They claimed that it was doubtful if all the complaints added together "would add up to one per cent of the whole membership in total and probably less than 0.5% of those registered for a ballot vote." The cock-eyed logic in this statement only becomes apparent when you read it twice! In fact, the number of envelopes returned undelivered by the Post Office was 1¾ per cent of the membership, and nearly 3 per cent of the electoral roll, and the other complaints far out-numbered that figure.

Among the oddities were:

● a ballot paper sent to a market gardener who had never been a member of the union;

● a ballot paper sent to a man who had been dead for five years;

● large numbers of papers sent directly to District Offices, instead of to members' home addresses;

● members who received ballot papers for elections in which they were not entitled to vote;

● members who received only an empty envelope.

Sister Nora Bance, herself a candidate for the post of General Secretary, had received a voting paper in the first ballot, but not in the second, likewise some of her colleagues, including her branch secretary. Others had received no papers at all, though they had been included in the branch secretary's returns. She claimed that a quarter of the members in her factory had received no ballot papers in the first ballot, and she declared in exasperation that nobody in authority wished to know about the muddle, or to rectify it. Her husband's papers had been sent to the wrong address, leading her to wonder how many other members who wanted a new General Secretary had had their addresses mislaid! The last straw was when her branch received a list of names and addresses from the General Office with a letter attached, saying "We have not got these names and addresses. Please will you send them to us."

Following the close of the elections, there were long delays before the results were announced. 'The Guardian' reported that "votes in one National Organiser ballot, which closed in October, have still to be counted." That was on 13th January 1973. This naturally led to speculation about the security of the procedure, which in turn led to further complaints. But even as late as 1978, the 'Engineering Gazette' thought it necessary to draw members' attention to the lack of democratic control, pointing out that "ballot papers are stored in cardboard boxes with no special security", although officially only the office concerned has access to the ballot room. The count takes weeks, and "the only scrutiny is by two EC members for a 2–3 hour check on spoiled papers, and a few spot counts." The 'Gazette' claimed to have received hundreds of complaints from members who did not receive ballot papers, and from many non-members who did receive them.

As a large number of elections took place at the same time, members would receive different selections of ballot papers according to which part of the country they lived in (e.g. in 1972, each member in Wolverhampton should have received papers to vote for General Secretary, Assistant Divisional Organiser 16 and the Wolverhampton District Secretary.) The General Secretary would be Returning Officer in all these elections **except his own,** but there was no provision for separating the papers in his election from the other papers, and the sorting and counting procedures took place in the same room. The counting took place over a period of weeks, and during that time scrutineers were present for only a few hours.

The holes in the system were obvious, although the Executive Council appeared to be unaware of all deficiencies and impervious to all complaints. One district secretary wrote on behalf of his District Committee, expressing deep concerns over the elections, pointing out areas which might be open to interference, and concluding with the statement that even Parliamentary election procedures did not go to the extent of issuing ballot papers to every elector by post, since such a system could "lead to abuse of democracy".

I was active throughout the period of the 1972 elections, not so much in electioneering on my own account, but in publicising the deficiencies of the new system. Picking up Lord Carron's injunction to members to 'Be Vigilant!', I wrote an article for the 'Voice' papers, pointing out that although some of the results were apparently decisive (I myself had lost to Jim Conway in the second ballot by 73,600 votes), the irregularities could have made an important difference where the majority was small – as low as 100, in some of the local elections. Nevertheless, when I took legal advice about the possibility of getting the elections scrapped, I was told that "the irregularities were marginal". One wonders whether similar irregularities would have been considered marginal in terms of a parliamentary election – if, for example, 40 per cent of potential voters were not included on the electoral register through no fault of their own, and a further 1¾ per cent were disenfranchised because the Post Office could not deliver their ballot papers! Other Unions run postal ballots, and without the turmoil of the scrutineers' efforts. Their elections are run efficiently and quickly by the Electoral Reform Society, which takes the whole procedure out of the hands of the union, and organises it from beginning to end under properly-scrutinised conditions. The Electoral Reform Society was consulted by the AUEW during 1971, but was not brought in to conduct the ballots. The Society made a public statement in January 1973, defending the principle of the postal ballot system, and saying in effect that the AUEW ballots had been poorly administered. Some members believed that the Electoral Reform Society should be given the whole job of organising the union's elections, especially as it became clear in later years that the problems of 1972 were not merely 'teething troubles'. But an amendment to Rule allowing the Society to be called in was turned down by the 1980 Rules Revision Committee, as were other proposals designed to tighten up security. (This has since been changed and the ballots are now conducted by the Electoral Reform Society).

Seeing that the chances of getting postal ballots scrapped completely are very slight, I concentrated on persuading the Executive to democratise existing procedure, and to that end I put before the Executive a list of suggested procedures, which included making each member responsible for his own inclusion on the electoral roll, instead of being dependent on his branch secretary; identifying all ballot papers by number, as in parliamentary elections; controlled destruction of surplus papers; separating the counts for ballots involving different Returning Officers; scrutiny by the candidates, or their chosen representatives, at any time during the count.

These were merely emergency proposals, designed to bail out a leaky boat, but they would not stop the boat from leaking. The only way to do that was to start from scratch: go back to the Rulebook. I worked out a method which would keep the postal ballot and at the same time satisfy all the demands of the Rulebook, and I maintained that this would be the most secure and democratic way of running postal ballots, and the least expensive. The system would operate this way:

- members would register themselves on a central electoral roll, as for parliamentary elections;
- ballot papers, numbered as for parliamentary elections, would be sent from the General Office to members on the roll;
- members would mark the ballot papers and post them to their branch, where they would be stored, unopened, until the appointed meeting night. Alternatively, members could deliver their sealed envelopes personally to the meeting;
- at the meeting, under the scrutiny of the elected tellers and officers prescribed in the existing rules, and before the eyes of members present at the meeting, the envelopes would be opened, sorted and counted;
- the results would be declared at the meeting, written into the minutes, and returns made to the General Office;
- envelopes and ballot papers would be stored in the branch for three months, as per Rule, in case any query should arise;
- the union's Half-yearly Report could publish the results from each branch, as required by Rule.

Assuming that a quarter of a million members voted, the 2,500 branches could cope happily with the count during the meeting hours on one evening, even if more than one election was involved, and this would reduce the cost of postal balloting considerably, as well as satisfying all the relevant Rules.

While the argument was raging inside the union, the world outside was also expressing its opinions, mainly in the newspapers. Following an article in the 'Financial Times' in November 1975, I wrote in reply:

Your labour editor John Elliott, writing (Nov 19) about AUEW elections, perpetuates the myth that postal ballots mean 'more' democracy. Yet if some members 'do not normally take an active part in union affairs', how can they be expected to cast an intelligent vote? They might as well pick out a candidate with a pin, or vote for the candidate their newspaper pushes. What kind of democracy is that?

The basis of the 'more democracy' idea is the 30% vote.... but if you express members voting as a percentage of total membership, you come out with a more realistic figure, only a few per cent higher than in branch ballots. Mr Elliott refers to 198,000 members in 26 weeks' arrears; this is roughly the same number as those who vote in postal ballots, that is, 17%....

Mr Elliott on the subject of democracy questions the union's 'cumbersome democratic procedures' which generally restrict efficiency. Efficiency is undermined, he says, by electing officials every three or five years, so that they suffer from 'excessive accountability' to the members and live in dread of being unseated if they don't behave themselves. I seem to remember something similar being argued in the case of Mr Reg Prentice. You know, people might almost begin to think your paper isn't in favour of democracy at all. That is, if democracy means accountability to the electorate, and acceptance of defeat when you cease to reflect their wishes.

The tendency of Mr Elliott's argument seems clear.... today, remove Left democrats and replace them with Moderates; tomorrow, persuade the Moderates to remove these cumbersome elections and replace them with appointments.

I have always maintained that democracy means more than a vote every few years. It means the active control by **all** of us, **all** the time, of the society in which we live. A union member who merely casts an occasional vote is not really exercising his democratic rights, but only proving how well the press has manipulated him. That is not to say he should not have a vote, but that he can hardly be casting his vote wisely if that is the only part he takes in the running of his union. 'Crucifer' made the point in the 'New Statesman' of 28th November 1975:

If newspapers can devote large photo-features to the various candidates – openly supporting some while seeking to undermine others – how is any but the most knowledgeable and active trade union member going to avoid having his vote determined for him?

This is especially true when the trade union member does not even have to go as far as a branch meeting in order to cast his vote. Small wonder then that the Thatcher Government proposed a system of postal ballots in unions, subsidised by public money – it would naturally be regarded as money well spent, since the Establishment could exercise vast influence over the outcome via the media.

At the end of 1981, a trial system was announced by the AUEW for appointing full-time, paid branch secretaries, responsible to the Executive

Council, to administer branches of between 7,000 and 10,000 members. The reason given was that some areas find it difficult to get members willing to do the job on a voluntary basis. However, if everybody knows that a lack of volunteers will mean a full-time job for somebody, the number of volunteers is going to dwindle to nothing, fast. Thus, instead of a body of elected branch officers, the union will have a system of appointment which will make branch secretaries rely entirely on the approval of the Executive Council for the continuance of their jobs. John Elliott of the 'Financial Times' complained about the 'excessive accountability' of officers to the electorate; would he complain similarly about branch secretaries' accountability to an Executive Council of seven members?

The closing lines of my letter to the 'Financial Times' in 1975 are beginning to look prophetic:

.... today, remove Left democrats and replace them with Moderates; tomorrow, persuade the Moderates to remove these cumbersome elections and replace them with appointments.

All in the cause of democracy, of course!

Leicester University Students' Union invited me to give their annual Woodcock Lecture, named after a former General Secretary of the TUC. The subject they chose was 'The fight for real democracy'. My talk was based on the ideas I put forward in my book 'Workers' Control', i.e. Democracy every day in the workplace, in the trade unions and the Labour Party; Democracy as the very basis of Socialism.

Chapter 5

In parliament, we are admonished on high authority that "the policy of a party is not the carrying out of the option of any section of it, but the general consensus of the whole", which seems to be a hierophantic manner of saying that the policy of a party is one thing, and the principle which makes it a party is another thing, and that men who care very strongly about anything are to surrender that and the hope of it for the sake of succeeding in something about which they care very little or not at all.
John Viscount Morley

1   Fight for democracy within the union
2   Left-wing pressure groups
3   International solidarity
4   Campaign for Labour Party Democracy
5   Founding of Campaign for Nuclear Disarmament
6   Institute of Workers' Control and Workers' Charter
7   Struggles for socialism within the Labour Party

Eddie Frow, a former full-time officer of the AEU, and his wife Ruth, suggested to me that we write a booklet on 'Democracy in the Engineering Union' in view of the continual eroding of the Union's democracy. I agreed. In the introduction of the booklet in 1982, we quoted the first President of the AEU:

In every trade union are to be found men occupying high official positions who prior to their appointment were militant and progressive-minded men; but, alas! what a change comes over these erstwhile militants when the mantle of responsibility is cast over their shoulders. What hitherto was bad becomes good; what was arbitrary becomes reasonable; what was near progressivism becomes extreme; what was wholesome criticism becomes unwarranted attacks. 'Be reasonable and

164

have implicit trust in your officials' is the lamentation of all the little-minded Caesars who are at the head of the Labour army.

JT Brownlie: Some Dangers Which Threaten Trade Unionism.

We referred to the illegal conditions in which trade unions met as described in the Huddersfield Branch of the Old Mechanics minute book of 1831 which showed that a Bible, a Pistol and Heavy Curtains had been bought. The heavy curtains were drawn, the new member placed his hand on the Bible, the pistol was pointed at his heart, and he swore not to disclose anything about the Branch. Such were the conditions under which workers organised into our trade unions.

Today the democratic checks and balances put into the constitution of the union by pioneers are being destroyed.

The principle of one member one vote in the election of delegates to the annual Trade Union Congress and the annual Labour Party Conference have been removed and delegates chosen by committees instead.

The booklet ended with the call:

Brothers and Sisters. It is time to stem the tide of reaction. Our union has had a magnificent history in the struggle to build a powerful and democratic Union. Let us continue to keep it so. The price of democracy is eternal vigilance!

By the time I left Coventry for the AEU headquarters at Peckham, I was 'doing' meetings at the rate of 365 a year, in addition to working full-time as a toolmaker. They were mostly a mixture of trade union meetings and City Council committees. But on arriving in Peckham, I found that, while the flow of engagements continued, their character changed completely.

The daytime meetings were officially-sanctioned ones, and were mostly run-of-the-mill matters of administration, such as negotiating details of the car scheme under which certain elected officers of the union were provided with a new car each year. On or two of the projects were of more interest; for example, the 'Million Membership Campaign', which I was given the responsibility of organising, in an effort to boost unionisation in the engineering industry.

The signing-up of the millionth AEU member coincided roughly with the opening of a new building extension at the Peckham Road officers, and the Executive gave a dinner to celebrate the joint achievements in

December 1961. Over three hundred guests sat down to dinner at the Piccadilly Hotel, including Hugh Gaitskell (leader of the Labour Party), Frank Cousins (General Secretary of the Transport & General Workers Union), George Woodcock (General Secretary of the TUC), a host of other assorted officers of unions, and Mr B Macarty of the Engineering Employers' Federation. Into this august assembly burst three angry AEU members who, according to press reports, "were led away to an ante-room before they could unfurl two placards" protesting at the waste of union funds and asking "Who's footing the bill?" The demonstrators, who went more or less unnoticed by the majority of guests, explained that they had no objection to the dinner in principle, but they felt that AEU members on the breadline would have benefited more from the largesse that was being distributed. They were particularly incensed at the presence of a member of the Engineering Employers' Federation. I, as usual the buffer between the Executive and an irate membership, left the dinner to talk to the protesters, who then left peacefully. I did not object to the holding of a celebration in the circumstances – although I too would have edited the guest list more carefully, given a chance.

Later in the Sixties, the Executive was again attempting to promote recruitment, this time with a film about the history and the present-day activities of the union, which they hoped would attract new members and also stimulate activity among existing members by explaining the meaning and function of trade unionism. I was made responsible for seeing the film through to completion, and I was closely involved with it at every stage. The film was made by ACT Films Ltd., the film unit of the Association of Cinematograph, Television and Allied Technicians (ACTT), which was the only film company in the world to be owned and run by a trade union.

'We are the Engineers' was released in 1970 to coincide with the union's 50th Anniversary celebrations, and it was still going out on loan to union branches more than a dozen years later. One of the spin-offs from the film was a record of the theme music, which was sold to members at 5/- a time. The words and music for 'We are the Engineers' were written by Ewan MacColl and Peggy Seeger, and told the history of the engineers in the lines of a marching song:

Two joined hands was our device when our banner first unfurled –
Hands that knew the feel of tools and helped to build the world.
Two hands became a million hands, and fashioned down the years
The machines that make the world go round,
The ships and planes and the diesel trains,
The weaving frames and the building cranes:
We are the Engineers!

We tamed the fire and harnessed metals, learned a thousand skills;
Our hands have made the tools men use in factories, mines and mills.
Ours the hands that throw the switch that puts the world in gear,
That make the ploughs that turn the soil
And the ships and planes and the diesel trains,
The weaving frames and the building cranes:
We are the Engineers!

Gaols and transportation hulks faced union pioneers.
Police and spies at every turn, a world of doubt and fear.
Our union sprang from poverty, from hunger, blood and tears,
But we fought the cruel laws and when
We lost, we rose to fight again,
For the right to work and live like men:
We are the Engineers!

We've stamped our feet in morning queues, known unemployment's toll,
Known hands go soft in idleness, the slow death on the dole.
The rusty lathe and the silent factory marked the hungry years,
And the grass growing clean on the shipyard floor,
And the endless beat of marching feet,
Men demanding the right to eat
And work as Engineers.

And we, the youngest engineers, now march to claim our rights,
For we have learned that nothing's ever won without a fight.
Every battle fought and won reveals a new frontier,
And a world to be won by those who build
The ships and planes and the diesel trains,
The weaving frames and the building cranes:
We are the Engineers!

On the 'flip side' of the AEU disc was a lively and witty song written
and performed by Peggy Seeger as a contribution to International Women's
Year: 'I'm Gonna be an Engineer'. I, who knew MacColl and Seeger

personally, had invited them to write the theme and incidental music for the film, and was delighted with the result.

Most of the activities in which I was involved during these years gave much less scope for creativity. I often found myself representing the union, the TUC or the Confederation of Shipbuilding and Engineering Unions at meetings of outside organisations.

Into all my meetings I brought the same conviction, that Socialism was the only answer. No palliative would work on the decaying shell of capitalism – only a complete change would solve the problems of the working people, in this country or any other. I took this attitude into all the bodies on which I was elected or appointed to serve, sometimes to the annoyance of employers and civil servants who served on those bodies, and whose object was to patch up immediate problems with conventional capitalist solutions.

I represented the Engineers in a variety of ways:

- I served for many years as the AEU representative on the National Executive of the United Kingdom of UNICEF (the United Nations Children's Fund) – not under any illusion that the Fund could bring lasting solutions to the starvation of millions of the world's children, but because the children could not wait for Socialism to ease their hunger.

- I represented the Confederation of Shipbuilding and Engineering Unions on the Health and Safety Executive's Joint Standing Committee on the use of Power Presses, protecting British standards of safety on these machines from being eroded by the less stringent regulations of the EEC countries, which now have the freedom to export their accident rates to Britain.

- I served as the AEU's representative on various City & Guilds sub-committees, responsible for arranging syllabuses for apprentices in various branches of the engineering industry, and arguing strongly against cutting back the length of an apprenticeship on grounds of cost to the employer, at the expense of a young person whose future career depends on present training.

- I was the TUC representative on the National Joint Council for Materials Handling, serving as Chairman of the Operator Training/

Accident Prevention Study Group, from which came the report 'Training for Safety'. On this body, I pressed persistently for the setting up of a Joint Committee for the research, development and display of materials handling equipment. This pressure helped to lead to the establishment of a government-sponsored research centre at Cranfield (although this still goes only a small way towards meeting the needs of industry).

• Work on this body was followed by appointments as union representative on a number of committees connected with the National Economic Development Council. As a member of the Electrical Engineering EDC, I worked on three Sector Working Parties, for Domestic Electrical, Heavy Electrical, and Electrical Industrial Equipment. On these committees, my voice was unorthodox and unwelcome. Sharing a table with the captains of industry such as Lord Nelson GEC, Ferranti, and Edwards of Rover, and government officialdom, I put an uncompromising case for the working class, and pricked the balloon of capitalist economics with unpopular regularity. But a lone voice on the Economic Development Council can do no more than cry in the wilderness. For this reason, as a member of the Mechanical Handling Sector Working Party, I agreed to become chairman of a small sub-committee which organised on an experimental basis a small step in the direction of industrial democracy. The object of the sub-committee was the experimental establishment of Company Action Groups, to involve trade unionists at factory-floor level in discussing and making decisions on pricing, exports, investment, development of new products, and other subjects which have in the past been the prerogative of management. Recognising that this was only a small step (and one which did not bear much fruit in terms of improved democracy!), I nevertheless saw it as a move towards bringing the Economic Development Councils and Sector Working Parties and other high-flown bodies down from the higher echelons of management and civil servants, and on to the shop floor where the job is done.

To those who would denounce such work as class-collaboration, I would say that these posts are going to be taken up by trade union leaders, come what may; better by far that they be taken by trade union leaders who are aware of the dangers, and can be trusted not to sell the workers they represent in return for personal honour or gain.

Not that the union ever let me get within striking distance of jobs where honour or gain might have ensued, or where I might have had any serious influence politically. The union posts I was given were mainly bland and innocuous, and the hope of actually achieving anything concrete for the members was remote.

Of course, in the evenings and at weekends, there were still meetings with AEU branches, districts and shop stewards' quarterlies. But for every one of these which was permitted by the Executive Council, several more were refused. However, the 'title' of Assistant General Secretary attracted requests and invitations from many organisations outside the union, and by accepting 'in a personal capacity' virtually any invitation that came my way, I built up a reputation for unstinting support of progressive causes.

It was at such meetings, at grass roots level, that I was happiest. I once referred to myself as "probably the least sectarian trade union officer". If a cause was worthwhile, I rarely stopped to ask "Who is organising this?" or "Can I afford to let my name be associated with it?" – I simply went ahead, regardless. Thus I found myself protesting against a police raid on the premises of the Workers' Revolutionary Party on the one hand, and supporting the 'Right to Work' campaign of the International Socialists on the other, although these groups did not see eye to eye with each other, and neither would fall over backwards to support the Labour Party. But I have always argued that the differences are less important than the similarities. If an organisation has got a good campaign going involving the united Left, join in with it – don't stand back on the grounds that you don't agree with that organisation 100 per cent on policy, therefore you can't allow yourself to agree on anything!

As a result of this attitude, I found myself speaking at such diverse meetings as the Adlerian Society of Great Britain's weekend school about 'Workers' Participation', and the National Organisation of Labour Students' fringe meeting at the NUS Conference; courses for lieutenants at the Royal Naval College, Greenwich, and the Chile Solidarity Campaign mass rally;

the Committee for Democratic Rights in the USA, and the Committee in Defence of Soviet Political Prisoners. As long as the inviting body did not attempt to dictate what I should say, I would go virtually anywhere that I thought might benefit from a bit of Socialist propaganda.

It would be impossible to give any comprehensive idea of the thousands of meetings, conferences, rallies, committees, enquiries and so on which I crammed into my life while at Peckham Road. A few examples, however, will serve to give a flavour of the immense variety of jobs I did and causes I supported in those years, and have continued to support since.

In the field of Human Rights alone, the following is a random selection of the campaigns and issues with which I was involved:

1959   Committee of African Organisations – sponsor of African Freedom Day.

1960   Campaign for the Release of Untried Prisoners in Belfast – signatory, with Bertrand Russell, Fenner Brockway and others, of a telegram to Lord Brookeborough, Prime Minister of Northern Ireland.

1962   Campaign for the Release of Morton Sobell – Sobell was sentenced in the United States to a sentence of 30 years, on the evidence of one self-confessed perjurer. He served part of his sentence in Alcatraz.

1962   Committee for Democratic Rights in the USA – spoke at a London meeting where I was billed as "the voice of Progressive Britain", against "the new McCarthyism".

1965   International Conference on General Amnesty for Iraqi Political Prisoners – after which I received a letter from Bertrand Russell, thanking me personally for my contribution.

1968   Committee for Peace in Nigeria – following a request for support by Fenner Brockway.

1968   Dubcek Appeal – to defend the right of Alexander Dubcek to hold his own political views (right or wrong!), free from persecution and harassment.

1970   Ruskin Kitson Committee – speech at Trafalgar Square Rally to demand the release of Dave Kitson, sentenced to 20 years' imprisonment in South Africa for his activities against apartheid.

1973 Spanish Young Socialists' Defence Campaign – amnesty for political prisoners.

1974 Chile Solidarity Campaign – mass rally.

1976 Angola Solidarity Committee – invitation to take part in an International Commission of Enquiry into mercenaries in Angola; permission to accept the invitation refused by AEU Executive Council.

1976 Campaign for the Restoration of Trade Union Rights in Iran – sponsor.

1976 International Tribunal on Britain's Presence in Ireland – sponsor.

1977 Agee-Hosenball Defence Committee – sponsor.

1977 Committee to Defend Czechoslovak Socialists – sponsor.

1977 Islington 18 Defence Committee Inquiry – jurist. The Islington 18 were a group of young black people, picked up by the police on charges of conspiracy or 'sus', with apparently little or no concrete evidence against them. The 'public inquiry' was set up to investigate police attitudes to black youth.

1977 Campaign in Defence of Soviet Political Prisoners.

1978 Campaign against a Criminal Trespass Law – a proposed law aimed at preventing peaceful picketing and occupation of premises.

1978 Committee against Repression in Iran.

1980 Don't Let the Irish Prisoners Die Campaign.

1981 Committee for the Defence of Democratic Rights in Turkey – chairman.

Of course, this list of causes is not exhaustive, even within the field of human rights. And each cause generally involved a series of meetings and committees spread over a period of months.

One of my first campaigns after coming to London was the newly-formed Campaign for Nuclear Disarmament. I have already made my feelings about nuclear armaments plain while in Coventry, and in the years that followed my arrival in London, I continued to campaign vigorously for unilateral nuclear disarmament in Britain, speaking at scores of CND meetings, and doing all I could to promote this policy within my own union and also in the Labour Party.

There were the inevitable clashes with the AEU Executive, of course, as for example over a Peace Conference called by the Ipswich & District Trades Council. The press began to call this the 'on-off-on conference'. The two speakers were to be Konni Zilliacus MP and me, both of whom were perpetually under criticism from right-wing circles. The choice of speakers was (according to the conference secretary in Ipswich) fiercely attacked by the TUC, who banned the conference, ostensibly on the grounds of a technicality in organisation. So while one group of Ipswich trade unionists was sending out letters and telegrams to delegates to say that it had been called off, another group was burning the midnight oil on another set of letters and telegrams to say that it was on. Zilliacus and I both declared our intention of speaking at the conference, banned or not, and we did. The conference was a success, despite attempts to stop it which were branded as 'sabotage' in certain quarters in Ipswich. But after the conference came a letter from Vincent Tewson, TUC General Secretary, to the AEU Executive, complaining about my part in the event, and there was then the usual exchange of acrimonious correspondence between me and the Executive about 'personal capacity' speaking.

The CND had considerable support among the public at large: meetings with titles such as 'How far can you run in four minutes?' (a reference to the four-minute warning of a nuclear attack) caught the imagination and fanned the flame of fear throughout the country. I took part in the CND's Nuclear Disarmament Week in 1959 when, as part of a team of speakers (including Michael Foot, Stephen Swingler, Canon Collins and Professor Rotblat), I spoke in Tonbridge on 13th September, Romford, Ilford and Dagenham on 14th, Hornsey, Stoke Newington and Wood Green on 15th, Kennington, Acton and Willesden on 16th, Wandsworth, Hammersmith and Staines on 17th, Dulwich, Greenwich and Dartford on 18th, Bristol on 19th, and finally at a rally in Trafalgar Square with Bertrand Russell on 20th September.

Also in 1959 I made a speech at l'Institut International de la Paix (the International Peace Institute) in Vienna, calling for concerted action by labour and trade union movements internationally to get governments elected which would be committed to unilateralist policies. At the commencement of my speech I said:

May I, on behalf of the CND, thank the members of the International Institute for Peace for this opportunity to describe the aims and activities of our organisation. This is of special importance because, whilst we demand that our Government unilaterally discontinue the Testing, Manufacturing or Storing of Nuclear weapons, we are also most anxious that the citizens of other countries too make similar demands upon their own Governments in their own countries.

We realise that Peace, like prosperity, is indivisible and that it must be internationally pursued by all people.

It was against this background that on the 16th January 1958, the Campaign for Nuclear Disarmament was born.

This put my neck on the block in no uncertain terms, as neither my own union nor the Labour Party was at that time in favour of nuclear disarmament, although there were strong lobbies in both organisations to put the pressure on for unilateralist decisions to be taken in their conferences.

In 1960, the AEU National Committee – the policy-making body of the union – gave its support to nuclear unilateralism, as a result of grass roots pressure, and the AEU block vote then assisted in getting a unilateralist resolution carried at the 1960 Labour Party conference. The CND was pleased with this progress, but could not afford to sit back on its laurels. The same year, I received a personal letter from Bertrand Russell, in which he talked of "the rapidity with which we are moving towards nuclear calamity", and the consequent necessity for a programme of civil disobedience to make the disarmament campaign effective. Russell asked for my support in this project, inviting me to join the 'Committee of 100' which he was forming.

This put me in a quandary. While being totally in sympathy with the aims of the proposed Committee of 100, my personal difficulties with the EC at Peckham Road were at such a pitch that I felt obliged to refuse Russell's invitation. My decision proved to have been the right one, for within a very few weeks of the AEU delegation casting its vote in favour of unilateralism at the Labour Party conference, there was a concerted effort to reverse AEU National Committee policy. (The interesting details of exactly how this was done can be found in Lewis Minkin's book 'The Labour Party Conference', page 190). This effort was successful, and led to the union helping to change Labour Party policy the next year, which would have left me, had I been on the Committee of 100, out on a limb. Although that would have been nothing new!

Of course I continued actively to support the CND, and sponsored the Direct Action Committee against Nuclear War. I had joined all the Aldermaston marches from the first one in 1958, and spoke from the plinth in Trafalgar Square at the conclusion of the march on a number of occasions.

The CND is still in existence, and still opposes the manufacture, stockpiling, testing, use and threatened use of nuclear, chemical and biological weapons. The public for a number of years were lulled into a false sense of security by the non-arrival of a nuclear holocaust, and the man-in-the-street became much more concerned about nuclear accidents than about nuclear war – although the threat of such a war is not lessened by public refusal to contemplate it. It seemed that we had learned to live with the bomb, and the CND's cutting edge became blunted. The new threats of the siting of Cruise missiles in Britain, coupled with the remarks of US President Reagan that a limited nuclear war could be confined to Europe without affecting the USA, led to a 1981 revival of CND activity, culminating in a massive demonstration against nuclear weapons involving nearly a quarter of a million people in London. This was timed to coincide with similar events in Germany, France, Italy and other European countries, to make an impressive "weekend of action" in September 1981.

During the years at Peckham Road, I was involved in scores of meetings about the Vietnam war, and my interest in that country has extended even into the nineties, as I ultimately became Chairman of the Britain-Vietnam Association.

There were countless meetings on the Common Market, which I opposed vigorously; I stressed the criminal stupidity of food mountains combined with high food prices, and the imbecility of milking a cow, only to turn the unwanted milk into cattle-feed to make more unwanted milk: "Why not just connect a tube from the cow's udder into its mouth?" I asked. But with the major parties united at parliamentary level in favour of the EEC, the anti-market lobby did not stand a chance.

There were, and still are, innumerable marches and demonstrations about all manner of domestic issues, from unemployment and wages to

175

trade union legislation and industrial democracy. One such issue which came to the fore in the seventies and is still with us, under governments of various political complexions, was the axing of the Health Service. I responded to this by becoming chairman of the Co-ordinating Committee against Health Service Cuts, bitterly denouncing vast increases in arms expenditure and – under the Thatcher administration in 1979 – huge tax-giveaways to the 'super-earners', which were carried out at the expense of the health of ordinary people.

Unfortunately, when protesting against cuts and prescription charges, I and my fellow protesters had to face the unpalatable truth that, after establishing a free Health Service in 1948, successive Labour administrations had been responsible for cutting health expenditure and imposing charges, and the actions of the Tories were only making a more savage job of what Labour had already started.

But the campaign of the seventies which provoked the most grass roots activity (and which put me in the unusual position of being on the same side of the fence as the AEU Executive, and of speaking at meetings all over the country without their interference) was the campaign against the Industrial Relations Bill. Again, Labour had started the ball rolling with Barbara Castle's 'In Place of Strife'; the Tories were simply taking it one step further. In February 1971, 50,000 workers demonstrated their opposition to this measure by marching through London; the following week, 2,000,000 engineers went on an official one-day strike against the Bill, and a couple of weeks later, the engineering unions called out 3,000,000.

But the Tory Government continued in its intransigence. The cry of "Kill the Bill!" which had resounded in demonstrations of millions of workers the length and breadth of Britain died out as the Bill became law. The new Industrial Relations Act's message to workers was: "Shut up and keep working!" The Labour Party conference of 1971 agreed without dissent that a Labour government should repeal the Act at the first opportunity.

The Act provided for registration of unions and vetting of trade union rules, and there were heavy financial penalties for non-registering unions. It also provided for cooling-off periods before strikes could take place, and compulsory ballots before strike action. The futility of such measures quickly became evident when the National Industrial Relations Court ordered a compulsory ballot in a railway dispute: 95 per cent of members voted, and 85 per cent of those voted in favour of strike action. That was the last that was heard of cooling-off periods and compulsory balloting until the 1980s Thatcher government, when compulsory ballots before strike action were made law.

The registration of unions was a more difficult nut to crack. All but twenty unions refused to remain on the Tory register and opted for de-registration, which laid them open to tax problems and heavy fines. The AEU took a decision that it would not only de-register, it would also refuse to recognise the National Industrial Relations Court. So when a man by the name of Goad claimed to have been improperly expelled from the union, the AEU failed to appear at NIRC to defend itself.

It did, however, send a circular to branches explaining the reason for Goad's predicament: he had a record of three expulsions already for heavy arrears in union dues, and an alleged history of blacklegging. He had then submitted a fourth proposition form for re-admittance to the union, which came with the cheerful threat that a refusal would be taken straight to NIRC.

When the AEU did not turn up to defend itself in the Goad case, NIRC seized £55,000 from union funds as a penalty. This was followed by further penalties of £100,000 and £75,000. Over half a million engineers stopped work in protest; 187 Labour MPs called for the resignation of Sir John Donaldson, President of the National Industrial Relations Court. But further seizure of funds followed, and the EC of the AEU called a strike which virtually closed down the engineering industry, until a donation (from "an unknown source", suspected to be a combine of Tory businessmen) paid the AEU's fines, and got the government off that particular hook.

By this time, with the whole of Britain reduced to a three-day working week as a result of the disastrous Tory Government led by Edward Heath, the electorate thankfully took the opportunity to bring back a Labour administration, and one of its first deeds was to scrap the Industrial Relations Act.

From the inception of the legislation in 1971 to the fall of the Heath Government in early 1974, I was involved in scores of meetings, demonstrations and marches, all aimed against the intervention of law in industrial relations. There was a certain amount of public disquiet (fomented by the media) throughout this period about the morality of using industrial action to oppose law. Even some members of the Labour Left came out against the use of "strikes for political ends". I, however, was never in any doubt about my own stance.

Checking back over a hundred years and more, I saw that, without industrial action, the law would have been used time and again to shackle workers. The very existence of the trade union movement is the result of workers combining 'illegally' to fight for their rights. Industrial action is the only way open to the mass of people to voice their dissatisfaction, and is therefore the correct course of action to take against a law which will act against the interests of the working people. Moreover, I do not draw a dividing line between industrial and political action: in my opinion, **every** strike is political, whether it is for a better canteen, higher wages, or the repeal of the Industrial Relations Act, because every strike is a means of heightening the political awareness of workers to the point where they can see that every aspect of their lives is affected by political issues.

Amid all the uproar caused by the Industrial Relations Act, other activities and campaigns were proceeding as usual. One of the areas which was always demanding attention was education. Not only were there campaigns against the cuts in the education budget; there was also a constant stream of invitations from educational establishments, from "both sides of the desk", since both teachers and students requested my services. I was often invited to speak to successive generations of schoolchildren and students, because the first visit generally proved provocative and successful. I was always pleased to speak to schoolchildren, especially, believing that not nearly enough is done in schools to alert children to the importance of politics in their lives, or even to teach them the very elementary principles of local and national government.

I spoke to children at the Isaac Newton School in West London on 'Why you should join a trade union'; I spoke to William Penn schoolchildren in South London on 'Social democracy in the trade union movement'; I addressed Manchester Polytechnic Students' Union on 'The Role of Troops in Northern Ireland' (or rather, the case in favour of bringing them out!); the University of Warwick Labour Club secretary wrote to thank me for my talk on democracy, adding that they had already put into effect one of my suggestions by "establishing a committee to investigate methods of democratising the university structures"; I spoke at Durham University with Len Murray, the General Secretary of the TUC, against the motion 'That this House believes that the power of the trade unions stifles democratic government'; I spoke to the Workers' Educational Association and the National Council of Labour Colleges; I addressed the Oxford University Labour Club and the Oxford Union on several occasions; and – biggest irony of all – as a Labour Party member banned for thirty years from contesting parliamentary elections, I was invited by the Labour Party Political Education Officer to address a residential course at Ruskin College on the theme of 'Introducing the Labour Party'.

Each year, a host of new committees and organisations springs up. Some of them are the work of a few weeks, some last a few months before their job is done. Where the need persists, the organisation persists with it, growing and developing sometimes over a period of years.

Such was the Movement for Colonial Freedom. As an individual member and then as the AEU representative on the Central Council, I saw the MCF develop from its original role in defence of freedom movements within the British Colonies, through the slow crumbling of the colonies and the establishment of independent states, to the support for national independence movements the world over. The MCF grew into 'Liberation' – a more suitable name for its new role, following the dwindling of the British Empire.

My interest in international affairs is all-embracing. Many trade union officers wear blinkers when it comes to their brothers and sisters overseas; I have always been an internationalist in the best sense of the word – fighting for the establishment of socialism throughout the world, not only within the confines of my own country. Typical of these aspirations is the membership of a little-known but valuable organisation called the British

179

Trade Union/SACTU Liaison Group – SACTU being the South African Congress of Trade Unions. The work of the group is an attempt to win for black trade unionists in South Africa the same rights from their British employers as are enjoyed by trade unionists in this country, seeking through the trade union movement in this country to improve the lot of black South African workers.

One of my deepest overseas interests has been China. From the time when I wrote to the press in 1936 protesting about the murder of Chinese Socialists by Chiang Kai-Shek, I have followed the development of political life in China with close attention. In 1965, I assisted in founding the Society for Anglo-Chinese Understanding, and was for many years on its Council of Management, as well as being one of the original trustees of its educational wing, The Anglo-Chinese Educational Institute. As in all spheres of life, I did not look on China with an uncritical eye, but what I saw was more often than not progress towards a new kind of society which I could admire. This judgement was based not only on hearsay, but on personal observation, for in 1965 I had the opportunity to visit China for a month, with other SACU members, as a guest of the Chinese International Friendship Association.

There were formal aspects to the visit – a state banquet with Mao Tse-tung, Chou En-lai and Lin Piao, for example, although there were so many others present that it was not exactly an intimate occasion. But much of the time the party travelled extensively and freely into schools and factories, and even – at my request – into the prison in Peking. The SACU party was small, the most eminent among them being Robert Bolt (playwright), Professor Hugh Trevor-Roper (Lord Dacre) and Mary Adams (TV director). This was the first such visit to China by Britons in many years, and it marked the beginning of a new era in Anglo-Chinese relations. Hugh Trevor-Roper repaid the hospitality of the Chinese by contributing on his return to England a two-page article to the 'Sunday Times', headlined "The Sick Mind of China". I myself had seen, not a sick mind, but the healthy bodies of millions who had formerly been starving, and the steady development of industries and services in a politically-conscious community which gave much hope for the future.

At about the same time as the birth of SACU in 1965, I was also assisting into the world another venture, the First Trade Union Country Club. The premises of the Club were at Plaw Hatch Hall, near East Grinstead in Sussex, a modest 'stately home' in 25 acres of ground, belonging to Joe Winter. Winter's idea was to hand over the premises by degrees to a co-operative venture composed of trade unions and other interested organisations, who would buy shares in the property and eventually take it over. In the meantime, the Club was to be run by Winter, in conjunction with a members' organisation, of which I was chairman. It was a fine plan: the hall and outbuildings would house seminars, schools and courses for trade unionists; there would be a conference hall seating 300, and accommodation for up to 300 on the premises. There would be facilities for golf, tennis, swimming and riding, and trade union members could bring their families for holidays at remarkably low prices.

The same idea flourishes in other European countries, notably in France. But in England, there was a long silence from the trade unions which were asked to contribute to Plaw Hatch on behalf of their members. The Transport & General Workers' Union has its own club, and so have one or two other unions. Perhaps there is not yet a sufficiently advanced feeling of brotherhood among them to join in a single venture of this kind. Whatever the reasons, Plaw Hatch now caters for the wider labour movement, offering a venue for conferences and courses, but most of its potential has never been realised – and the trade union movement is the loser.

There are many trade unionists who have too much leisure, but not enough resources to spend that leisure in the stately home atmosphere of Plaw Hatch. They are the people who have leisure forced upon them: the unemployed. When the Right to Work Campaign was launched by the International Socialists (now the Socialist Workers' Party), I gave it my full support. In the absence of a concerted campaign in the Labour Party and the TUC, it was a straw to clutch at for the unemployed, and the Campaign organised some effective demonstrations; lobbying the TUC and party conferences, for example, and marching to London for a mass meeting of thousands of young trade unionists in the Albert Hall, where I was one of the speakers. The march was marred, however, by a clash between police and marchers in Hendon, as the marchers were approaching London after three weeks and three hundred miles of peaceful demonstration. In the clash, thirty-five marchers and nine other trade unionists were arrested. The marchers claimed that the police had provoked a confrontation, and photographs of the event published at the time certainly indicate that rather more force than necessary was used to 'contain' eighty marchers who had walked peacefully for three hundred miles. I was invited to be treasurer of a fund which was set up in defence of the arrested marchers, to pay their legal costs, and I received one or two messages from prominent people who ought to have known better, asking why I associated my 'respected name' with those International Socialist ruffians. The answer was that they were workers, and they were suffering not only unemployment but the added burden of prosecution for something they claimed not to have done. One of those arrested was the energetic and courageous fighter on behalf of the unemployed, John Deason, who seemed to be a prime target for arrest, and about as likely to get a job in engineering as I myself was forty years ago!

While the Right to Work campaigners lobby the outside of the Labour Party Conference, largely ignored by the delegates within, those same Labour Party delegates are busy inside the building taking decision which are very likely to be ignored in their turn by Labour Governments.

One such decision was Conference's instruction to the Labour Party National Executive to institute an investigation into expenditure on armaments. Conference was concerned that arms expenditure seemed to be always on the increase while cuts were being made in vital health, education and other services. They instructed the NEC to set up a study group on defence expenditure, the arms trade and alternative employment, the most important factor being the alternative employment of the armaments workers whose jobs would disappear in the projected cut of millions of pounds in the arms budget. I was invited by the Labour Party NEC to take part in this study group, under the chairmanship of Ian Mikardo. The group met over a period of three years, and its only tangible results were a report to the NEC, and Ian Mikardo's book, 'Sense in Defence'. The Labour Government chose not to act on the Report. And

until Party Conference decisions are made binding on Labour Governments, as I have been advocating along with others in the Campaign for
Labour Party Democracy, much good work will be instituted by rank-and-
file members at Conference, only to be politely ignored when the Party
gets into office.

In fact, Party Conference has enough good material on hand to keep a
Labour Government supplied with Socialist legislation for years to come.
But seeing that this was not enough to tempt a Labour Government into
action, I went into action on my own, sending to Harold Wilson MP, prior
to the 1964 General Election, a wide-ranging Industrial Charter. I pointed
out to Wilson, then leader of the Parliamentary Labour Party, that if he
became Prime Minister in a Labour Government, he would become
Britain's biggest employer, and therefore he and the Labour Party should
state quite clearly what they, as employers, were prepared to do for their
employees.

I set out some of the possibilities in my 'Industrial Charter for Labour',
including:

1 The Government setting a good example to other employers on wages,
   especially for the low-paid and for women. No wage-freeze.
2 A 40-hour week for all, with progress towards 35 hours.
3 Training for young people, to ensure that there are no dead-end kids in
   dead-end jobs.
4 Government employees to have a minimum of three weeks holiday
   with pay.
5 Adequate pensions and sick-pay.
6 A Labour Government to be a model for private industry through
   workers' participation in the control of all local and central government
   industries and services.

Wilson received the Charter coldly, saying that he felt that one of its
weaknesses was that it was 'limited' to the public sector. I felt that if such a
charter were operated 'only' by the public sector, there would be room for
rejoicing – and a substantially better chance of reducing the private sector
by increased public ownership with the full co-operation and control of the
employees.

The Charter was widely publicised in the press. It was plainly my own initiative. Of course, even though the Charter made no proposals outside the union's own policy, the AEU Executive Council did not take it lying down, and they lost no time in saying so: not at a private meeting, but at one which would be sure to find a place in the newspapers. Thus the 'Daily Express' announced, under the modest headline "AEU Rebel on Carpet":

> Mr E Roberts, Left-wing rebel of the AEU, has been 'carpeted' by union president, Sir William Carron, over the personal plan for an industrial charter which he sent to the Socialist Party chiefs last week.

> Sir William picked a meeting between the union executive and the AEU's 10 sponsored MPs to rap Mr Roberts for announcing the scheme without reference to the union.

What, one might well ask, is 'rebellious' about a Socialist Charter from a member of the Labour Party, which does not overstep the mark of AEU or Labour Party policy in any way? And why should an AEU member be obliged to have his ideas vetted by his union's Executive Council before making them public?

Not long afterwards, in 1968, I was joining my voice to those of other like-minded trade unionists in the Institute for Workers' Control. The leading organisers in this movement were the prolific writers on trade union and industrial affair, Ken Coates and Tony Topham, with Ken Fleet as secretary.

The IWC was funded by the Bertrand Russell Peace Foundation, with which it shared a home in Nottingham. It produced a mass of literature in the form of pamphlets and bulletins (my own contribution to the series was 'The Fight Against Unemployment', written in 1972). It held national and regional conferences, which grew bigger each year. It discussed "work-ins, sit-ins, demonstrations, workers' control of hiring and firing, work-sharing, overtime bans, lobbies, solidarity actions.... a full employment policy for the labour movement." It held conferences for the industries individually (e.g. the motor industry) and for particular problems (e.g. unemployment). It discussed anything and everything to promote the control of workers of their own lives in all spheres, especially political and industrial.

The Institute flourished still in 1990. It has had a well-known – some would say notorious – band of supporters behind it, including Joan

Maynard (former MP), Audrey Wise MP, Tony Benn MP, Bill Jones and Walter Kendall. Its main driving force is Ken Coates and Ken Fleet. Its big disadvantage has been that, while able to draw crowds to its seminars and conferences, it has had less appeal as regards individual and affiliated membership. The aim of the Institute is to attract its membership from as wide a political spectrum as possible. It does not attempt to draw people away from their own parties and organisations, because it does not function as a party, but as a forum, as the nature of its conferences has consistently shown.

I have been a contributor to IWC conferences since the Institute's foundation. I have therefore not escaped the criticism which has been heaped on the heads of the Institute and all associated with it by its detractors – for example, the persistent attacks by the 'Workers' Press', an ultra-left newspaper which denounces IWC as "reformist and revisionist", a front organisation for worker-directors. I view the organisation in a different way: whereas 'Workers' Press' envisages a workers' party (its own, of course) leading the workers to revolution, I see a long haul ahead before the workers will even contemplate such a revolution, and I look on organisations such as IWC as a force drawing workers towards a Socialist society through political education, rather than fobbing them off with something second-rate.

One of the pre-requisites of a Socialist society is the control by workers of their own political parties and working-class organisations. I have explained the theory behind this full in my book 'Workers' Control', and have been fully involved in the practice of my theories, both in my union and in the Labour Party, throughout my political life.

With Clause 4 of the Labour Party Constitution in mind (about common ownership of the means of production, distribution and exchange), and with a leadership ever sliding Rightwards, leading left-wing members of the Party came together in 1958 to try to halt the move away from Socialist ideals and away from the Constitution. They formed a group called Victory for Socialism, which was born of disillusionment. Its object was to work within the Party, not outside it – not against the Party but for it, and for its rapidly disappearing principles. But it was lambasted in the

Party, in he trade unions, and especially in the Tory press, as disruptive and subversive. The Tory press had no reason to protect the Labour Party. Had they really believed that VFS meant destruction to Labour, they would no doubt have encouraged it wholeheartedly. The truth was that it meant new life and new democracy in the Party, and for that reason the Right-wing and the press came together in an unholy alliance to defeat it.

The VFS manifesto spelt out clearly the direction for Labour: renunciation of nuclear weapons, public ownership (with industrial democracy), free social services ("the cost of improved social services is not a burden on the community; it is the contribution society makes as an insurance to safeguard the life of the people"), and the sanctity of Party Conference decisions. It did not call for the election of Party Leader, but pointed out that Labour MPs have "the obligation of ensuring that the leader is one who is willing to abide by Conference decisions on policy". In that respect, VFS showed a touching faith in human nature.

The biggest outcry against Victory for Socialism came when, in 1960, it called for the resignation of Hugh Gaitskell, the Party Leader, who, it was claimed, was "a source of weakness, confusion and disunity". This did not endear the leading lights in VFS – Sydney Silverman (chairman), Jo Richardson (secretary) and the two vice-chairmen, Ian Mikardo and myself – to the leadership of their Party, even though VFS boldly spelt out its Labour-based objects: one of its clauses repeated word for word Clause 4 of the Party Constitution, and another called for VFS "to make the greatest possible contribution to the Labour Party".

The newspaper 'Socialist Review' was not impressed with the VFS record despite, as it said, "the importance of having Ernest, whose contribution is not to be sneezed at". There was pressure on all sides to call it a day – particularly from the Right-wing who, in the warm-up period before a possible election, saw the possibility of persuading VFS to wind up, so that the Party could present a 'unified front' to the electorate.

That was precisely what happened. In a deal with the Right-wing organisation 'Campaign for Democratic Socialism', VFS agreed that both groups should cease operations. Michael Foot and Stephen Swingler, among others, supported the move; I stood out against it. My argument was that the Campaign for Democratic Socialism had nothing to lose by winding up. Its Right-wing supporters already controlled the Party machine, and by getting rid of VFS they got rid of a thorn in their flesh. VFS, on the other hand, had everything to lose and nothing to gain by the agreement. I was outvoted, and the VFS group disbanded.

It was not long before the loss of the organisation began to be felt. There had been a rather half-hearted attempt through an 'Appeal for Unity' to get Party leaders to accept conference decisions as a basis for Party policy, but this met with no success at all: plenty of support from the Left, and complete indifference from the Right.

The Labour Government which was elected in 1964 worked on a shoestring of votes, tailoring its policy to suit its tiny majority. Re-elected in 1966 with a three-figure majority, the Wilson Government proceeded to jump with both feet into the job of making capitalism work better. Old Tory policies, dusted and polished were brought out to serve a Labour administration, and Labour's Left – both in parliament and out of it – were incensed at this misuse of their Party. For Government backbenchers life was made especially difficult, as they were reduced to lobby-fodder, expected to march through the right lobby (and it was 'right' in both senses of the word) when it came to a vote, and their position recalled the words of WS Gilbert in 'Iolanthe':

> When in that House MPs divide
> If they've got a brain and cerebellum too,
> They've got to leave that brain outside
> And vote just as their leaders tell 'em to.

Harold Wilson reinforced this when he reminded 'his' backbenchers that they could have their licences revoked like dogs if they stepped out of line.

The period 1966–1970 was a time of despondency throughout the country, as the electorate saw a Government which it had elected with something approaching euphoria in 1966 gradually sliding down a miserable slope towards wage-freeze and depression. For Labour Party members who really believed in Clause 4 of the constitution, this period was one of misery and frustration.

It was this disillusionment which led to the birth in 1968 of Socialist

Charter, successor to Victory for Socialism, and involving many of the same people. Like VFS, it was born of frustration; like VFS, it pledged itself to work in the Party, for Party democracy and unity; like VFS, it was vilified by Tory press and Labour right-wing alike.

I was invited by Ian Mikardo to join the first published group of sixty-six Chartists, who included such prominent Party members as Frank Allaun, Audrey Wise, Jack Jones and Lawrence Daly. The published Charter made it clear that the Chartists were not setting up an alternative to the established Party, but a front within that Party, whose central principle was the accountability of the Government to the electorate.

The original Chartists in the nineteenth century had called for "one man, one vote". The new Chartists maintained that a vote every five years is not enough; it must be backed up by a fully accountable government. The eight-point Charter included economic independence for Britain, Socialist planning, public ownership, redistribution of wealth, and full accountability with "growing democratic control by workers and employees over the decisions which determine their working lives."

The Chartists failed to make much impression on the Wilson Government, which fell in the ignominy which its policies deserved in 1970. These policies were, nevertheless, markedly better than the ones advocated by Edward Heath, whose Government came to an equally ignominious end in 1974. But in those years of Conservative mis-government, the Chartists failed to press their cause within the Labour Party, turning their attention away from putting their own house in order in favour of fighting a battle against Heath.

The weakness of Victory for Socialism, which was repeated in the Socialist Charter, was its failure to see that it is useless to attempt to promote the policies of Socialism in a Party in which the leadership does not behave in a Socialist manner, and does not hold itself accountable to the membership for its actions.

The only way of dealing with the problem is at the root, by altering the Constitution of the Party in such a way that the leadership risks being replaced if it fails to follow Party policy, and Party policy is determined democratically by Annual Conference. This is the reason why the

Campaign for Labour Party Democracy, which took these factors into account, stood a much better chance of succeeding in its aims than VFS or the Socialist Charter.

Like them, it grew out of a disillusioned membership. Like them, it supported the true aims of the Labour Party, as exemplified in the Constitution. And like them it has been pilloried and maligned by those who stand to gain by its demise – on the one hand, the 'free' press, whose object is to weaken the Labour Party by encouraging its present trend towards the Right, and on the other hand, those on the Right within the Party, who have everything to lose if the CLPD succeeds in all of its aims.

The principles of the Campaign for Labour Party Democracy are grounded in one belief: that the growing tendency to concentrate decision-making inside a small group of people at 'the top' must be reversed. Democracy means carrying out the will of the majority, and the will of the Labour Party majority is expressed at Party Conference.

The tendency to concentrate decision-making into 'top-level management' in the Party has been slow but marked. The Labour Party was established as a democratic body whose allegiance was to its members, and whose policy grew out of the members' decisions at Conference. This was acceptable to everybody in the Party until Labour MPs began to be elected in large numbers to the House of Commons, at which point Conference became an embarrassment. After all, Socialist policies need a Socialist government to carry them out, but the newly-arrived Labour members were rather nervous of rocking their parliamentary boat by pressing for the implementation of the progressive policies which Conference was advocating. Thus the concept of the Parliamentary Labour Party (PLP), as distinct from the Party at large, was brought into existence, and this was promoted as a body which was better able to take decisions than the mass Party outside Parliament – on the grounds that the Parliamentary Party was closer to the hub of government, and would therefore know what was the best and 'most statesmanlike' course of action to take.

So the PLP was set up as a higher authority than Conference, and those Conference decisions which the PLP did not like were conveniently swept under the carpet. However, in spite of the election of large numbers of political opportunists to the PLP, there were also some Socialists who made their way into Parliament, and were determined not to let go of their Socialist principles. Gradually, the authority of the PLP went into decline, and the National Executive Committee was the new oracle. The NEC was in a strong position. It could influence Conference, often decisively, by exercising its right to command a very high proportion of Conference time with its own speakers; it had strong pulls with the trade union elites, and could pull off deals with them in order to quash progressive motions; and if all else failed, it could always ignore unfavourable decisions, as the PLP had done before it.

The NEC was elected by Conference. It was by and large a right-wing body because, in spite of what the press would have us believe to the contrary, Conference itself was also largely right-wing. (Indeed, it was a curious paradox in Labour Party Conferences that the delegates consistently voted for mainly left-wing policies, and then proceeded to vote for mainly right-wing representatives who would not carry those policies out.) But disillusionment slowly seeped through to the Party membership and there was a gradual shift of opinion among both constituencies and trade unions, leading to a miniature revolt against the established order, as the Labour Party moved so close to the Conservative Party that the electorate began to talk of 'Tweedledum and Tweedledee'. Over a period of years, the Left began to gain seats on the NEC, and a split developed between the Leadership (appointed) and the NEC (elected).

Decision-making had first passed from the Party at large to the Parliamentary Party – from many thousands to a few hundred. It had then passed from the Parliamentary Party to the NEC – from a few hundreds to fewer than thirty. Now, not even the NEC's decisions are sacrosanct; they must be vetted and approved by the Leadership (that is, the Leader of the PLP and a small number of close advisers). The NEC is now attacked by the press as a divisive element, whereas in more right-wing days it was hailed as the fount of all wisdom!

The Campaign for Labour Party Democracy does not view these developments as a disease, but as symptoms of a disease, the disease being the readiness to accept that 'they' know better than 'the likes of us'. So the

CLPD designed its policies to put power back where it belongs – with ordinary members, through Conference. The four pillars of CLPD policy were:

- the automatic re-selection of MPs;
- accountability of elected representatives to their electorate;
- the election of Party Leader by Conference;
- sanctity of Conference resolutions.

'Automatic re-selection of MPs' is perhaps an ambiguous phrase. What it amounts to is that MPs should **not** be automatically re-selected – that is, that an MP should not automatically continue to be the candidate in his constituency in election after election, simply because he is the sitting tenant.

I have spelt out my reservations on the selection of new parliamentary candidates in my book 'Workers' Control' (see pp 233–243). Human nature being what it is, constituencies will no doubt go on making mistakes in their choice of a candidate, and finding that the one they selected with such high hopes falls short of their expectations. This may happen within the lifetime of a parliament; it may happen after fifteen or twenty years.

Until 1979, when a constituency was dissatisfied with its sitting Member, the Party provided a procedure for 'retiring' that Member at the end of a session ('Workers' Control' p.243). The trouble with this procedure was that it was cumbersome enough to be little used by constituencies, and it was hedged about with safeguards to protect the MP's job. The result was that the procedure was rarely invoked, and was even more rarely successful, even though many constituencies were visibly and volubly dissatisfied with their MPs.

The CLPD policy was to have a system of re-selection before each election, in which the sitting 'tenant' should stand against other nominees and prove that he/she still has the confidence of the constituency party. The advantage of such a procedure is that the CLP can exercise judgement on the job which its MP is doing, and he/she must therefore always work with the constituency in mind. The disadvantages put up by the right-wing are that the MP must have 'job security', and that an MP represents the electorate, not only the Constituency Labour Party. CLPD supporters dismiss the 'job security' argument by saying that only safe seats have job security anyway and, in any case, why should an MP have security of tenure to do a job badly? The MP certainly represents the electorate, not the CLP: but only a very tiny proportion of the electorate vote for a candidate because of personal reasons, the bulk voting for the party the candidate represents. Therefore, when an MP ceases to act in accord with Party principles, the Party should be able to replace him/her with somebody who will do so, in order to protect the electorate, who elect a party representative, not an individual.

The automatic re-selection procedure was adopted at the 1979 Conference and would have ensured in part the accountability of elected representatives, which is the second pillar of CLPD policy. The right-wing of the Party maintains that elected representatives must be free to act in accordance with the wishes of the electorate, and not be 'tied down' by the dictates of the local Party. Since elected representatives cannot possibly 'know' the inclinations of the whole electorate, they feel free to follow their own consciences; and it is truly amazing how often an MP's conscience reflects the policies of a right-wing Party Leadership.

Thus, the right-wing supports the freedom of Labour MPs to behave as they choose following their election, even though they have been elected on a Labour ticket as a result of the support and sheer hard work of the local CLP, and the votes of Labour supporters for stated Labour policies. The Left, on the other hand, believes that an MP has a duty to carry out the wishes of the local Party in Parliament, thus reflecting the views of Labour opinion in the constituency. When an MP ceases to be accountable to the CLP, that MP should cease to be their candidate, if that is what the CLP decides.

Automatic re-selection has been stopped by the NEC who insist that if the sitting MP receives 75 per cent of the nominations, there shall not be a selection conference. In by-elections the NEC can impose a women only selection for candidate. They can dictate to the CLP and remove any local candidate or even impose a candidate on the CLP. The principle of one member, one vote is rejected.

The third tenet of CLPD policy, the election of the Leader and Deputy

Leader of the Party – rejected at the 1979 Conference but carried in 1980 – was the issue which caused most dissent within the Parliamentary Party, and most defections to the newly-formed Social Democratic Party. The right-wing says that the Parliamentary Party knows its own ranks better than the mass Party, and it is therefore better equipped to choose its own leaders. The CLPD believes that, if accountable to Conference for re-election, the Party Leader is less likely to flout the mass Party and ignore Conference decisions.

On past showing, the Party cannot rely on the goodwill of any individual when it comes to carrying out Conference decisions. These decisions are made by the mass movement through their elected delegates, and are made to be acted upon. If Labour leaderships persist in regarding Conference merely as a **guide** to policy, whose resolutions can be safely ignored, then the Party might as well scrap Conference and save the money it costs for some more worthwhile cause. Conference delegates showed in 1981 that they were **half**-convinced of this, when they agreed to make the Manifesto, based on Conference decisions, binding on the Party, but then refused to give teeth to this decision by voting **against** writing it into the Constitution.

The sanctity of Conference decisions has been opposed vigorously, the nub of the opposition being the belief – widely held on the Right of the Party, and even subscribed to by some on the Left – that the block vote is undemocratic. I take an uncompromising stand in favour of the block vote; the unions created the Labour Party, I maintain, to be the political voice of the trade union movement. Union members are to a large extent the paymasters of the Party. For these two powerful reasons, the unions are entitled to a significant say in Party policy. My own experience of the misuse of the block vote in my own union has not in any way affected my assurance of the correctness of the block vote principle in a Socialist party, and I defend it:

1   There were, in the 1970s, 6,000,000 block votes cast by affiliated unions, compared with 600,000 votes cast by constituency parties. Because of variations in policies from one union to another, the block votes are not all cast the same way, and are divided 'for' and 'against'

motions, in the same way that CLP votes are divided in the annual conference.

2 It is wrong to make an artificial distinction between trade union votes and CLP votes; individual members of the Labour Party are almost invariably also members of trade unions, and each one has a personal responsibility to carry his opinions into his union, to ensure that issues are fully debated there, and to see that the final vote cast by the union delegation agrees with the majority decision.

3 There is considerable discussion within unions at all levels – branch, district, division, etc – before policy decisions are taken. Most unions operate their procedure in a democratic way, and it is up to individual members to see that (a) decisions are democratically made and then followed through to Party Conference and (b) as many union members as possible are involved in the decision-making process. In any case, a higher proportion of members are involved in making union policy decisions than are generally involved in deciding how CLP votes are cast.

4 In cases where votes are required on issues where a union has no fixed policy, the delegates should reach a democratic decision among themselves as to how the block vote is to be cast, based on their knowledge of that section of the union membership they represent. There is usually a pre-Conference delegation meeting to decide on such issues within each affiliated body, and where a snap decision is required in Conference, it is quick and easy to pass a 'For and Against' pad round the delegation to ascertain the majority view. Compare this with what usually happens in a CLP: because of lack of time, only a very few Conference motions are discussed, and the delegate is mandated on these issues. On other issues – the majority – he uses his individual judgement as to how his CLP would have wanted him to vote. If operated properly, therefore, a union block vote in Conference can be more democratic on more occasions than a CLP vote.

5 If a union casts a million votes on behalf of its million affiliated members, it is a truism to protest that not all those million members would hold the same view on any given issue. But no more is it true to

say that a thousand votes cast by a CLP delegate represent a thousand individual members who all think the same way. The difference between the two votes is one of **size,** not of **kind.** Indeed, taking into consideration that a CLP **must** affiliate on a minimum of a thousand members, even though its actual membership may be much smaller than this, the 'voice' of the CLPs is disproportionately **large** in the total vote at Conference, not – as CLPs often claim – disproportionately **small.**

6   It is true that union members who pay the political levy may belong to parties other than the Labour Party. The very small number of people in Britain who are individual members of any political party (13 per cent of voters is a generous estimate, many of whom would not belong to a trade union anyway), plus the fact that most other parties encourage their members to contract out of paying the political levy to the Labour Party, means that any 'external influence' wielded in the Labour Party through the block vote must be infinitesimal. In any case, members of other parties, while they are free to pay the political levy if they wish, are not eligible to contest any position in the Labour Party, and may not even be delegates to CLPs or to Conference. During the many years in which a majority of block votes were cast for the right-wing, the possibility of 'external influence' was not considered worth mentioning. It has only become an issue since votes have started to swing to the Left. Shirley Williams, for example, was not disturbed by the fact that it was a majority of the 6,000,000 block votes which kept on electing her to the NEC each year.

In 1993 the Labour Party decided that the Trade Union block vote of each union must be divided equitably among all members of their delegation and so permit each TU delegate to cast his portion of the TU vote in the way that the members who elected him would want him to do. This means that the millions of TU block votes will be used as the individual delegates of all the unions think best.

The amount of support for the CLPD has caused fear among the ranks of the Right, whose safe jobs are much less safe than before. As with Victory for Socialism and Socialist Charter, opponents inside and outside the party have been using all their influence against the CLPD campaign.

The press denounces CLPD as a takeover-bid by the Left. I, as former CLPD Vice-President, see a world of difference between 'democracy' and a 'takeover-bid'. Although I would be only too pleased to see left-wing policies succeed in the Party – that is, the kind of policies the Party Constitution upholds – I would not wish this to happen against the will of the majority of Party members. What the CLPD can achieve is the handing back of power within the Party to the people it belongs to – the mass membership. If they are happy to continue the drift to the Right, then that drift will continue. If not, then they would have the means to change the direction of the Party, instead of leaving the steering-wheel in the hands of a few powerful individuals. The right-wing (ably assisted by the media) persist in maintaining, however, that the Left – and particularly the latest scapegoats, the Militant Tendency (all of whom are primarily Labour Party members, and only secondarily supporters of Militant) – wish to take over the Labour Party, with a view to overthrowing the parliamentary system.

To establish who are the 'goodies' and who are the 'baddies' in the saga of Labour Party life which has become virtually a media soap-opera, it is necessary to look carefully at what the Labour Party says about itself. The essence of Labour's political intentions is contained in Clause 4 of the Constitution, which was accepted by Conference in 1918:

> To secure for the workers by hand and by brain the full fruits of their industry and the most equitable distribution thereof which may be possible upon the basis of the common ownership of the means of production, distribution and exchange.

Since 1918, members have resisted all attempts to replace Clause 4 with something less exacting, and this Clause has been so central to Labour Party philosophy that it is printed on every Party membership card – including the cards issued to Shirley Williams, Roy Jenkins, Bill Rodgers, David Owen (the gang of four of the SDP) and others who have since denied all belief in Socialism.

For, make no mistake about it, Socialism is what Clause 4 is all about. Let those who have doubts on the subject refer to Sir Stafford Cripps MP, that most moderate of Socialists, who was reported in 'The Observer' of 7th February 1932 as saying that:

> the first lesson of the recent election defeat was that the real issue was now between reactionary capitalism and Socialism. The second was that it was impossible to have

a slow and gradual transition. On gaining power, they must be prepared to end the power of the House of Lords, nationalise the land, break down the capitalist control over money, and the strangle-hold of private ownership, and place industry under social control.

With this view of Labour Party objectives in mind, the words of Bernard Levin in 'The Times' of 12th March 1980 take on a new meaning. Writing of Shirley Williams, prior to her defection from Labour, he asked:

Will she tell us whether, should she find herself invited to speak on the same platform as Mr Ernest Roberts, Labour MP for Hackney North & Stoke Newington, she will be willing to do so, or – if she is not – that she will tell those who have invited her precisely why, rather than, say, pleading a prior engagement or a bout of flu?

Levin's argument was that Williams represented the 'old original' Labour Party, whereas I was one of the band of infiltrators intent on taking over and smashing the Party. Bearing in mind Sir Stafford Cripps and Clause 4, the reverse interpretation more nearly approaches the truth.

The intentions of 'moderates' had already been made clear prior to the 1979 election; as a group calling themselves the Social Democratic Alliance, they had gone to press a month before the General Election, urging voters not to vote Labour in 59 named constituencies (including Hackney North & Stoke Newington), where they considered the candidates to be too far to the Left. Dr Stephen Haseler and Douglas Eden, leading lights of the Social Democratic Alliance, were threatened with expulsion from the Labour Party following this gross act of disloyalty, but they were reprieved by the National Executive, and maintained their Party membership.

The Social Democratic Alliance proceeded in July 1980 to issue a hit-list of 27 MPs (again including me) against whom it intended to field candidates in a future election, and their organisers went on to say that they had dropped Labour Party membership as a condition of belonging to the Social Democratic Alliance. No action was taken against this right-wing group, even though they were breaking basic rules of Party membership.

It is worth noting at this point that when the Militant group was accused of breaking some of those same rules, the NEC, urged on by Michael Foot, instituted an official enquiry with a view to expelling Militant members en masse, although Militant had never gone so far as to threaten to field alternative candidates against official Labour ones, as the Social Democratic Alliance had done. In fact, Militant supporters were among the most zealous in fighting for and campaigning on behalf of whichever candidate is selected by their CLP.

The witch-hunt of Militants has continued and in 1992 Labour MPs Dave Nellist (Coventry) and Terry Fields (Liverpool Broadgreen) together with the suspension of their constituency parties took place. Following this, a section of the Militant members decided to run candidates against the officially recognised candidates of the Labour Party, thus breaking the rules of the Party, resulting in their expulsion from the Labour Party.

After the special Wembley Conference in January 1981, at which the method of electing the Leader and Deputy Leader was finally decided, a new grouping emerged, calling itself Solidarity. With the departure of many members of the Social Democratic Alliance, led by the Gang of Four, to the newly-formed Social Democratic Party, the remaining right-wing and some of the centrists came together in the cause of 'Unity, Fraternity and Democracy', called themselves the Labour Solidarity Campaign, and proclaimed that "we should be uniting to attack the Thatcher government, not squabbling among ourselves." I roundly condemned Solidarity's motives, in an article for 'Labour Weekly' on 20th March 1981:

Recent Labour governments have promoted membership of the EEC, expanding defence expenditure, wage restraint and cuts in public spending. All these policies have also been Tory policies, and all go against conference decisions.

Now that some of the key proponents of these anti-working-class policies have left the party, members of Solidarity begin to tell us that 'we should be uniting to attack the Thatcher government, not squabbling among ourselves'.

They say that, right or left, pro- or anti-market, 'we know that nothing can be achieved by a party weakening itself through division, bitterness, disorganisation.'

But the only thing that **can** come out of Solidarity is division. The very basis of its existence is bitterness – bitterness because the grass-roots is waking up from its disorganisation, and slowly getting organised.

For what is the top priority of the Solidarity programme? It is to 'seek to change the Wembley decision' on the election of the Party leader.

Solidarity supporters talk about unifying the party, but in fact they are unsettling it by trying to overturn a conference decision which has not even been given a trial; moreover the means they have chosen to fight the decision are unconstitutional.

I went on to say that most Solidarity MPs would not dare to put up a motion to their own CLPs to reverse the Wembley decision, which would be the constitutional way of approaching the matter. Then:

Solidarity's second objective is a mass membership which will not be 'dominated by any clique or group.' Strange, isn't it, how 'domination' was never mentioned as long as the Right was dominant?

Why should the media constantly refer to 'a Left takeover'? What is happening is simply that the party is reverting to type. After years of dabbling with capitalism, the grass-roots is at last drawing the party back to its first socialist principles. And this is what Solidarity calls 'domination by a clique'.

But what is Solidarity itself, but a clique, mainly composed of MPs, whose object is to continue that domination over the party which the mass membership is at last determined to break?

....They talk of returning to 'the traditional virtues and loyalties'. Loyalties to what? To that conglomeration of policies which we have shared with the Tories, which have been forced on us by parliamentary cliques....?

No! Our loyalty now should be to the party, its constitution and its socialist principles....

The membership at large is now all set to establish firm control over the party's democratic machinery – so that it can be used in the way it was originally intended, as the foundation of a socialist society.

We **do** want a united party: a party united behind socialist policies. A new-look Labour Party would give the electorate what it needs, by breaking out of the Tweedledum-and-Tweedledee mould, and giving socialist policies a real chance for the first time since 1945.

The attempt to put the Labour Party back on its original Socialist road is an uphill fight; this is not only because of the struggle put up by the right-wing to maintain their power, but also because of the support given to the Right by the media, whose reporting of developments in the Labour Party is riddled with what Churchill might have called 'terminological inexactitudes' – which the Left would call at best 'distortions' and at worst 'lies'.

Chapter 6

For a newspaper must live, and to live it must please, and its conductors suppose, perhaps not altogether rightly, that it can only please by being very cheerful towards prejudices, very chilly to general theories, disdainful to the men of principle.

John Viscount Morley

1   The role of the media and workers' press
2   'Voice of the Unions'
3   Libel actions
4   'The Way'
5   Workers' Control

> *You cannot hope to bribe or twist –*
> *Thank God! – the British Journalist,*
> *But seeing what the man will do*
> *Unbribed, there's no occasion to.*

The trouble with newspapers is that people are inclined to believe everything they read in them. In cases of libel, the wheels of the law turn exceedingly slowly, and by the time the editor is persuaded to print a retraction, it is usually too late to undo the damage. Over a period of forty years, I have taken successful legal action on many occasions over statements of the "Roberts is a known Communist" variety, but the words still keep being written. Perhaps this is because journalists, as Arnold Bennett wrote, "say a thing that they know isn't true, in the hope that if they keep saying it long enough it **will** be true" – or at least it will be believed.

During my period at Peckham Road, I gained something of a reputation amongst members for being the one who would always meet a deputation and listen to their case. Many were the times when workers with a grievance came down to the AEU General Office by the bus-load, and ended up having a demonstration outside the building because the Executive Council refused to speak to them. But I would always talk to them. In 1961, a couple of hundred workers from Rootes engaged in a 'siege' of the General Office because they could not get a hearing from the Executive. I went outside, talked to the strikers, and received a petition from them, after which the demonstration broke up. Police had been hovering in the background to disperse the men forcibly if necessary, since they were causing an obstruction, but their 'services' were not needed. Next day, 11th October 1961, the 'Daily Sketch' printed the following account of the incident:

> A Rootes strikers siege of union headquarters ended last night before police could interfere. 'We'll have to consider moving demonstrators bodily if no action is taken,' warned AEU Assistant General Secretary, E Roberts.

A month passed, punctuated with brisk exchanges of letters between the paper and myself, before the editor agreed to print an explanation of the error: the word 'police' had been omitted before 'warned', thus reversing the attribution of the statement.

Corrections can only be made, however, if the victim sees what has been written about him. One case only came to my attention through the vigilance of Audrey Wise, when she was MP for Coventry South-West, who spotted a reader's letter in the 'Stafford Newsletter' of 7th September 1979, alleging that I had had "repeated contracts" with a Czech intelligence officer. In other words, I was a spy. This allegation arose out of the unfounded accusations made by Stephen Hastings MP in the shelter of the House of Commons' privilege. A long argument took place between the editor, the newspaper's solicitors, myself and my solicitors, as to the precise wording of the retraction. The editor could not understand why his own wording was unacceptable: he wanted to say that the mistake had been a typographical error – it should have been "contacts", not "contracts". This was hardly satisfactory to me, since the amended version of the letter still accused me of meeting a Czech intelligence agent repeatedly, even if there had been no "contracts" between them. In the end, my version of the retraction won:

> Mr Roberts has informed us that, when a trade union official, he met Labour attaches at the Czech and other embassies, but he has never had contacts or contracts with an intelligence officer.

This was a hollow victory. The original letter was printed in September 1979, but the retraction did not appear until August 1980.

Libel, though comparatively frequent in my experience, is still rare in comparison with the twisting of ideas which, while offensive and misleading, is not actionable. Such distortion is an almost daily occurrence, with letters from 'Outraged of Oswestry' and 'Shocked of Shepherd's Bush' being a regular feature of correspondence columns. The unfortunate fact is that although papers often do print such letters, they are not legally obliged to do so, even when the facts of what they have written are in dispute. Most of the letters and articles which I had published in the press have been prompted by some previous article which I could not let go unchallenged. Often my reply has been ignored by the editor, but having a fairly well-known name, I have been able to bulldoze unwilling editors into granting me what I believe every individual should have: the right of reply.

Some individuals have claimed the right of reply by writing directly to me in terms which no editor would dare to print. After I had written about AEU ballots in the 'Financial Times' in 1975, I received a reply quite startling in its frankness, explaining in graphic detail what the writer would do to me and the "no-good bastard 'Still-factories' Scanlon", should they be fortunate enough for him to meet me – presuming that he happened to have a red-hot poker with him at the time, and that his victims stood still long enough for him to apply it to the places mentioned. At least the gentleman concerned was honest enough to put a name to his letter. Most of the invectives came unsigned.

There were some publications which continually baited me, and which never seemed to catch on to the fact that I would take legal action against them every time they overstepped the mark. One such was 'East-West Digest', a publication dedicated to witch-hunting in one form or another, and edited in the early seventies by a then Tory MP, Mr G Stewart-Smith, who had defeated George Brown in his Belper constituency. I had written a pamphlet called 'The Solution is Workers' Control', which had been published by the Bertrand Russell Peace Foundation, and in January 1972, 'East-West Digest' reprinted the whole of Section 5 of the pamphlet, which dealt with the control of the Labour Party. The Peace Foundation took up the case as a breach of copyright, and the 'Digest' was forced to print an apology for their 'inadvertent' error, and also to pay £60 in damages. The Foundation benefited in the end, as they used the £60 towards the printing costs of another of my pamphlets, this time on unemployment. But it was only five months later that the 'Digest' attacked again.

In a long article on the AEU election for General Secretary, there were a number of references to 'Communist support', and the fact that I had been refused endorsement as a Labour candidate, but their conclusion was blatant:

> A Communist General Secretary in place of Jim Conway.... would be disastrous for the AEU.

So I went after them again, this time on the much more serious charge of libel.

There was likewise continual baiting by 'IRIS News'. Industrial Research and Information Services had been set up in 1956 "to draw attention to the Communist menace in the trade union movement", although it has always extended its scope to include attacks on any number of the Left. There were suspicions about the source of its funds and its political connections, but these were never verified until a 'Daily Telegraph' article reported that Common Cause was acting as the channel by which money from industrialists was passed to IRIS. (Common Cause is an extreme right-wing organisation, dedicated to the eradication of Communism and the promotion of Toryism, in the pursuit of which it receives substantial cash handouts from the same big-business companies which support the Tory Party.)

The 'Daily Worker' seized upon the Telegraph's article, and re-stated it for the benefit of its readers: here was a supposedly trade union orientated organisation, about which there had long been doubts on the Left, openly revealed as receiving cash from what was effectively a Tory body. IRIS responded by sending a 'personal and confidential' letter to its readers, the contents of which were not printed in 'IRIS News'. The letter said, contradictorily, that Common Cause was a "non-political, non-sectarian, anti-Communist" organisation. There was no mention of its strong financial backing from Tory businesses. Common Cause had, continued the letter, given financial assistance to IRIS – but, they insisted, without strings. Strings were hardly necessary, since IRIS was already following a policy of attacks on the Left which must have been heartily approved by Common Cause.

The IRIS letter was unsigned. It was not their policy, so the letter said, to give prominence and use valuable space in 'IRIS News' to publicise directors or staff. In any case, perhaps the readers of 'IRIS News', who were led to believe it was a trade union publication, might have been put off by the names of those who were involved in its production.

Conscious of the overwhelming odds against the Left's point of view ever reaching the average reader, I have made determined efforts over a period of thirty years or more to redress the balance. With all the capitalist press against Labour and the trade unions, supported by strong fringe organisations and publications such as 'IRIS News' and 'East-West Digest', along with the insidious effects of television and radio coverage, what chance did the Left stand of putting over its policies to the man in the street?

One way of tackling the problem was to write to the capitalist press myself, and this I did as often as possible, when necessary shaming the editor into printing a short article or letter in reply to some blatantly anti-Labour propaganda. I also contributed, often at their request, to sympathetic publications such as 'Tribune' and 'Labour Weekly', and sometimes to so-called 'revolutionary' papers which did not hesitate to make their opposition known in no uncertain terms – papers like 'Workers' Press' and 'Socialist Worker', where I was usually taken to task for promoting Socialism via the Labour Party, which they regarded as a reformist organisation.

Looking back on my writings over the past forty years, it is their single-mindedness which is most striking. For all those years I have been writing about the Labour Party, trade union democracy, unemployment, wages and inflation, disarmament, public ownership and workers' control, and the ideas I am putting forward now are precisely those I was putting forward at the beginning of my political career. Individuals come and go, but the principles remain; as I said in 'Workers' Control', "the game's the same, only the names change." It would be quite possible to pick out some of the early articles, change the names and statistics, and reprint them without anyone knowing that they were written during, say, the MacMillan government or the Attlee leadership.

An article headed "Principles before Personalities" appeared in the 'Daily Worker' of 11th January 1960. It said:

> It has always been my opinion that the Labour Movement does not exist to give unquestioning or uncritical support to leaders, but rather to give unflinching support to the principles of the movement....
>
> The party supported an expanding arms programme which led.... to the undermining of the very welfare state services which Labour had established. Cuts in health services, charges for teeth, spectacles, etc., cuts in housing, holding back of education services....
>
> The policy of wage-freeze which the Labour Government tried to operate led many workers to become opposed to us, and they either voted against us in 1950, or abstained.
>
> So our party's policies in the 1950, 1951, 1955 and 1959 General Elections became less and less Socialist, and more and more indistinguishable from that of the Liberals and muddled, mixed-economy politics.
>
> I do not accept the statement of a prominent trade union leader that 'irresponsibility among union members helped the Conservatives to win the last election....'
>
> The people of Britain are desirous of a full, free, secure and happy life. The Labour Movement can create such a life – if it rids itself of the disunity, the witch-hunting bans and proscriptions which the Tories foster and encourage.

Change the dates of the elections and you would have an article equally applicable to the 1980s and 1990s.

Anyone reading the body of literature produced by me must inevitably be struck but its repetitive nature: the situation has not changed, the solutions are still the same and have never been tried, so I have no hesitation in hammering home the same arguments time after time, in the firm belief that some day people will listen and take the appropriate action.

An isolated article, five or six times a year, buried under the mountain of anti-working-class, anti-Labour propaganda was not enough, and I realised this early in my political career. I therefore gathered together a small group of friends and with their support formed the Labour Publishing Society. This group met originally in my hotel room during the Labour Party Conference at Scarborough in 1948, and this meeting resulted in the birth of a newspaper called 'Socialist Outlook'. Those present at the Scarborough meeting included Konni Zilliacus and Sidney Silverman, and among those who officially formed the Labour Publishing Society were Coventry councillor Arthur Waugh, John Lawrence (a London councillor who on one occasion chained himself to the railings outside St Pancras Town Hall in protest against Civil Defence), and a man called Gerry Healy who later became leader of the Workers' Revolutionary Party.

An editorial board was elected in Scarborough, and I was commissioned to write "an article on workers' control by 8th December" – the earliest extant reference to my interest in the workers' control movement. The object of the paper originally was to keep the Party's constitution, and its Conference policies, before the eyes of the readership, so that any deviations by the right-wing leadership would be self-evident. It would also put forward arguments for policy-changes which, we hoped, would be taken up by the constituencies. 'Outlook' itself said that it was "an expression of left-wing Labour Party opinion, which could not be linked with the Communist Party, but which could to some extent be critical of official Party policy."

It was not long before I became disenchanted with the paper which I had helped into the world, and which was showing every sign of growing into a monster. I had, as I thought, produced a paper for the ordinary Labour Party member. After a year or so, I found that it had grown into a publication for an intellectual audience, propounding political theories quite unsuited to its original purpose. Losing interest, I ceased to be active in its production, as did others of the founding group, and eventually Gerry Healy was left in control of the editorial board, which he maintained until 'Socialist Outlook' was proscribed in 1954, as being inimical to the interests of the Labour Party. Healy then founded the Socialist Labour League, which functioned within the Party until it, too, was proscribed by Harold Wilson in 1964, whereupon Healy and other ex-Labour Party members set up the Workers' Revolutionary Party.

The 'Outlook' was a popular paper, and had progressed from monthly, to fortnightly, and then to weekly production. It was proscribed as part of a general witch-hunt which included by implication anyone who put forward a policy similar to that of 'Outlook'. The paper clearly had support from many who were just ordinary Party members, and Morgan Phillips, the Party's General Secretary, put out a private circular to the NEC in which he said that the Party had received 150 protests from constituencies opposing the proscription, and only one – from North-East Leeds – in favour of it. 'Socialist Outlook' was the outward sign of an evil which the Party leadership was trying to suppress in all possible ways – the evil of Socialism. It was even rumoured that the NEC was planning to disband certain London CLPs which expressed vigorous support for the paper.

'The Backbench Diaries of Richard Crossman' reveal something of the fear which gripped the leadership at this time; in his entry for 24th March 1955 (after the proscription of 'Outlook') he retails a conversation with Hugh Gaitskell, in which Gaitskell makes clear that 'Tribune' is to be the next target, saying that "It's read everywhere in the constituencies. It's the single most important factor which our people on the Right complain about." After a brief tirade against Nye Bevan, Gaitskell concluded that "if Nye went out of the Party, the main Tory propaganda for the next election campaign would be killed," although Crossman argued that "the Left would not be smashed by Nye's expulsion, and indeed it would only increase the division." The 'Diary' continues:

> He said, "Of course we shall have to do some cleaning-up in the constituencies," and remarked what a nice time he'd had in Exeter, where the 'Socialist Outlook' had been successfully cleaned up. I said, "But do you really think that cleaning up Bevanism is like cleaning up the 'Socialist Outlook'? Look at Coventry, where if you don't look out, they will select another candidate instead of Burton." "Oh," he said, "we may have to clean up Coventry too." I said, "What do you mean?" And Gaitskell said, "We've cleaned up the shop stewards' movement before now."

I had long ceased to take an active part in 'Socialist Outlook', but I was nevertheless strongly opposed to its proscription, representing as it did a strong and legitimate strain of Party opinion in the constituencies.

It was 1962 before I next founded a newspaper, 'Voice of the Unions'. This time it was in the trade union sphere, although it promoted left-wing Labour policies, and strove to bring out the vote for Labour at election times.

I sent out a circular to drum up support for a new paper, and received much encouragement, although there were some who thought I was biting off more than I could chew. George Doughty, for example, then General Secretary of DATA, wrote:

.... you are undertaking a pretty phenomenal task involving a tremendous amount of financial responsibility.

Which turned out to be true, although the financial responsibility fell on other shoulders. An old friend, Alf Hack, of the AEU, commented:

I am returning your enclosure without much enthusiasm. During my career I have seen a lot of left-wing publications come and go. I remember over 50 years ago a militant publication (weekly) on which Fenner Brockway was sub-editor, but the 'Labour Leader' has been extinct for many years. Then there was 'Clarion', edited and conducted by Robert Blatchford. Personally I feel that no publication of the kind suggested would have any chance at all unless it is at least weekly....

Hack was wrong about 'Labour Leader', which was still in production in a small way. Undeterred by Hack's pessimism (as apparently was Lord Brockway, who contributed an article on unemployment to the first issue of my new paper), and understanding that a weekly publication was a non-starter because of financial considerations, I floated the idea of a monthly trade union paper at a press conference on the eve of the TUC Congress in 1962, and followed it up with a conference to discuss "a new friend for 'Tribune'. Sponsors of the project at that early stage included eight trade union general secretaries, thirteen Labour MPs and twenty full-time trade union officials. The conference was chaired by Anthony Greenwood MP, and the participants argued over the nitty-gritty of name, size, price and finance, as well as establishing the aims of the paper. It was agreed that the paper would be called 'Voice of the Unions' (picking up the name of an earlier paper, long-deceased), and it would cost sixpence and be issued monthly. The first issue was to appear on 1st February 1963. The objects of the paper were simple:

- to work for the return of a Labour Government;
- to struggle for the implementation of Clause 4 of the Party Constitution;
- to aim for Peace and Socialism.

In fact, it was to do the same job in the industrial field as 'Tribune' did in the constituencies. Amongst its first sponsors were Ian Mikardo, Richard Briginshaw, Hugh Scanlon, Frank Allaun and Bill Jones. There was also one who was to feature prominently in the development of the paper, Walter Kendall, whose principal involvement, apart from his connection with USDAW, was with research at Nuffield College, Oxford.

The paper had a good reception from its readership, but was not well-received by union hierarchies, particularly in the engineering industry. The reason for this was plain: the paper was opposed to the established order, and in favour of change. Typical of the response was the AEU convener who wrote to order a regular three dozen copies, then contracted his order to fifteen: the workers had received the first issue with enthusiasm, but certain full-time officers were making enquiries into whether the paper was acceptable to the powers-that-be, and were advising members not to read it, so the salesman was obliged to 'go underground'. 'Voice of the Unions' survived and is still going strong in 1994 – that is 31 years later, thanks to John Spencer and a voluntary editorial board, and in 1965 was joined by a sister publication, 'Engineering Voice'. Edelstein and Warner write, in 'Comparative Union Democracy':

> 'Voice' conferences on workers' control were held during 1964 and 1965. Soon after, in 1965, a special 'Voice' journal for the engineering industry appeared, called 'Engineering Voice'.... This seemed to be a force for unity in the broad left in the engineering industry.... It held separate conferences for workers in the automobile and aircraft sectors, and the union actually threatened its shop stewards with disciplinary action for attending these meetings. It helped to publicise Scanlon.... and to rally the anti-Carron forces. The unity of the broad left was also assisted by the reaction against the three-year 'package deal' which Carron, the President, put forward, and against proposals for rule-book changes made by Conway, the General Secretary – all opposed by 'Engineering Voice', which was superseded by the 'Engineering Gazette' by Les Ambrose and other left-wing union members and is still going in 1994.

Despite the 'broad Left' nature of the conferences, the paper itself is, and always has been, run by members of the Labour Party, and this to some extent hampered the opposition to it from the right-wing. Which explains why Carron was anxious to make a splash with his 'Be Vigilant!' campaign, in which he could link the paper with the Communist Party, and tar the paper with the Communist brush.

When the paper was four years old, I asked for my name to be withdrawn from the list of sponsors which appeared in every issue. The reasons behind this request were connected with the union. 'Voice' had been active in promoting left-wing candidates in AEU elections, which it was perfectly entitled to do, in the same way that 'IRIS News' did for the Right. I could not afford to allow my name to appear among the sponsors, especially during periods when I was myself up for election. There was no disagreement between me and the editorial board, but inevitably there was some misunderstanding of his motives. A friend wrote angrily:

> It makes it very difficult for the ordinary member like myself to gain active support for those who are being victimised by our ruthless bureaucracy, if the victims appear to be unwilling to challenge the tyrants.

This was galling indeed to me, who had been engaged in challenging the tyrants for thirty years, and was now making only a tactical withdrawal.

The format of 'Voice', as agreed at the 1962 conference, allowed for at least a full page of each 8-page issue to be given over to letters, undoctored and uncensored. There were signed articles from various sources, expressing views which the editorial board did not always agree with. The chief feature of each issue was a two-page article in the centre-spread, designed as a wall-newspaper which could be lifted out and pinned on a factory notice-board. I contributed a number of these in the early years of the paper: in April 1963, I did an analysis of "Who gets what?" in society; in June I tackled "The Commanding Heights of the Economy"; and in July, the relationship between the unions and the Labour Party.

As often happens, the hard work involved in producing each month what is, it must be admitted, a very professional paper, tends to get concentrated into fewer and fewer hands – not because the few want it to be that way, but because it is easy to offer passive support, but much more difficult to maintain an adequate level of active involvement. Then the 'willing-horse syndrome' comes into operation, and when things go wrong, abuse is heaped on the heads of those very willing horses who have carried the bulk of the work on their own backs.

In this case, while there was an active editorial board which discussed each issue, the bulk of the work fell to Walter Kendall in the 1970s, and slowly it began to look as if the paper were growing into a vehicle for Kendallism – in particular, his own style of pungent anti-Communism, and criticisms of the Institute for Workers' Control, some of whose organisers were closely connected with 'Voice' and the many offshoots which had by this time sprouted from it – 'Engineering Voice', 'London Voice', 'Teesside & Cleveland Voice', 'Labour's Voice', 'Northern Voice' and so on. In 1970 an open quarrel broke out when the Institute wrote to Kendall complaining about certain critical items in the paper and asking why such attacks had been made. Even the readership began to pick up hints that all was not well, noticing that many of the articles bore Kendall's name. One reader wrote angrily, "Haven't you got any other writers?" – rather an unfair criticism, since 'Voice' had no writers at all, and was dependent on voluntary articles; what Kendall did was to fill up the blank spaces.

The quarrel was stitched up on the surface, but the wound beneath did not heal. Kendall had other worries, besides making sure that there was enough copy for each issue. 'Voice' had managed to survive financially until 1965, when 'Engineering Voice' was first brought out. It was questionable whether the movement could support two papers, especially when much of the material from 'Voice of the Unions' also appeared in 'Engineering Voice', along with items of specific interest to engineers, so that readers did not need to buy both. By the time the second issue of 'Engineering Voice' was published, Kendall was complaining that those who had taken copies to sell on the shopfloor were not paying up promptly, that 'Voice' was in debt to the tune of £220, and operating on £50 of Kendall's own money. The financial position was never secure, and the 'Voice' papers always ran on a hand-to-mouth basis. This became increasingly true as the parent paper gave birth to little editions on a geographical or industrial basis, and finally

Kendall took the step of closing down the satellite editions, a decision which the editorial board said they had not been consulted about.

In May 1976, 'Voice' carried a front-page shock: "OUR LAST ISSUE". On page 2 were various articles, all unsigned, which were "of an obituary character". So said the editorial board in their news-sheet 'What happened to Voice?', printed in response to the May issue. For no-one was more surprised than the editorial board to find that this was the 'last' edition of the paper. A normal paper had been prepared, and the board had vetted and approved the printer's proofs. Then out came the paper, headlined 'Last Issue', with part of the approved copy removed to make way for the unapproved explanations. The editorial board claimed:

> For the last eighteen months the editorial board has sought to resolve the unsatis-
> factory situation in which it received no financial information, and has no control
> over, nor responsibility for, financial administration.
>
> The statement that publication of Voice Newspapers was to cease was made
> unilaterally by the business management of the paper.

Kendall responded with a statement that one way or another 'Voice' had cost him £10,000.

As with Mark Twain, reports of Voice's death were an exaggeration. After a brief hiccup in June, the paper reappeared in July 1976, and is still fighting fit in 1994. For this, thanks are due to John Spencer, an untiring fund-raiser and chaser-up of contributors, and to the volunteer editorial board, who assumed responsibility for the revitalised paper in both editorial and financial spheres.

'Voice of the Unions' was not the only newspaper I launched in 1963. Eight months after 'Voice' appeared, I edited the first edition of an 8-page tabloid called 'The Way', an official publication of the union which was financed by the AEU and distributed free to its target group, the women and youth of the union.

There were probably a good many readers who did not appreciate the significance of the name: 'The Way' was for **W**omen **A**nd **Y**outh. Certainly many publishers interpreted it as an ecclesiastical journal, and sent copies of their religious books to 'Father Ernie Roberts' for review. Unlike 'Voice', which could barely afford 10,000 copies, 'The Way' started with a circulation of 80,000, which later increased to 90,000.

The aim of the paper was "to organise and inform" on wages, hours, conditions and other issues of interest to women and young people. The first issue, in October 1963, was typical of later ones in content: unemployed youth, nurseries, Junior Workers' committees, equal pay, training and articles by Arnold Wesker (playwright), Miriam Karlin (actress), and Harold Wilson MP, formed the bulk of the 'serious' material, backed up by correspondence, book reviews, fashion (for men and women), a legal column (about insurance wins for members injured on the job), and jokes. Some of the jokes made sharp points in a light-hearted way:

How hard is it for a rich man to enter the kingdom of heaven concerns us less than how hard it is for a poor man to remain on earth.

and:

All his working life he took benefits won for him by the union, but he refused to become a member. Then on his death-bed he told his wife, "Darling, please do something for me. I want union members to be my pall-bearers." When his wife asked why, since he had never been a union member, he answered, "My dear, they've carried me this far, they might as well carry me the rest of the way."

I was unhappy about 'women' and 'youth' being lumped together, picked out from the rest of the membership as if they were a species apart. For this reason, I tried to make the paper as full of general interest material as possible, while including enough copy directed to women and younger members to satisfy the Executive, who vetted each issue before it went to press.

But you can't please all the people all the time. While some readers were writing to 'Voice' to complain that there was no 'lighter material' to leaven the politicals, others were writing to 'The Way' to complain about the fashion and the football. I did not object to a little light-hearted rubbish, believing that people would be more inclined to read the paper if it looked interesting, and when they had read the light stuff, they would very likely pass on to the more serious items. One member was not so optimistic:

Page 2, instead of having a pop column, there could be basic socialism of Marx, Engels and Lenin.

Chance would have been a fine thing! While I had control of the whole paper, from collecting copy through laying out the page-proofs to vetting the proof copy, the Executive still had a veto on material they did not like. Basic socialism of Marx, Engels and Lenin, indeed! It was as much as I could do to get away with 'basic socialism of Ernie Roberts' on the front page editorial, and I only achieved this by sticking rigidly to National Committee Policy.

Nevertheless, the front page was usually an eye catcher, especially after a change in format in January 1970 reduced the page-size of the paper and made me re-think front page policy. I was always against a mass of unbroken blocks of text, believing that people approached a paper with more interest if the text was interspersed with pictures and arranged in an asymmetrical fashion. I asked myself why the 'Daily Mirror' appealed to workers more than 'The Times', and came to the conclusion that the layout and chatty style had as much to do with it as the content. If it was good enough for the 'Mirror', it was good enough for 'The Way'. In later years, the front page editorial was often either a brief but hard-hitting text with a relevant photograph or cartoon, or it was a diagrammatic layout of facts or statistics making a political point. There was much sloganising but no jargon. A typical front page was that of the November 1976 issue, headlined "Contradictions". On the left of the page, a fact; on the right, a consequence or conclusion:

206,700 construction workers without a job	=	millions of bricks, tons of cement, surplus. One million homeless!
9,000 hospital staff unemployed	=	500,000 patients on hospital waiting-lists
20,000 fully-trained teachers want a teaching job	=	hundreds of schools with over-size classes; nurseries closing
Standard of living down	=	profits up.
British Government borrows £10,000 million		But British investments abroad are £23,400 million

The keynote was simplicity.

Unlike the AEU Journal, 'The Way' did not contain many contributions from the Peckham Road hierarchy or the Labour Party right-wing, and was probably all the more popular for that. A questionnaire confirmed that the paper was well-liked, and I did all I could to keep it that way. Nevertheless I often found myself in the same situation that Kendall was in with 'Voice' – with a deadline approaching, there were gaps to fill, and the only person to fill them was me.

I got an occasional bouquet for my efforts, as when Hugh Scanlon wrote me a personal letter complimenting me on "an interesting and well-balanced" issue of the paper. I was far more likely to get brickbats, and 'The Way' was closely watched from the Right, to check that it did not get out of line. On one occasion when the galley-proofs were a little later than usual, I received a pencilled note from John Boyd, then on the Executive Council, brusquely asking where his copy was, and reminding me of his reputation as the Executive's MI5 man.

In the circumstances, I got away with as much as I could in the way of political propaganda, and from the letters I received when I gave up the editorship on my retirement, my efforts did not go unnoticed among the members. I was congratulated on providing "many interesting hours of reading", on doing "a first-class job of work.... useful and helpful in attracting and recruiting women and youth", and on editing "the only inspirational literature to come from the Engineering Section for a very long while". The Acocks Green Branch wrote to Boyd, who was by then General Secretary, and asked him to print their tribute in the Journal, thanking me "for the services rendered to our society in his editing of 'The Way'. The letter continued:

It is a sad goodbye. We will always remember Ernie Roberts and 'The Way' in the engineering industry. Thanks again, Brother.

In my 60 years' membership of the union, this appears to be the only commendation of my work which ever appeared in the Journal, with the exception of a review of my book, 'Workers' Control', which was written by the ex-AEU head of research who was a friend of mine, George Aitken.

Since my early days of involvement with Civil Defence and the peace movement, I have been proud to number myself among the friends of Bertrand Russell. Russell had been involved, with the Bertrand Russell Peace Foundation, in establishing a new magazine, 'Spokesman' of which I was on the editorial board. At Christmas 1969, I had been given the Russell autobiography, which I sent to Russell for his signature. Russell, born in 1872, was then in his 98th year, with a mind as active as ever, though his body was weak. As the world entered a new decade, Russell was asked if he had anything to say about the seventies; "Which seventies?" was his reply. When I got back my parcel of books, I found not only a signature on the flyleaf, but annotations in the margins. A paragraph of one of the Russell letters, written on 28th December 1916, was marked for special attention:

> I hate the world and most of the people in it. I hate the Labour Congress and the journalists who send men to be slaughtered, and the fathers who feel smug pride when their sons are killed, and even the pacifists who keep saying human nature is essentially good, in spite of all the daily proofs to the contrary. I hate the planet and the human race – I am ashamed to belong to such a species – and what is the good of me in that mood?

A few days later, Bertrand Russell died.

The magazine which he had helped to found, 'Spokesman', was first published in March 1970, and it was the 'Spokesman' publishing facilities which started me in the serious pursuit of Workers' Control. I had had the ideas for many years, but they had found expression in diverse movements, often with no apparent connection. The Bertrand Russell Peace Foundation provided the opportunity to bring these diverse ideas under one roof, when I was invited to write one of the series of Spokesman Pamphlets: 'The Solution is Workers' Control' which dealt with the issues of the Upper Clyde strike. Working on this 16-page, quarto-sized booklet made me realise just how much there was that I would not have space to write. So came the idea of the book, 'Workers' Control'.

All the elements of the book were present in the pamphlet's five sections: Capitalist Crisis, The Right to Work, Mergers and International Capital, Workers' Control within the unions, and Workers' Control of the Labour Party.

It seemed so logical to me that the evils of society could never be righted until workers took control of their own destiny, which meant gaining control of the organisations which they had set up – the unions and the Labour Party – organisations which had been insidiously taken over by people whose end was not Socialism, who had twisted those organisations to serve opportunistic purposes of their own.

There was nothing academic about 'Workers' Control'. It arose from a non-academic source – a man whose formal education had terminated at the age of thirteen – and was intended for non-academic readers. It attempted to analyse some of the problems of society and to suggest how working people could bring about Socialism, the solution to those problems, by taking control of their own lives. There was no attempt in the book to write a blueprint for how such a society should operate, and this was picked out as a weakness by some reviewers who expected 'Workers' Control' to be something on the lines of William Morris's 'News from Nowhere' – a fanciful attempt to describe a perfect society of the future. Firmly believing that the workers themselves, not some author who has only had experience of capitalism, will decide the detailed operation of Socialist society, I avoided predictions and prescriptions; my only excursion into the realms of imagination was a tantalisingly brief account of an indus-trially-based parliament.

On reading through the reviews of 'Workers' Control', one might begin to question whether some of the reviewers had read the book at all. The best review – not the most favourable one! – was by Tony Benn in 'Labour Weekly'. He tackled the book fairly, even though it was sharply critical of himself as Minister of Technology in the Wilson administration, a criticism which he wryly alluded to in his review.

Most of the national newspapers gave the book a fair amount of space in their review columns – naturally enough, since a political creed from a serving trade union official is something of a rarity. As was to be expected, their coverage was none too complimentary. The 'Coventry Evening Telegraph', which had a special interest because of my former connection with the city, wrote a scathing attack under the heading "The Gospel according to Roberts". But the most vicious broadsides came from the extreme Left – from the very people with whom I have frequently been accused of fraternising. I was not dismayed about this, feeling that if the capitalist press slated me from the Right and the revolutionary press slated me from the Left, I must have hit the right note!

The 'International Socialism' paper, instead of commenting on the book, simply denounced me as a hypocrite:

Anyone in doubt should have seen this official critic of union officialdom last autumn at the Fine Tubes conference, where he sat advising the chairman against taking resolutions calling for local support committees for the strike.

The Fine Tubes strike lasted three years in all, and foundered eventually on lack of solidarity from the unions concerned. The remark in 'International Socialism' about my part in it was unfair and ill-informed. I had been instructed – much against my better judgement – by Fine Tubes strike leaders **not** to take resolutions from the floor and **not** to take a collection for the strike fund. "Anyone in doubt" – to quote the International Socialists – should read the commendation of me in the official book recording the history of the strike, as the only national trade union officer to give complete and consistent support throughout the strike; they might also read the letter from Fine Tubes Strike Committee thanking me for doing "a wonderful job on our behalf", following the conference which the 'IS' criticised.

The 'Morning Star' attacked from a different angle. 'Workers' Control' argues that every battle won by the working class is a step in the direction of full control. The 'Star' reviewer took this to be "a reformist approach", denying the need for "revolution". He missed the point. He had perhaps not read on page 29:

It is.... naive to imply that, come the Revolution, all the workers' problems will be solved. The working class taking power is the point at which they tip the scales in their favour. The method by which this is done depends wholly on the workers and the problems they are trying to solve, but there can certainly be no clearcut before-and-after dividing line. There will be an uphill struggle before and after the balance of power changes.

The collapse of Communist governments in Europe is proof of the criticisms I made in 'Workers' Control'.

Just as I forebore to write a blueprint for a socialist society, I forebore to tell the workers what form the revolution should take: "The method by which this is done depends wholly on the workers...." The point which I insists upon is a matter of common sense: the working people are at present content to grumble and grouse, but to let capitalism take its course. They are not ready for a revolution, even of a very minor kind. Without the step-by-step progression of small victories, the working class will never see that it is strong enough to take the big, final step to break the old system and establish the new. Of course, for those who believe that 'revolution' can be imposed by the few on the many, this is sheer idiocy: you can have a revolution as soon as you can muster the military strength to topple the existing regime! I believe, however, that change must come from the mass of the people, the result of a constant process of political learning through their own experience. How they use their power to achieve ultimate workers' control is not for any **individual** to dictate.

'Red Weekly', organ of the International Marxist Group, took the same line as the 'Morning Star', although it is difficult to believe that their reviewer had actually read 'Workers' Control', and not merely nibbled at odd pages of it. He certainly did not read with any great attention, accusing me of believing that "workers' directors should receive the same salary as other directors", when in fact I was merely quoting, with strong disapproval, the conclusions reached by a Study Committee of the nationalised airlines, in their report, 'Industrial Democracy in the Nationalised Airlines'.

'Workers' Press', speaking for the Workers' Revolutionary Party, spent several thousand words in two consecutive issues of their paper attacking me for daring to suggest that Lenin's opinions might not be wholly applicable to today's struggle in Britain. They generously allowed me to write a lengthy article in reply (headed "Roberts revises Lenin again") and then followed this up with another long tirade by their reviewer, Royston Bull. I felt quite gratified that they considered my book worthy of such detailed attention.

The 'Socialist Worker' – newspaper of the Socialist Workers' Party – spent half of its review criticising that "fake organisation", the Institute for Workers' Control, and deals with my book almost in passing. Their strongest criticism is one repeated in a number of 'revolutionary Left' reviews:

> Ernie Roberts tells us again and again that the fight for workers' control is a political fight and to carry it through we need "a political party which has a real revolutionary theory of Marxism". Good. What can we do about it? We work, says Ernie, for "a revolutionary leadership in the Labour Party".

> Incredible? Well, there it is in black and white on page 223.

Several other papers found this view 'incredible', too, holding that the one true revolutionary party was the one they happened to belong to. They were condemned out of their own mouths – fighting as they were over which of them should lead the masses on the road to Socialism, like so many children fighting over a toy which none of them actually possess. None of the so-called 'revolutionary parties' contain the miracle ingredient which is in the hands of the Labour Party: the confidence of an average twelve million voters, most of them working class. What's the point, I say, of starting again from scratch? Far better to work inside the existing movement, to bring it back to the socialist principles which the founders wrote into its constitution, and elect a leadership which will for the first time carry out the decisions of the members. If the Labour Party is not a Socialist party, it is the fault of the Socialists: both those inside the Party who have failed to convince fellow members of the correctness of Socialist policies, and those who are outside chanting slogans. In spite of my criticism of the SWP, I have united with them on the issues of anti-fascism and unemployment.

I have never had much time for those who stand outside the mainstream of working-class politics, decrying labour leaderships – whether political or trade union – for not handing out the guns. I might well have said, along with Marx:

> The minority puts a dogmatic view in place of the critical, and an idealist one in place of the materialist. They regard mere discontent, instead of real conditions, as the driving wheel of revolution. Whereas we tell the workers: you have to go through fifteen, twenty, fifty years of civil wars and national struggles, not only in order to change conditions, but also to change yourselves and make yourselves capable of political rule; you, on the contrary, say: "We must come to power immediately, or else we may as well go to sleep."
>
> Mark-Engels Works, Vol 8.

Marx was also clear in his attitude to the evils of sectarianism, and would undoubtedly have applied the following remarks to some of the 'revolutionary' parties of today which call themselves 'Marxist':

> The first phase of the struggle of the proletariat against the bourgeoisie is characterised by the movement of sects.... Isolated thinkers undertake the critique of the social contradictions and want to remove them by fanciful solutions which the

mass of the workers has only to accept, propagate and put into action. It is in the nature of the sects which form around such pioneers that they alienate themselves from the trade unions and, in a word, from every mass movement. The mass of the proletariat remains indifferent or even hostile towards their propaganda....
Originally a lever of the movement, they became an impediment to it as soon as they are overtaken by it. Then they become reactionary.

Ein Komplott gegen die Internationale Arbeiterassonziation.

Marx himself did not prescribe methods of revolution; the peace or violence of revolution would depend on the stage of development of the working-class movement which brought that revolution about. If I am a reformist, a step-by-step revolutionary, so then was Marx, who spoke of the advances made by workers and the fears of the establishment as "signs of the times":

They do not signify that tomorrow a miracle will happen. They show that, within the ruling classes themselves, a foreboding is dawning, that the present society is no lead crystal, but an organism capable of change, and which is constantly changing.

Das Kapital, Vol 1

On the collapse of the so-called Communist Governments in Europe, my comment was "you can no more blame Christ for the misdeeds of Christians than you can blame Marx for the misdeeds of the Marxists." The Japanese workers movement published 'Workers' Control' in Japanese and their press gave it a good welcome.

Chapter 7

It is a very great mistake to imagine that mankind follow up practically any speculative principle, either of government of freedom, as far as it will go in argument and logical illation. All government, indeed every human benefit and enjoyment, every virtue, and every prudent act, is founded on compromise and barter. We balance inconveniences; we give and take; we remit some rights that we may enjoy others,.... Man acts from motives relative to his interests; and not on metaphysical speculations.

Burke

1   Labour's heresy hunting 1945–1990s
2   Reds in the bed
3   Labour leaders' attack on the Left
4   Parliamentary candidate for Stockport
5   Parliamentary candidate for Horsham

The war years had turned the national consciousness away from 'the management of the country' and towards 'the management of the war'. Yet I had never lost sight of the fact that government was still going on in the everyday spheres of life as well as on the military front, and that sooner or later the coalition would break up and the electorate would be asked to choose a new single-party administration to replace it. For people like me, the end of the year seemed to be the perfect opportunity to ensure that the new government would not be cast in the same mould as previous ones had been. It was the chance to break away from old patterns of conservatism and bring in a new, adventurous Labour Government with Socialist policies which would provide prosperity, not for the few but for the masses.

And I wanted to be there when it happened. As a Labour Party member, I stood for election to the Parliamentary Panel of the AEU in 1944, so that I could offer myself as a sponsored candidate whenever the General Election came. Out of a field of eighty in an AEU ballot, I came second. The first six were endorsed by the AEU as members of their Parliamentary Panel.

Even at the beginning of 1945, when the end of the war was hardly in sight, an early General Election seemed a possibility, although there were murmurings in the press about the inadvisability of rushing into an election when constituency boundaries were still being redrawn, and many constituencies were without candidates. Nevertheless, rumours of an election were strong enough for large numbers of local Labour Parties to put their selection procedures in motion by March 1945.

My name, together with the names of other successful members of the Parliamentary Panel, had already been sent to Transport House, the Party's national headquarters, and had been added to the 'A' list of trade union sponsored candidates, endorsed by Labour's National Executive Committee.

Cannock, close to Coventry and part of the West Midlands Region of the Labour Party (of which I was on the Executive), began to make up its shortlist. I was among the nominees and was shortlisted. I attended the Cannock selection conference with the blessing of my union, as a sponsored candidate, and with the blessing of my Party, which had endorsed me on 21st March 1945. In Cannock, I was unfortunate to come up against a candidate who had already served a term in parliament; pitted against such experienced opposition, I did well to come second in the selection ballot to ex-MP Jennie Lee, who was elected for Cannock in 1945, and went on to be a minister in the Wilson administration in the sixties, before becoming Baroness Lee of Ashridge.

However, even before the Cannock selection took place, I had been nominated for two other seats, and the AEU Executive had approved of my proceeding with both nominations. This was possibly the biggest mistake in my political career.

Coventry, until 1945 a single constituency, was about to be split into two under the boundary reorganisation. Coventry East and Coventry West were the two seats which the AEU had authorised me to go after. Among the other contenders for nomination were Dick Crossman for Coventry East, and George Hodgkinson for Coventry West. Crossman had already been the Labour candidate in Coventry before the war, and he and Hodgkinson were old friends. George Hodgkinson would never have stood against Crossman, but with the constituency now divided into two, he was anxious to get the nomination for the second seat. As Mayor of Coventry, he would have been the Returning Officer in any election held during his period of office, and in March 1945, he took the step of publicly delegating his powers as Returning Officer so that he would be free to accept nomination for the Coventry West seat.

However, there was another obstacle in his way which led to his being refused endorsement by the Labour Party NEC. He was the full-time Labour Party Agent in Coventry, and the rules of the Party forbade the selection of agents as parliamentary candidates. This put his nomination quite out of the question, and the NEC formally vetoed him as a candidate for the shortlist on 30th May 1945 – although his statement printed in the 'Coventry Evening Telegraph' nine days later did not refer to the technical necessity for his withdrawal from the contest at all, but stressed the aspect of 'moral duty':

> The best part of my life has been devoted to the working-class movement, and it would have been the proudest moment of my life were I elected to represent part of this famous city in Parliament. Circumstances, however, are such as to make my candidature difficult, including the strain on health and energy, and a choice had to be made between civic and other claims.

> After careful thought, I came to the conclusion that.... it was my duty to see my year of office as Mayor through to completion.

So Hodgkinson was out of the running as a candidate, but he still continued to act as Agent.

After losing to Jennie Lee at Cannock, my selection in Coventry was, if not a dead cert, at least a more than even chance. I was nominated for both seats. In fact, I received more than thirty nominations for Coventry East. My workmates were so sure of my winning one or other that they presented me with two suitably-inscribed books, one being Marx's 'Das

Kapital', the other a Guide to Parliament. Perhaps they thought that Marx would keep me on the right political road when the Mother of Parliaments was trying to guide me elsewhere!

The Cannock selection was on 14th April 1945. The two Coventry selections were scheduled for the first week in June. But on 25th April, the first bombshell dropped in the form of a letter to me from the AEU Executive Council. It seemed that a person or persons unknown had been spreading poison, being apparently anxious to prevent my selection in Coventry. The Executive Council named no names. They simply said that "it had been reported" that I was a member of the Communist Party and had only recently resigned from it. They pointed out that I had signed my acceptance of nomination for the AEU Parliamentary Panel in 1944, declaring that I was not a member of any organisation proscribed by the Labour Party. The list of proscribed organisations included the CP. The Executive demanded to know if the allegation was true, and if it was, why I had falsely signed the declaration. The tone of the letter suggested that the EC had already mentally found me guilty of secret membership of the Communist Party!

My reply was frank: I was not at that time a CP member, nor had I been when I signed the declaration. On 16th May, dangerously close to the selection conferences in Coventry, the AEU Executive wrote accepting my statement and admitting that there was no evidence to the contrary. They also wrote to the Coventry 54th Branch of the AEU agreeing to my nomination for both seats, and advising the branch to put in the nomination schedules without delay.

With less than three weeks to go, the way seemed clear. I was short-listed, and my name was sent, with the others on the shortlists, to Transport House for endorsement prior to the final selections being made.

Then came the second bombshell. Less than a week before the selection conferences, and with the General Election about seven weeks away, the Labour Party NEC refused to endorse my nominations. It was 30th May – in the same meeting at which George Hodgkinson's nomination was also rejected on the technicality of his being also the Party Agent. But whereas the NEC made an explanation of its refusal in Hodgkinson's case, in the case of me the NEC minutes simply stated that it was:

RESOLVED: that the candidature of Mr E Roberts be not endorsed.

Neither the Coventry Labour Party nor I had any more information than that. The AEU, whose sponsored candidate I was, got no information at all, not even a letter advising them of the decision.

So the selection conferences went on without me and without Hodgkinson: Crossman was selected for Coventry East and was subsequently elected with a majority of 18,749 in a four-way contest with Conservative, Liberal and Communist candidates; Maurice Edelman was chosen in Coventry West, and had a majority of 15,013 in a straight fight with Captain Strickland, the Tory who had held the seat for Coventry until the boundary change.

What had gone wrong for me? The NEC had had no hesitation in putting me on the 'A' list of candidates on 21st March. They declared my nomination valid at Cannock, and I attended the selection conferences there. Less than a month later, however, the AEU had been approached by someone who was anxious to prevent my candidature in Coventry, and it seemed likely that it was the same person who, having failed with the AEU, then proceeded more successfully to lay the same poison at Transport House.

On the evidence available, it seems that if I had gone for a seat elsewhere – any other seat would have suited! – I would have been endorsed without hesitation. The mistake was in attempting to win on my home ground, where certain persons had an interest in keeping me out of the running.

The NEC's action in banning me did not go without protest in Coventry. During the election campaign, my supporters had handed a petition on my behalf to Harold Laski (Chairman of the Labour Party), who visited Coventry on a whistle-stop tour, but that petition never again saw the light of day. One of those who had a suspicion that the Labour NEC had not been entirely impartial in its decision wrote to the local press about the 'MacDonaldism' that was still prevalent in the Party. The writer, Jack Carr, expressed his amazement at the NEC's apparent power to ride rough-shod over the wishes of the local party, and defended the choice of me as one of the AEU's six sponsored candidates:

We have in this area one of the most progressive persons of the whole of the labour movement, one who has all the qualifications that justly go forward with progress.... He has been recently awarded the Tom Mann Gold Medal, presented to the most energetic and ardent trade unionist in the Coventry area. He is President of the largest trade union in this city, and was elected by the engineers in the whole of Britain to be one of their six representatives in the election.

This eulogy from committed admirer was matched by sympathy and support even from less likely quarters: Dick Crossman, one of the successful candidates told me confidentially that he believed that I had been penalised for not attacking the CP after my expulsion. If I had gone to the press with vitriolic denunciations of the CP, Crossman maintained, my endorsement by the Labour Party would have been safe.

The AEU did not wait until the election was over before lambasting the Labour Party NEC in an uncharacteristically pro-Roberts letter. With 'indignation' and 'amazement', they protested at the NEC decision, declaring that my credentials and qualifications had been vetted by the AEU Executive and approved 'unanimously'. They demanded that reasons be given for the refusal of endorsement, and were anxious to know what would happen in the event of my being selected for another constituency. (At this stage, the election was still more than a month away.)

By the time the NEC got round to considering the correspondence, the election was long gone, and the AEU's complaint had been joined by demands for an enquiry by the Coventry Divisional Labour Party, and by me. On 19th September, the Labour Party Organisation Sub-Committee recommended the NEC to conduct an enquiry into the affair, and this was arranged for 15th November 1945, in Coventry.

The enquiry was conducted in a manner which no court of law would have tolerated. Those present were representatives of the Labour Party NEC (RT Windle, who later became National Agent, and H Wickham, West Midlands Regional Organiser, in addition to the Secretary and Vice-Chairman of West Coventry DLP), and a representative of the AEU Executive, Mr Kirkpatrick. Witnesses were interviewed in ones and twos by this group, under the chairmanship of Mr P Heady (NEC representative). The only major figure who was **not** invited to be present throughout was me. Accordingly, when I was at last brought into the room and asked what I had to say for myself, I simply asked, "About what? The weather?"

This was taken to be bravado by the investigating committee; in fact, it was quite genuine amazement. I had been told only that my endorsement had been refused. No explanation had been offered. The witnesses had been interviewed in my absence, and I had therefore no knowledge of their allegations against me. I had not been asked to provide any witnesses in my defence, and even if I had been, I would not have known what they were to defend me against. The only clues were the AEU's own investigation into my alleged 'secret membership' of the CP, together with Crossman's hints on the same lines.

When the questions began, they were all indeed about membership of the Communist Party, of which I was not a member. But still I had no idea of the precise nature of the allegations made against me.

Following the enquiry, there was a couple of months' silence. Then the Elections Sub-Committee of the NEC recommended that "Mr Roberts be informed that it cannot approve of his selection as a Labour candidate." The same bald decision went to the AEU Executive. No-one outside Transport House saw the report which was made to the NEC on the enquiry, and there was no way of finding out exactly what was said against me there, nor on what grounds I was excluded as a candidate. That the grounds were not very strong was evident. If anyone had been able to supply proof of my disloyalty to the Labour Party, the NEC would rightly have insisted on my expulsion from the Party. But there was no proof because there had been no disloyalty, not even so much as a minor infringement of Rules. So there was never any suggestion of expulsion.

The Report of the Coventry enquiry was filed away with the NEC Minutes at Transport House. I had my suspicions about who had done the scare-mongering at the AEU, and strongly suspected the same persons to have been at work blackening my character with the NEC. But it was not until 34 years later, researching for this biography, that the Report came to light, and my suspicions were confirmed.

The preamble to the Report, like the letter from the AEU, mentions no names, merely stating that the enquiry took place "following the receipt of information" about my association with the CP, but there is no beating about the bush when it comes to the evidence offered by witnesses. The accusations amounted to:

1 that in 1943 I had failed to give an assurance to the first witness that I was not a member of the CP.

2 that, according to the first and third witnesses, I had come second in the national AEU Parliamentary Panel election, and "the natural inference" was that I must have had CP support to popularise my candidature, since I was unknown outside the Coventry district.

3 that the third witness knew of my appeal against expulsion from the CP and "naturally assumed" that I had continued my membership of the CP after winning the appeal.

4 that I was regarded by the third witness "as a person carrying out the policy of the Communist Party", including supporting a CP member who was standing as a candidate in the AEU elections.

5 that, as the CP publication 'Coventry Organiser' had published a statement in May 1945 that I was not a CP member, "it was fair to conclude" that I had been a member up to the time of that statement.

6 that, according to the fourth witness, "it was the opinion of the majority of active and loyal members of the AEU that I still maintained association with the Communist Party." No information was offered on how this "majority opinion" was obtained.

7 that I was "believed to be reporting for the 'Daily Worker'" in the opinion of the final witness, who also declared:

8 that "so far as he knew" I had continued with CP membership, "though soured by the attitude of local CP members" and:

9 that "his speeches on 'unity' indicate that he supports a close alliance" with the CP.

These inferences, assumptions and opinions, backed up by not one solid fact, were the sum total of the case for the prosecution. The witnesses giving this evidence (virtually all of which would have been inadmissible in a court of law) were indeed an interesting collection:

Witness No 1 was Bro McKernan, an AEU member whom I helped on certain occasions with industrial problems which he had. I was unaware until I first saw the Report of the enquiry in 1979 that McKernan had spoken against me, believing him until then to have been a friend. McKernan had, according to the NEC Report, stood as a candidate in municipal elections against the official Labour candidate, and had then "resigned his membership of the Labour Party rather than face expulsion".

Witness No 2 was Bro H Morgan, another AEU member, who appears to have accompanied Bro McKernan merely to rubber-stamp his statements. The Report stated bluntly that McKernan and Morgan "could not be described as reliable witnesses".

Witness No 3 was Bro WH Stokes, a former CP member, who apparently played the part of 'poacher turned gamekeeper' in this enquiry. It was he who had proposed me for membership of the AEU in the early thirties. In 1945 he was a Divisional Organiser in the AEU.

Witness No 4 was Bro C Taylor, Secretary of the Coventry District Committee of the AEU, who continued his bitter opposition to me throughout my tenure of the Assistant General Secretary's post at Peckham Road.

Witness No 5 was Alderman George Hodgkinson, who did not appear personally at the enquiry, but submitted a detailed written statement which is quoted extensively in the NEC Report. Hodgkinson, also a member of the AEU, was a would-be candidate in the same election for which I had been refused endorsement. I would have been standing against Hodgkinson's friend, Dick Crossman, in Coventry East, and against Hodgkinson himself in Coventry West, although Hodgkinson's own candidature was quashed by the NEC at the same meeting which refused my nomination.

The Report contains an admission by Bro McKernan that he had sent out a circular to Coventry and District AEU branches, warning them not to vote for me in the election for the Parliamentary Panel. He had also written to the AEU suggesting that I was not eligible to be a Labour candidate because of my alleged CP associations. But this letter was written on 27th April, and the AEU's own letter to me accusing me of CP connections was written two days before, on 25th April. It therefore follows that someone else had sent a similar letter, and it seems not unreasonable to suppose that the writer of such a letter would appear among the witnesses against me.

After the four witnesses had appeared, and the statement of the absent Alderman Hodgkinson had been read to the Committee, I was called in to answer the allegations I had not heard. I took with me a friend, Bro Harry Brennan, not to give evidence, but simply to witness the proceedings.

According to the Report, I gave a brief outline of my relationship with the Communist Party, stating that I had not paid any contributions to the CP since 1941. Therefore, although I had not tendered any formal resignation, my membership would lapse because I had not paid my contributions. I produced my CP membership card, showing the last payment being made for the week ending 14th June 1941, and I produced my Labour Party cards for the previous two years.

I 'admitted' that I had continued on friendly terms with the CP since 1942, and that I was in favour of the affiliation of the CP to the Labour Party, but this policy was in fact also the policy of the AEU, so the same charge could have been made against any AEU-sponsored candidate.

I apparently "failed to give satisfactory answers" as to why neither I nor the CP had made clear before May 1945 that I was no longer a CP member. The answer was self-evident: the question had never arisen until them. In any case, I considered that I **had** made my non-membership of the CP very clear when I:

1 signed a declaration on joining the Labour Party that I was not a member of any proscribed body;
2 signed a similar declaration in 1944 when I was nominated as a candidate in the AEU Parliamentary Panel election;
3 sent yet another declaration in writing to the AEU on 28th April 1945, when I first heard of the accusations made against me in the union.

How many more declarations did they want?

As to the printed declaration in the 'Coventry Organiser' in May 1945, the explanation of that – I said at the enquiry – was probably that the CP, having already chosen their own candidate for the election, and knowing that I had formerly been a CP member, wished to dissociate themselves from my possible Labour candidature. This, of course, was pure speculation on my part. I was being invited to explain something which I knew nothing about, and this seemed the most likely explanation. However, the true reason for the appearance of that statement in the Communist press is actually stated in the Report, and was apparently ignored by the Committee of Enquiry, although it told substantially in my favour: Alderman Hodgkinson had **asked** the CP for such an assurance, and George Morrell (secretary of the Coventry CP) promised Hodgkinson that he would publicise my position, which he did in May 1945. The statement was therefore printed at the request of one of the witnesses against me, George Hodgkinson, who was of course acting in his role of Party Agent.

My final gesture was to present the Committee with evidence of my loyalty to the Party and of my own standing in it:

- I represented Coventry Labour Party on the West Midlands Regional Council;
- I had been elected to the Executive Committee of the West Midlands Regional Council;
- I produced a personal letter from Dick Crossman MP, thanking me for all I had done during the election, and complimenting me on my loyalty to the Party "in rather trying circumstances";
- I referred to my being awarded the Tom Mann Gold Medal in 1944; the award was made by a committee including many Labour Party members, the most notable of whom in the circumstances was Alderman Hodgkinson;
- I submitted a copy of a letter dated 3rd September 1944 which had been circulated to AEU branches prior to the election of the Parliamentary Panel. The letter "invited AEU members to vote for Roberts.... saying that Roberts would be a very suitable candidate for one of the Coventry divisions." This letter had been signed by, among others, Alderman Stringer (Leader of the local Labour Party). It was also signed by Alderman Hodgkinson.

This was the sum total of the case presented to the NEC. The conclusions reached by the Committee of Enquiry were three:

1 That the evidence obtained as a result of the enquiry confirms the evidence on which the National Executive Committee decided to refuse endorsement of the nomination of Mr Roberts in connection with the Coventry candidature.

2 That the evidence submitted by responsible people referred to in this Report supports the opinion expressed by Mr Hodgkinson.... that up to May 1945 Mr Roberts endeavoured to retain support of the people with whom he worked while a member of the Communist Party, and at the same time endeavoured to establish himself as a loyal member of the Labour Party.

3 that there is no evidence that since May 1945 Mr Roberts has been actively associated with the Communist Party.

There was no evidence for the period between June 1941 and 1945 either. The concrete evidence points the other way. Even Hodgkinson's evidence, which was against me in the extreme, contained the following:

> Bro Roberts has done useful propaganda work for the Labour Party at open-air meetings and in other ways, and he was largely responsible for the creation of a group of individual members of the Labour Party in the Daimler No 2 factory.

Of course I had remained friendly with CP members. Many were workmates, and most would be AEU members. Why should I shun them? Crossman was probably right: if I had attacked the CP openly, I would have saved myself 32 years of almost unbroken blackballing by the Labour Party NEC.

The accusation that I won the AEU ballot through having CP support was entirely unfounded. I had been District President in an area with 30,000 members. I had already stood for national office in the AEU, so was not unknown outside the area. Therefore, although a relative newcomer to national politics, I had massive support in the West Midlands Region, and the other 79 candidates on the ballot paper were not exactly household names, either! In any case, even if the CP had commanded vast numbers of the votes in the AEU – which it did not – it was ridiculous to suppose that such support would have had a favourable influence in a **Labour Party** ballot. Quite the reverse, in fact.

When the secretary of West Coventry DLP reported back to the local party's General Management Committee after the enquiry, Alderman Cresswell (who had been the first Labour Lord Mayor of Coventry, and who well knew the intrigues and machinations of some of his colleagues) listened to the report and then held up a bag with some coins in it, saying

"All that for thirty pieces of silver". But he did not pick out the Judases by name.

The NEC's decision to uphold its refusal to endorse me was made in the following January. I protested again. My protest was 'received', without comment.

Unwilling to take no for an answer, I put the pressure on for a further investigation, and Mr Windle made another journey to Coventry to meet the General Management Committee on 24th May 1946. The GMC decided at this meeting to endorse my candidature and put my name on the new panel of candidates. There was another silence from the NEC, followed by further correspondence with the National Agent, Mr G Sheppard.

This cat-and-mousing went on for some months. By January 1947, Windle had replaced Sheppard as National Agent, and I visited him at Transport House on 11th January. According to the note in my diary, made at the time, Windle then said that I was "free to be nominated by any constituency".

I appear to have viewed this rather optimistically as a sign from Above that future nominations would be considered sympathetically by the NEC, but apparently the unspoken end to Windle's sentence was: "....but you won't necessarily be endorsed even if you're nominated."

By the time the constituencies began to bestir themselves before the 1950 General Election, Windle seemed to have forgotten his conversation of 1947, for when Nottingham Broxtowe received a nomination for me and asked to have it sanctioned, he replied to the effect that there had been no review of my position since my endorsement was last refused, and in his opinion nothing had happened to make the NEC change its mind, should I be nominated again.

In the 1950 election, I had to be content with speaking at election meetings (in fact, I continued to speak on behalf of Crossman and Edelman in Coventry even after I moved down to London in 1957), and chauffeur-ing electioneering cars.

Once back on the AEU Panel, however, several nominations came my way. In 1953, I was nominated yet again for Broxtowe, and received an optimistic letter from Dick Crossman:

I have had a word with the office and I can see no reason whatsoever why you should not be endorsed automatically if you win the Broxtowe constituency. With Reg Underhill asking you to let your name go forward, and your record on the City Council, I think you can confidently regard the past as closed.

I was shortlisted for Broxtowe, but William Warby was the candidate finally selected. Also in 1953, Reg Underhill (West Midlands Regional Organiser and later National Agent of the Party before being elevated to the peerage) suggested my nomination for Sutton Coldfield, but that came to nothing, as did Holborn & St Pancras. 1954 saw a nomination for Aberdare and for Perry Bar, where I was shortlisted and came second to CA Howell in the selection conference. Howell and I shared 55 of the 57 votes between us – I got a respectable 22.

The trend was certainly optimistic. A candidate must be validated by the NEC before getting even so far as a selection conference, and I had now been to two selection conferences.

In 1955, there was bound to be another General Election on the horizon, but nevertheless a 'surprise' announcement in April of a May election caught a number of constituencies napping. I was involved in a flurry of selections, in Stamford and in Walsall South, neither of which got as far as the selection conference, and in Meriden. Here I was nominated by a CLP ward and was not standing as a sponsored candidate so, as I wrote to a friend, "my chances of getting it are small." In fact, I was shortlisted, and lost the selection by only two votes to R Moss.

I recall that, after Moss was elected, we met at Euston Station when I was travelling back to Coventry and Moss was going to Rugby. We got on the same train. A ticket inspector punched my ticket, then examined Moss's Parliamentary Rail Pass. "Where are you getting off?" he asked. "Rugby". "Well, mind you don't break your bloody neck," said the inspector casually as he moved off into the next compartment, "the train doesn't stop there."

One of the constituencies caught on the hop was Stockport South, where there had been a by-election only two months before. The Labour candidate had been beaten then by two and a half thousand votes. Stockport had never had a Labour MP, nor even a Labour Council, and, with only five weeks to go before the General Election, Stockport South did not even have a Labour candidate! (Labour got a majority on the Council for the first time in 1955, in the municipal elections which took place just before the General Election.)

Nominations were hurriedly called for, and the Stockport District AEU nominated me. My nomination was validated by the AEU, I was short-listed, and was selected as the candidate for Stockport South on 28th April. I was later told that the NEC representative at the selection conference had warned them that "Roberts had Communist tendencies". "That's good enough for us," they said, and promptly selected me.

There had been no time for the CLP to get endorsement of the shortlist from the NEC, which was the normal procedure. They simply forwarded the name of their chosen candidate to Transport House after the selection conference, and kept their fingers crossed. Five days later, there was a special meeting to discuss three candidates "about whose political position there was some doubt." One was Konni Zilliacus, who seemed to be in and out of trouble with the NEC all his political life; the second was Frank Allaun, who has since served the Party admirably in the House, and was Chairman of the Party during 1978/79. The third man was me.

The Elections Sub-Committee included Clement Attlee, Edith Sumer-skill, Hugh Gaitskell and Herbert Morrison – none of whom would have been inclined to give Zilliacus, Allaun and me a clean bill of health. Fortu-nately, three weeks before the election, the sub-committee delegated its responsibilities to three NEC members, one of whom was Ian Mikardo.

Writing of the dossiers on left-wing members compiled in the National Agent's office under the reign of Len Williams, followed by Sara Barker, Mikardo said that these MI5-style files were trotted out at the special meeting to discuss the endorsement of Allaun, Zilliacus and me. In the cases of Zilliacus and me, Mikardo said:

Sara Barker opposed their endorsement and produced her dossiers on them to support her case. I told my colleagues that if the endorsements were withheld on the basis of that procedure I would immediately resign from the NEC and announce publicly why I had done so; and that was the end of that. Ron Hayward has told me (and others) that on the day he took office as national agent he found a four-drawer filing cabinet full of these dossiers, and he burned the lot of them.

'New Socialist', March/April 1982.

236

Zilliacus and Allaun were both endorsed and then, "after a long discussion" (according to the sub-committee minutes), I also received the seal of approval.

There was no full NEC meeting to consider these decisions until 22nd June, and all three candidatures were confirmed at that meeting. The NEC could hardly have done anything else, since the election had taken place a month before.

I entered into my campaign with gusto. Although I had never in my life worn a hat, I was persuaded that I could not be seen without one in a hatting manufacturing constituency, so I bought one at the local Co-op and carried it in my hand throughout the campaign. I drew the line at kissing babies, but fitted factory-gate meetings, public meetings and walkabouts into my already tight programme of door-to-door canvassing. Three weeks is not a long time to get to know your constituency, nor for the electorate to get to know you.

Coming from a flourishing new city, in the process of being virtually rebuilt after the blitz, I, as the candidate for Stockport South, was horrified at the appalling housing conditions in Stockport, and I estimated that, at the Tory rate of house-building, it would take twenty years simply to house those who were on the waiting-list in 1955. Yet in spite of these conditions in which people were living, I came across considerable Tory support amongst those who were worst off. A pensioner in one of the poorest areas, beside the rat-infested River Mersey, put it into words: she intended to vote Conservative because the Conservatives had the money – that Labour lot didn't have any, so what good could they do? How, in three short weeks, could you convince 40,000 voters that Conservatives have the money because their principal object in life is to prevent anybody else from getting their rightful share of it? How, in three short weeks, could you convince the electorate that Socialism does not mean communal living, the abolition of home ownership and confiscation of corner shops?

Under the slogan of 'BE SURE TO VOTE, and to be SURE, Vote Labour', I campaigned on the abolition of Health Service charges, the withdrawal of National Service, the introduction of comprehensive education, and peace. Peace was my principal platform: stopping the H-bomb tests, peace negotiations with the Soviet Union and China, opposition to German rearmament, and redevelopment of some of our own arms expenditure into better old-age pensions and a reduction in the cost of living.

The local newspapers were determined to give Socialist policies as little publicity as possible. The 'Stockport Express' columns of correspondence were filled with Tory contributions from people who for some reason preferred not to put names to their letters –'Right', 'Housewife' and 'Reddish Conservative', to name but three. But a correspondent who had the courage to sign her letter – one Mrs Annie Sixton, who had been a Tory candidate in the recent municipal elections – drew forth columns of derision from Labour supporters, one of whom put his scorn into verse:

O list to the sad lamenting story
Of a poor misguided Tory.
She obviously finds too much to bear
The colour of flowers in Mersey Square,
And in a manner forthright and blunt
calls it an electioneering stunt.
Shall we make our town the poorer
By banning our displays of flora?
Do we truly want it said,
We shunned the rose, for it was RED?
We'll have to see what we can do,
And next year make the tulips BLUE.

The campaign was far from light-hearted, however. The Stockport Tories had been 'digging' in Coventry, and brought the results of their spadework into my public meetings. I was asked why I had opposed the building of Coventry Cathedral, and answered that the City had 10,000 people on its waiting-list for council houses and I thought it was more Christian to house the homeless. Then questions came thick, fast and searching:

"Have you ever been a Communist?"

"Are you a political agitator?"

"How many times have you been sacked?"

I said publicly that the Tories, unable to attack Socialist policy, were reduced to smear tactics on the candidate. The two local papers, the

'Express' and the 'Advertiser', had a field-day with these meetings, and splashed articles over the last two issues before polling-day. They had little room for Socialist policy, but plenty of Tory mud-slinging, although the 'Advertiser' fairly reported:

> Mr Roberts remained calm throughout the examination, frequently smiling as he replied to his examiners and his replies received rounds of applause from his supporters....

and:

> A man in the audience remarked, "Active trade unionists are either bought over by their employers or victimised." He added, pointing at the candidate, "You are good enough for me; you shall have my vote."

One of the characteristics of a good public speaker is the ability to rise to the occasion when faced with abuse. After repeated accusations from Young Conservatives of being "a Communist fellow-traveller", I quickly began to turn their smears to my own advantage, as when I opened a speech by saying what a great pleasure it was to meet the Tory fellow-travellers once again – "I mean those who have been travelling about with me on this campaign with their questions and tarbrushes."

I won my seat on the council in the municipal election in Coventry, which I had been fighting simultaneously with the General Election, but was less fortunate in Stockport, although I received a creditable result in view of Labour's poor showing nationally, and in view of the smear tactics which had featured largely in the campaign against me. The result was:

HM Steward (Con)	20,698
EAC Roberts (Lab)	16,612
Con majority	4,086

One of the first to commiserate with me in my defeat was Hugh Scanlon (at that time active in the Manchester District of the AEU, of which he later became National President, subsequently becoming a peer), who wrote in praise of my campaign:

> In contrast to some of the other constituencies where the merits of the price of bacon, sponsored television, etc., have been hotly debated, in your case the points of peace, German rearmament, H-bomb, etc. have really been brought home to the electorate.
>
> I know from my discussions with the lads on the AEU District Committee that

they feel they have in you a candidate who can ultimately win the constituency. Whilst, therefore, it is a matter of regret that you were not successful, I am sure a basis has been laid which augurs well for the future.

The Stockport South CLP had clearly been satisfied with my services, for I was re-selected as their candidate in 1956, and as I had already fought one election with their blessing (grudging as it was) the NEC could hardly refuse to re-endorse me.

I was a frequent visitor to Stockport throughout the next two years, spoke at Labour Party meetings, and entered into the life of the constituency as far as was compatible with a full-time job and a seat on Coventry City Council. But I was elected as Assistant General Secretary of the AEU late in 1957, and then felt that I would not be able to give sufficient time to my candidature. In February 1958 I tendered my resignation which was accepted with genuine regret by my friends in Stockport South.

A couple of years' experience at Peckham Road was enough to make me change my mind about the onerous nature of the duties placed upon me by the Executive Council and I rejoined the AEU Parliamentary Panel again in 1960. Once again, nominations flooded in: Coventry South, Small Heath, Billericay, Maldon, King's Lynn, Central Norfolk, Bedford, North Norwich, Epping, West Lewisham, Stroud, Yardley, Norwich South, Burton, Lambeth, Nottingham Central, Croydon South, Huddersfield West, Yeovil, Heston & Isleworth, Isle of Thanet, Dover. I was invited to all of these during 1960 and 1961, sometimes by my union, sometimes by the Constituency Labour Party, but I refused them all for one reason or another. One of the reasons was that I already had enough to cope with in the way of aggravation at Peckham Road, and my suspension from office during the same period.

At the latter end of 1961, however, I had a special reason for refusing further nominations – I had been nominated for Horsham in Sussex, and had been selected as their candidate. I was originally nominated by the Crawley Branch of the National Union of Sheet Metal Workers and Coppersmiths; my own union also nominated me, but not as an AEU-sponsored candidate, because the union was naturally only prepared to put its money into seats which Labour had some chance of winning. Horsham definitely did not come into that category, being solidly Tory. The selection conference took place on 22nd October 1961, **after the Labour Party NEC had validated my nomination,** and my name was sent to Transport House as Horsham's selected candidate. Within a month, I received a summons to attend at the House of Commons, where I was to be interviewed. The interview was conducted by Len Williams (National Agent and Deputy General Secretary of the Party), Harry Earnshaw, Ray Gunter MP and George Brown MP. (Ray Gunter and George Brown were both on the Right of the Party; Gunter became a Director of Securicor in 1969, and resigned from the Labour Party in 1972; George Brown accepted a peerage in 1970, and resigned from the Labour Party in 1976.)

At the interview, Gunter referred to a list of events at which I had spoken, and which was causing the Party some concern:

March 1958	National Conference of British Youth, Festival Committee
March 1958	Student Labour Federation Weekend School, Cambridge
June 1958	London TU and Old-Age Pensioners Joint Campaign Committee, Trafalgar Square Demonstration
October 1958	'Labour Monthly' Conference
November 1958	'Irish Democrat' Conference
June 1959	'March for Life' demonstration
November 1960	London Peace Campaign Demonstration, Trafalgar Square
February 1961	Yorkshire Peace Conference, Doncaster
March 1961	Midlands Peace Conference, Birmingham

Nine meetings. I estimated that in the period from March 1958 to March 1961 I had attended about 400 public meetings, in addition to my trade union ones. Moreover, the meetings picked out for criticism seemed to be a singularly innocuous collection. As I pointed out, none of the meetings was called by or sponsored by an organisation on the Labour Party's 'proscribed' list. I further pointed out that I had stood as a candidate in the 1955 election and was re-adopted in 1956 and no-one had had cause to complain about my behaviour. I produced letters of commendation from various sections of the Labour Party in Coventry (written when I left the city) and Stockport (when I resigned my candidature), and reminded the investigating committee that the NEC had validated my nomination for selection conferences on several occasions, including for Horsham, without a quibble. The report of this investigation went before the Organisation Sub-Committee on 12th December 1961. Thirty-five candidates had been selected by various constituencies, and all were endorsed at that meeting with the exception of me.

Horsham was solidly Tory. In the 1959 election, the Conservative had a majority of 13,263 in a straight fight with Labour. At first sight, it would seem to serve the NEC better if I fought Horsham, where I had no chance of winning. They must have seen a danger in the future, however, that once endorsed at Horsham I would sooner or later be offered a safe seat elsewhere, and Horsham must therefore be considered as the thin end of the wedge.

Dogged to the end, I fought the ban, with the full support of Horsham CLP, and after discussion of the case had been deferred by the NEC for a couple of months, I was eventually informed that my name had been withdrawn from the 'A' list of trade union sponsored candidates and, although any nomination would be considered by the NEC on its merits, I had little reason to hope that any future attempt to stand for another constituency would meet with any greater success.

As I had been one of their candidates, the AEU was naturally concerned that I had been banned from standing, but their concern on this occasion (in contrast with Coventry in 1945, in which they had been genuinely helpful) seemed mainly to be that of getting the problem of Ernie Roberts out of their hair. They had chained me to my desk (with only limited success), suspended me from office (with no success at all), 'shopped' me to Transport House over the 'Daily Worker' conference in 1960, and now here I was again, causing trouble as usual.

The Labour Party NEC was told by the sub-committee that although "there had been consultation" with the AEU beforehand, the approval of the union had not been sought before my name was removed from the 'A' list. Not surprisingly, the AEU retaliated under such cavalier treatment – not because the Executive Council regretted the NEC decision, but because the AEU National Committee, which had endorsed me for the AEU Parliamentary Panel in the first place, was likely to complain. The NEC agreed that George Brown and Morgan Phillips should meet Messrs Carron, Hallett and Boyd of the AEU to discuss the matter.

That meeting took place in June 1962, and a report of it was minuted by the NEC Organisation Sub-Committee. It was perfectly clear what support I could expect from my union:

> Mr Brown reported that, as agreed by the NEC, the General Secretary and he had met the officers of the AEU concerning Mr EAC Roberts. After a long discussion, the officers of the AEU stated that, having heard the statement of Mr Brown and the General Secretary, they had no comment to make.

From the time when the NEC's refusal to endorse was first made public, the press had been having a field-day, exploiting the "split in Labour's ranks". The event was seen as the first step in a purge of 'Red' elements and the promotion instead of a "nicer type of candidate" in readiness for the next General Election. 'The Sussex Evening Argus' leapt with glee on the Party's endorsement of an ex-Fascist, Derek Lesley-Jones, with a sixteen-year fascist record, including deputising for Oswald Moseley, and coupled it with the rejection of me, pointing out that Jones was a convert to Gaitskellism, whereas I was anti-Gaitskell. 'Tribune', in two articles on the Labour Party's modern version of 'The Star Chamber', stressed the fact that the NEC had refused Horsham CLP an explanation of the ban on their candidate:

> What a howl would go up from those members of the Parliamentary Labour Party if they heard of such a thing happening in another Party.... No court of law can get away with sentencing a person without giving the reason for so doing.

'Tribune' went on to put its finger right on the main issue:

> What in effect they are doing is to say that constituency parties have no longer the right to select their own candidates. Transport House will continue to veto them until they get someone who is suitable to their purpose.

But if the NEC kept its opinions on me to itself, the Tory press had no such inhibitions! They gave a variety of reasons for my rejection, ranging through membership of the CND, membership of Victory for Socialism, sharing a platform with communists, sharing a platform with Bertrand Russell, and general left-wingery. The truth was probably a cocktail of all these, plus a generous helping of personal animosity. On the union front, Bill Carron was widely reported as accusing me of having created "a deliberate hullaballoo" over the issue. Presumably he was of the opinion that rejected candidates should turn the other cheek. When I wrote privately to the Executive stating my case and asking for their support, the Executive published their answer everywhere from the 'Daily Telegraph' to the 'Yorkshire Evening Post' – NO!

The press, the union and the NEC were unanimous in their opposition. But enormous support came from the grass-roots of the Labour Party. Horsham circularised all constituencies with the facts of the case. Nearly 250 constituencies sent resolutions to the NEC deploring its decision to withhold endorsement. They were told that the NEC had been advised by lawyers that they were not obliged to say why they had rejected me; whereupon the constituencies themselves took legal advice and were told that the NEC must give this information if pressed. There were so many complaints that Transport House began to send out duplicated letters in reply to constituencies. Slowly, CLPs came to the frustrating realisation that there was no remedy: the only way they might pressurise the NEC to give reasons for the ban was by taking them to court, and Transport House was better able to finance a court case than the CLPs were.

Crawley Labour Party (part of the Horsham Constituency) declared that they would not accept any candidate the NEC cared to foist on them, and stated their intention to ask me to stand as an Independent candidate if necessary (which I would never have done). At least one long-standing member of the Party who had never met me or even heard of me prior to the Horsham incident, resigned from the Party in disgust at the NEC's actions.

A flood of trade union branches and CLPs asked me to stand for their constituencies instead of Horsham – Liverpool Scotland, Luton, Salford West, Hendon North, Hertford, Kingston-upon-Thames, Chertsey, Chelsea, Walton, Basingstoke, Croydon North-West, South Bedfordshire and Poplar among them – but I refused them all. I was no longer on the list of sponsored candidates, and if I could not get endorsement at Horsham there was no reason to suppose I would be more successful elsewhere.

Many constituencies submitted motions on the case to the 1962 Party Conference, demanding that at the very least the NEC should be obliged to give reasons for any refusals to endorse candidates. Horsham CLP had a "Message to all Conference Delegates" printed, bearing a photograph of me and a very restrained record of the situation, asking for the delegates' support. The object was to get the reference back of the paragraph of the NEC Report dealing with parliamentary candidates. The reference back was moved by Horsham CLP in the closed session on the Thursday of Conference week. I was not present. I had written to the Conference chairman, Harold Wilson MP, asking to be permitted to speak in my own defence, but this was not allowed since I was not a delegate to the Conference. Ray Gunter replied to the debate on the reference back, and although there is no written report of his speech (the published Conference Report dismissed the whole debate in one brief paragraph), notes taken at the time suggest that his main themes were the need to protect the Party from infiltration by people who would wish to harm it, coupled with my activities with 'strange organisations'. The Horsham CLP wrote a blistering letter to Len Williams, the General Secretary, denouncing the Party's gross injustice: they had made public the reasons for the ban, which should have been made public long before, but since nobody had known in advance what was going to be said, there had been no opportunity to prepare a defence. The CLP asked for a copy of Gunter's statement to Conference and for a deputation to be allowed to meet the Organisation Sub-Committee. The NEC reply was short and to the point: the matter was now closed.

In December, after more than a year's wrangling, I admitted defeat. I resigned as Horsham's candidate (in the NEC's opinion, I had never been their candidate anyway!) and two days later, I resigned from the AEU Parliamentary Panel.

However, the mid-sixties found me again trying to get on the Panel, and in 1967 my name was submitted once more for inclusion on the 'A' list. The NEC didn't think very highly of me, but they must surely have given me full marks for persistence. Yet again, the NEC called me up for a grilling, and on 12th February 1968 I was facing another investigation, this

245

time chaired by Joe Gormley (later Lord Gormley) of the NUM. Yet another catalogue of grievances emerged, suggesting that the NEC knew at least as much about my diary as I did myself. This time there were two main complaints, one concerned with a meeting organised by the Bertrand Russell Peace Foundation in 1967, the other about my connection with the Society for Anglo-Chinese Understanding. I maintained that I had neither spoken nor agreed to speak at the 1967 meeting, and later obtained a letter from the Peace Foundation confirming this. As for SACU, I provided the NEC with a brochure of its aims, to which they could not possibly have taken exception, and – more importantly – a list of its sponsors, which included MPs of all three major parties.

The reason for the sudden activity at Transport House was the possibility that I might be selected as the candidate for Oldham West. However, as Transport House dillied and dallied over whether to put me back on the 'A' list, the threat receded, as I was not shortlisted for Oldham West, and subsequent nominations for Bradford South and Bristol South came to nothing. In North Paddington I was shortlisted but did not go to the selection conference, backing down in favour of Jock Stallard (later Lord Stallard), an AEU man who succeeded in getting the nomination and winning the constituency in 1970. At last, in mid-1969, the NEC took the plunge and put me back on the 'A' list.

But as the Labour Party relented slightly, at least one person had strong reservations about the advisability of pursuing a parliamentary seat. Walter Kendall wrote to me:

> My view would be that the position you now hold is far more important and influential from the angle of the socialist and working-class movement than a place on the backbenches.... I realise that you may well prefer MP to the drudgery which must be involved with some of your work, but wonder if you have discussed it with any of the others in Parliament to discover just how empty their own role is and how much meaningless waste of time is involved there, too?
>
> .... Additionally, you ought to ask, I think, who would take over if you left? Would it be a respected left-winger like yourself, or a CP-er or someone in their pocket?

Kendall's good advice was hardly necessary. Even if I were offered a good seat on a plate, it seemed very unlikely that the NEC would scotch it

– after all, I had been on the 'A' list before, only to be knocked off as soon as a seat was in the offing.

But then came a curious development. On 3rd April 1970, 'The Times' carried a substantial item in its Diary column, with the headline "Ernie Roberts Cleared". According to this article Transport House had lifted its ban on my endorsement. There was no seat on offer, no hint of a candidature in the air, no reason for such a decision out of the blue. But 'The Times' Diary put its finger on an important factor: at 57, I was too old to stand much chance of a parliamentary seat. I was not a danger any more. (Perhaps that was why they did not even write and tell me that they had lifted their ban, but left me to read it in 'The Times'!)

PENGE & BECKENHAM TRADE UNION & SOCIALIST FORUM

Programme: 1961-62

SEPTEMBER 26th, 8 p.m.

"Which Way British Youth?"—an "Any Questions" panel comprising: JOHN DELAHOY (Comm.), Cllr. FRANK COOKE (Cons.), GEORGE JERROM (Lab.) and DAVID GARNER (Lib.), will deal with the questions.
Chair: Mimi Silver.

OCTOBER 17th, 8 p.m.

"Berlin—The Role of the United Nations." This problem discussed by OMO OLOFIN (Nigeria) and other speakers.
Chair: Jack Simons (*President, A.S.L.E.F.*).

NOVEMBER 21st, 8 p.m.

"The Common Market—Britain, IN or OUT?" JACK DUNMAN of the "Country Standard" discusses this problem with COLIN BEEVER—Author of book on Common Market.
Chair: Ernie Roberts (*Asst. Gen. Secretary, A.E.U.*).

DECEMBER 19th, 8 p.m.

"The Trade Unions and Working-Class Culture." The subject discussed by ARNOLD WESKER (Robin Hood Choir).
Chair: George Bowden (*London Dist. Secretary, Bakers' Union*).

JANUARY 16th, 8 p.m.

"Democracy In the Trade Unions—Are Changes Needed?" ERNIE ROBERTS . . . presents the facts.
Chair: Don Pullen (Nat. E.C., A.S.L.E.F.).

FEBRUARY 13th, 8 p.m.

"A Road to Socialist Britain—Is Socialism Really Necessary?" BILL ALEXANDER (Asst. Gen. Sec., Communist Party) poses the question and suggests a few answers.
Chair: Dan Huxtep (U.S.D.A.W.)

MARCH 13th, 8 p.m.

"Education In Britain—Is It Adequate for a Modern World?" RON DEADMAN (School Teacher, N.U.T.) presents the problem from the inside.
Chair: George Jerrom (Y.S.)

APRIL 24th, 8 p.m.

"Defence for What?" The greatest problem of our age dealt with by SYDNEY SILVERMAN, M.P.
Chair: Ernie Roberts (A.E.U.)

The programme for the Forum I founded in Beckenham Library in 1962.

Chapter 8

Truth, said Bacon, has been rightly named the daughter of Time.
Burke

1   Breaking the fascist menace
2   Forming the Anti-Nazi League
3   Accused as KGB agent
4   Fall of Callaghan government
5   Chosen for Hackney North & Stoke Newington

As a result of my own experiences, I fought against the expulsion of Labour Party members which was taking place to an increasing degree during the 1980s. This heresy hunting by the right-wing of left-wing members was doing electoral harm to the Party and destroying its socialist content.

Together with Joan Maynard MP, Reg Race MP and Keith Lichman, Hackney North Secretary, we convened a conference of members to form an organisation 'Labour Against the Witch Hunt'. I was elected as Chairperson. Together we supported those in various parts of the country who were under threats of expulsion. But because the right-wing controlled the machine of the Party, the Right most often got away with their attacks on the Left.

The last occasion I was able to oppose witch hunting was as a delegate to the 1990 annual conference of the Labour Party, where it was recorded in the Annual Report that 200 left-wing members were to be expelled or disciplined. I urged the conference to be democratic and tolerant and not to agree to expulsions. I reminded them of how tolerant the right-wing had been towards the 'gang of four' MPs, Prentice MP, G Brown MP and others who were not expelled. However, the conference was not allowed to discuss the matter and my objections were dismissed.

In the 1990s the witch hunt continues. Left-wingers like Dennis Skinner MP and Tony Benn MP are removed from the NEC of the Party. Dave Nellist MP for Coventry, P Walls MP for Bradford, and Terry Fields MP for Liverpool Broadgreen were expelled. The right-wing is still heresy hunting members and is doing great harm to the Party.

Transport House had lifted its ban on my endorsement in 1970. But with invitations to accept nominations for 59 constituencies already under my belt, I had an ability to come back when least expected. I retired from the AEU Assistant General Secretary-ship in 1977, aged 65. And within a couple of months up popped Constituency Number Sixty, unexpected and certainly not sought after – Hackney North & Stoke Newington.

I did not regard my retirement from the union as being in any sense 'the beginning of the end'.

At 65, I am sure I looked much younger than my years, was physically strong and active, and mentally agile.

When the challenge of Hackney North arose, I therefore took it up keenly. I was far from confident of success, having learned from bitter experience of the slips which can occur between cup and lip, but I had no doubt of my ability to do the job, given the chance.

The sitting tenant in the constituency was David Weitzman QC, then 79 years old, who had been a barrister for 55 years and an MP for 32 years since his election in 1945. A write-up in the 'House Magazine' (published for MPs) labelled him as "one of the quiet elder statesmen of the House", who had "pursued a legal career, eschewing great political ambition."

Weitzman was to retire at the next General Election, and when nominations were invited for his replacement, over a hundred willing volunteers came forward. I was nominated by a member of Springfield Branch, Councillor George Armstrong, and was asked to attend an interview at a special branch meeting. Five others were also shortlisted in Springfield, and each candidate made a ten-minute speech, followed by a ten-minute question-and-answer session, after which there was an exhaustive ballot to decide the branch's nominee. Each invited candidate provided brief biographical details, and any other interested party – even though not invited – could put in a biography for consideration by the branch. In addition, members were free to nominate extra candidates to go into the ballot, so that nobody who wanted to enter the contest was excluded. I won the Springfield nomination.

Meanwhile the other branches and affiliated organisations were also making selections. The final list comprised sixteen nominees, all of whom were thoroughly investigated by the Executive Committee of the constituency (an elected body consisting of 27 members) in eleven and a half hours of interviews spread over a period of three days. Each of the six branches in the constituency had selected a different nominee, and there were also nominations from affiliated union branches, the women's section of the party, the Co-op, and from Poale Zion (a Jewish Socialist organisation). One of the trade union members was Alf Lomas, who had been secretary of the Stockport South CLP when I fought the 1955 election there; Lomas went on to become a strictly anti-Common Market member of the European Assembly in the first round of EEC elections.

My political biography could rival any of the others with its wealth of political experience, and there could be no possible doubt about where I stood in the political spectrum. The statement I made to the Springfield Branch and then to the Executive Committee explained how I felt about the Labour Government of the day: "What we need are leaders who will implement our great Socialist aims and principles," I told them.

I had expected opposition on the grounds of my age, and was prepared for it. When asked "How old are you?" I replied "Chronologically 65, biologically 25," and I invited members to inspect my busy diary as evidence of how active a life I led.

My views matched the mood of the Executive, and I was one of the shortlist of six to appear before the General Management Committee (consisting of about 70 elected representatives from branches and affiliated organisations) in the final selection conference, where I was chosen as the prospective parliamentary candidate for Hackney North & Stoke Newington.

Those who have never been involved in a Labour Party selection procedure may be surprised at how far-reaching and comprehensive a survey of Party talent it is, putting interested candidates through a variety of hoops before one finally emerges the victor. This is the procedure which the Left was anxious to extend, to apply not only when a sitting MP dies or chooses to retire, but prior to every General Election, so that the CLP can be sure that it is still getting the best person for the job. It is this procedure which is denigrated by the Right as being one in which some unrepresentative clique of extremists can force a candidate on an unwilling CLP. In Hackney North, a typical selection procedure, over two hundred members of the Party were involved in the selection from start to finish. Some clique!

Even after my selection, I was not over-confident about my chances of fighting the next election, I had been selected as a prospective candidate in Horsham sixteen years before, but the NEC had refused to endorse me. For the next three weeks I attended a hectic round of Party meetings, still unsure of my official position. Then came the letter: my selection had been endorsed.

That year's Party Conference, 1977, yet again proved a fertile breeding-ground for new movements. It was here that I met with Peter Hain, Liberal-turned-Labour member, elected MP in 1992, and Paul Holborow of the Socialist Workers' Party, to found "the fastest-growing political organisation of 1978", the Anti-Nazi League.

The fascist National Front was gaining support in Britain, and Hain, Holborow and I took the initiative to found an organisation which would highlight the similarities between the National Front and Hitler's Nazis. We were particularly anxious to combat the television-time which the Front would 'earn' by fielding large numbers of candidates in the General Election, and the Founding Statement declared:

> This must not go unopposed. Ordinary voters must be made aware of the threat that lies behind the National Front. In every town, in every factory, in every school, on every housing estate, wherever the Nazis attempt to organise they must be countered.

The ANL took off in the early months of 1978. Forty Labour MPs were among the first sponsors; people from the entertainment world, such as Glenda Jackson, Miriam Karlin, Annie Ross, Jack Rosenthal, Ron Moody, sports personalities including Brian Clough, Jackie Charlton and Terry Venables, writers, scientists, barristers, professors, peers, all put their names to the founding statement.

Donations and subscriptions amounting to £120,000 in the first year enabled the League, with me as Treasurer, to publish vast quantities of leaflets, some of it generally anti-fascist, some aimed at specific sectors of the community. There were leaflets for teachers about Nazism in schools, for women, for gays, for engineers.... for practically any group you could think of. The literature was good. Posters with photographs of concentration camps carrying the slogan "NEVER AGAIN!"; a close-up of Hitler superimposed on a picture of a National Front march, with the words which became almost a hypnotic chant in ANL demonstrations, "The National Front is a Nazi front: stop the National Front"; giant swastikas covered with the ANL's 'red arrow' logo. Graffiti appeared on walls overnight:

NF = No Fun
    No Freedom
    No Future

The most spectacular evidence of the ANL's success in reaching a wide audience was the series of carnivals which attracted massive crowds from all over the country. Only four months after its founding, the ANL drew together 80,000 people in a rally in Trafalgar Square, followed by a march to Victoria Park in Hackney for a kind of political rock-concert. It was very gratifying to the organisers that the vast majority of the 80,000 were young people who clearly were not swallowing the NF line on racism. The rally was addressed by Ian Mikardo MP and Ray Buckton, ASLEF leader, with me in the chair. None of the speakers could have addressed a crowd quite like this before. Dressed in assorted garb of leather and satin, with hair of green or purple or pink, the teenagers gave them an enthusiastic welcome.

Far from approving of this sign of unity and integration among young people, the national press denigrated it roundly. The most virulent attack came from Colin Welch, in the 'Daily Telegraph' of 5th May, who said that the march was made up of "Communists of every sort", although even a conservative estimate classed 80 per cent of ANL participants as non-political, the majority of the remainder being Labour Party supporters. Welch describes the marchers as "militants, anarchists, punk rockers and their bands, freaks, children of every colour and the usual sinister perverts attracted thereby." He continued:

> More sinister even than these.... was a most respectable dressed elderly man, with a smart red tie, not unlike Bill Fraser or Enoch Powell, though with a rather coarser face. He stood on the plinth of Nelson's Column and appeared to be master of these bizarre ceremonies.

> This turned out to be Mr Ernie Roberts.... One would give a lot to know what this grim teetotal monolith thought of the decadent tide which ebbed and flowed at his bidding, a tide of which he in his heart must have harshly disapproved but from which he presumably hopes to derive some benefit.

Why should I have disapproved? I had worn some pretty outlandish clothes in my time and so am not in a position to point a finger at anyone else's display of personal taste. Apart from the clothes, there was nothing to disapprove of. Welch went on to express what seemed to be disappointment at the peaceful nature of the day's events, perhaps because that left him nothing concrete to complain about except the fashion.

This carnival was the first of many to be held in different parts of the country. A minority of the more political ANL events ended in clashes with the Front or with the police, but 99 per cent of ANL activities have been peaceful, and that is how they were intended to be.

Before long however trouble arose on two scores. First, the Jewish community, in the form of the Board of Deputies, took exception to what they believed to be the anti-Zionist inclinations of the ANL, and in vain did the three founders try to convince them that the ANL as a body had no policy on Zionism, which was not in its province anyway, nor did it have control over the views of individual members. The basis for the complaint was that the ANL was a Socialist Workers' Party front, an was led by anti-Zionist SWP members. The ANL stated categorically that the bulk of its support was Labour, that nine of its twelve steering-committee members were Labour, and that it was an anti-fascist organisation and nothing else. The two sides agreed to differ.

The same accusation of SWP control was the cause of a much more serious development – the withdrawal of some of the more prominent sponsors in a blaze of publicity, valuable sponsors such as Lord Willis, Jackie Charlton and Michael Parkinson. Part of the trouble began when the SWP themselves claimed that the ANL was their brainchild – a claim for which there is no foundation in fact – which led some of the sponsors to believe that they had been conned into lending their names to a SWP front organisation. There grew to be some foundation to the contention that the SWP 'controlled' the League, mainly because a steering committee of busy politicians cannot run an organisation on a day-to-day basis, and so the responsibility falls upon those who are prepared to beaver away at the practical jobs beneath the surface of top management. The SWP are rather good at being beavers. I tried to get Labour Party members working in the same way, but without success. There was wide coverage of the defection of a few well-known sponsors, but nothing like the same publicity when the National Front burned down the ANL's London headquarters, and forced it to 'go underground' for fear of further attacks.

The Anti-Nazi League had, like Topsy, 'just growed'. Then a conference was held to decide national policy and to elect a steering committee to replace the original one. I, who chaired one of the conference sessions, went away disillusioned and disgusted by the way in which certain of the delegates had sought to impose their own sectarian interests on the League, which ought to have remained a broad-based anti-fascist organisation. There was criticism of the way the old steering committee had run the ANL, but whatever the rights and wrongs of the original set-up, the League has never since equalled the achievements of the first year of its existence, in part because of internal squabbling about ways and means, but also because the rout of the NF at the 1979 General Election led members mistakenly to believe that the fascist menace had been overcome. And whatever the protests to the contrary, the ANL was built on the impetus and support of those Labour Party members who took up its cause.

Throughout my association with the League as its Treasurer, I had been getting threatening letters and phone calls from NF members and other fascists. The letters I gave to the police; the phone calls became so abusive and disruptive that I went ex-directory. Since I ceased to be ANL Treasurer, the abuse has not reduced in volume. I get 'warnings' of what will happen if I speak at meetings of black people, but do not let that stop me from speaking. And there are still letters.

On the occasion when Michael Foot was scorned for his lack of sartorial elegance on Remembrance Sunday 1981, I initiated a Commons motion, pointing out that Foot had done a great deal over a long period in the cause of international peace, and it would be more appropriate to condemn the insulting use of the Cenotaph by British fascists who are admirers of Hitler. The following letter, signed "Yours racially....", was the result:

> The millions who have died are far more insulted by having Trotskyite skum like you polluting the House of Commons, than they are by the National Front patriots honouring them on Remembrance Sunday.
>
> The BRITONS who died did so for a free country – not a Zionist/Communist multi-racial CESSPIT.

There is one consistent admirer who does not let a Christmas go by without a greeting:

> Black Greetings and Evil Wishes for Christmas and the New Year.
>
> May those who will benefit from your death receive their inheritance early in 1982.

I am not disturbed by such evidence that I am hitting the National Front where it hurts. The only emotion it arouses in me is sorrow for the twisted minds which resent Jewish parentage or a different colour of skin so much that their whole lives are soured by hatred.

The fascist menace in Britain was not completely defeated. In spite of the loss of their headquarters in Hackney and their internal division which weakened them, they have again raised their ugly heads under the title British National Party involved in racial confrontations. therefore, in January 1990 the three of us who initiated the ANL, Peter Hain, Paul Holborow and myself, decided to re-launch the ANL. We collected sponsorship from MPs, trade union leaders, sportspersons, artists etc., and I was asked to become National Treasurer as before. The ANL has organised demonstrations, conferences and street opposition against the BNP. The fascists are putting up candidates in local elections in May 1994, so the ANL are exposing the Nazi face of the BNP as we did in the 1970s elections which blocked their efforts to appear respectable.

While the Anti-Nazi League was still in its infancy, storm-clouds were brewing on another front, although the storm proved to have been brewed in a tea-cup. The story appeared on the front page of the 'Daily Express' on 15th December 1977 as "MP's Amazing Red Alert". The MP involved was a Tory, Stephen Hastings, who had announced dramatically in the Commons that there were "links between those in responsible positions in this country and foreign Communist Intelligence Services". Those in "responsible positions" were Hugh Scanlon, Jack Jones, Lord Briginshaw, the late Lord Hill, and myself. Hastings used as the basis for his allegations a book called 'The Frolik Defection', which had been published in London in 1975. It contained a series of disconnected anecdotes about the attempts claimed to have been made by Josef Frolik, a Czech defector, to recruit 'agents' in Britain. As Frolik kept on pointing out, the laws of libel prevented him from naming names; Stephen Hastings was not hampered in the same way. He had heard, he said, tapes made by Frolik in which the names were not censored, and in the House of Commons, protected by parliamentary privilege, he spilled out all he had heard.

He was reprimanded once by the Speaker for calling into question the honour of a member of the House of Lords, but there was no check on his allegations against those who were outside the House, and who had no opportunity to defend themselves. Once Hastings had spoken, the media had a field day. While they could not have printed the names on their own account, they were free to retell what Hastings had said, and this was "legitimate reporting", whether it was true or not. The victims discovered the accusations against them through television programmes or in the newspapers.

Neither Frolik nor Hastings claimed that any of the five trade unionists had actually become agents for Frolik or anybody else. The accusation was simply that Frolik had tried to recruit them – and failed. That subtlety was not made much of in the press, and the overwhelming impression created was that Hastings was calling for an investigation into five British spies.

All the press carried accounts of the story, repeating large slices of Frolik's story – but with the names filled in – and the 'Daily Telegraph' even dredged up the Labour Party's ban on my candidature in 1945, and the fact that I had written on odd occasions for the 'Morning Star'.

The story told by Frolik about me was well-imagined, and much more detailed than the allegations against the other four, but there was one serious error which Frolik had overlooked. In all his supposedly intimate knowledge of me, and the visits he is supposed to have made to my home, he apparently never discovered that the union official he was trying to cultivate was **a teetotaller**. At an embassy party, Frolik claimed, he was introduced to me and afterwards and we went back to Frolik's flat to continue drinking. As I was leaving, I was supposedly given a bottle of brandy by the sympathetic Frolik, with whom I was by this time "on a first-name basis":

> He looked so poorly dressed that I thought I was doing him a favour by giving him the drink.

Poorly dressed? Surely not the dapper Ernie Roberts?

Three weeks later, claimed Frolik, his new friend invited him home to a party. He was amazed to find that I lived in "a real villa of the type once owned by the richer classes in my country." I occupied the ground-floor flat of a large, converted house bought by the union, which customarily provides London homes at low rent for elected officers.

Frolik sat down "to enjoy a few drinks" with his host. Apparently the visit was repeated on many occasions until, "one night, when we had had a lot to drink, and the rest of the company had left", I said with a knowing wink:

> Joe, I know you're disappointed in me.... I've realised what you were here for from the very start.

At this point, so the story goes, I offered to introduce Frolik to Hugh Scanlon, President of the AEU – an odd offer, since Frolik, in his capacity of Labour Attache, would have met Scanlon at embassy functions in the same way that he might have met me. Nevertheless, Frolik claimed that I said:

> "At the next most convenient occasion, I shall introduce you to him."

> Thus, leaving me suitable mystified, he dropped the subject and we concentrated on the more satisfying business of emptying a bottle of Scotch together.

At one point in Hastings' recital, Hugh Jenkins (then MP for Putney, now Lord Jenkins) shouted across the floor of the House that Ernie Roberts was a teetotaller; this was not reported in the press.

Interviewed on Radio 4's 'PM' programme, I said that, while I could easily have met Frolik in his capacity as Labour Attache, the allegation that I had entertained Frolik at home was a lie, and I invited Hastings to "come outside and say that". I discounted the whole incident as a "red scare" of the usual kind used by the Tories in the run-up to an election, to discredit Labour and the trade union movement.

Even the media grew tired of the story after two days' saturation coverage, and the Prime Minister's statement that the five trade union leaders had been given the once-over by MI5 and cleared of the allegations was accepted. Naturally, defecting diplomats have to provide some evidence to pay for their sanctuary – even if they have to invent it.

Towards the end of 1977, the electorate was beginning to wonder how long the Callaghan Government would hang on, and expectations of a General Election in October 1978 were high. Many Labour Party members thought an October election would be advisable, since the price that the ordinary people were paying as a result of Callaghan's efforts to bring down the inflation rate was swinging more and more votes away from Labour. Up to the autumn of 1978, Callaghan had carried the unions with him in an all-out attempt to hold back wages; it would have been advisable to go into an election at that stage, before the explosion came which was the inevitable result of restraining wages while prices rose mercilessly. After a "winter of discontent" on the wages front, combined with rapidly rising unemployment, Callaghan's success in bringing the inflation rate into single figures was but a poor victory.

Although I had been selected as an unsponsored candidate, I naturally approached the union afterwards to obtain their sponsorship, which I obtained in May 1978, and this brought considerable financial benefits to the constituency. The CLP was therefore able to contemplate an election from an unaccustomed position of financial security, and could put all its efforts into Party work instead of fundraising.

Callaghan's hand was forced in March 1979, when the issue of devolution became his downfall. The Scottish Nationalists, whose only chance of devolution lay with Labour, nevertheless voted against Callaghan on 28th March 1979. The loss of this motion by a single vote precipitated a General Election, which spelt the end of devolution prospects for the Nationalists;

Callaghan quipped that it was "the first time turkeys had voted for an early Christmas."

The Labour Party Manifesto when it emerged did nothing to life the sinking spirits of Socialists. The proposals of Labour's elected National Executive were wiped out by a sub-committee appointed by Callaghan. Callaghan's men took out nationalisation of banking and insurance, the abolition of the House of Lords, public ownership of the drugs industry, and plans for withdrawal from the Common Market. What was left was a mere shadow of the document worked out by the NEC, with platitudes about fighting unemployment, reducing Common Market food mountains, and a renewed commitment to Scottish devolution.

Hackney North used the official Party publicity, and published a selection of their own to add to it, including exhortations to 'Vote Labour' in Greek, Turkish, Gujerati and Urdu, covering the four principal non-English-speaking minority groups in the area.

The only piece of literature which went into every home was my election address, which I wrote myself and had cleared by the CLP before going to press. It consisted of brief statements on a number of important issues, plus a message of support from the retiring MP, David Weitzman, and a short letter from me:

> The Tory Party is representative of Big Business, supporting the haves at the cost of the have-nots. They are the business Millionaires against the working Millions. Working people need a **Socialist** Labour Government to protect their interests....

Thus I distanced myself from the government which had just fallen, and aligned myself with that minority of candidates who still believed in the Socialist ideals of the Party's constitution.

The Tories' national campaign was based on the accusation that the Callaghan Government had been an extreme-Left administration. Their rather negative slogan, "If you care about Britain, keep it out of the red", appeared on massive posters the length and breadth of the country, and the narrow strip at the bottom was temptingly within reach of saboteurs: originally reading "Support the Conservatives", it was frequently amended to "Deport the Conservatives", or – mindful of the need to improve the balance of payments, perhaps – "Export the Conservatives".

The Hackney North Conservative candidate was no more positive than his party, devoting a substantial part of his address to an attack on the Labour candidate, and leaving a large area blank – symbolic, of Tory policy.

Some of the Tory leaflets were about housing, outlining a "Tenants' Charter" which the Tories proposed to bring in to "give us a greater say in the way our homes are managed." This was neatly countered by a Labour leaflet, put out by Transport House, which reprinted a letter sent from Margaret Thatcher's office to an elector only two months before the election:

> I hope you will not think me too blunt if I say that it may well be that your Council accommodation is unsatisfactory but considering the fact that you have been unable to buy your own accommodation, you are lucky to have been given something which the rest of us are paying for out of our taxes.

The chief qualification of the Liberal, Tudor Gates, seemed to be that he was Hackney born-and-bred. His loudspeaker car sailed through the constituency full of raucous adolescents whose message to the people of Hackney was:

> Don't vote for the Labour candidate who lives outside the constituency – vote for Tudor Gates, the Hackney man.

There was also a National Front contender, Sylvia May, whose election leaflet proposed repatriation as a remedy for the "MILLIONS of immigrants" with whom our country is "flooded" – hardly calculated to win those of Asian, African and West Indian origin whom Sylvia May blamed for the "alien, nightmare world" of Britain today.

The Communist Party had agreed on a policy of not opposing candidates on the Labour Left, so I was surprised and pleased when the Communist Monty Goldman stood against me. Pleased, because Goldman's candidature took away the mainstay of the Tory argument that I was a Communist in Labour clothing.

Then in 1978, Hackney acquired a new title. It was dubbed the "dustbin of England" by the Transcendental Meditation movement, which claimed to be able to solve Hackney's problems by training one per cent of the population in Transcendental Meditation – TM – which would reduce unemployment, alleviate poverty and wipe out crime. They also claimed to teach TM trainees to fly. All this could be done, said Hackney's guru, John

Windsor, by applying £100,000 to the cause of training the one per cent of the population in TM methods.

I had very different ideas on reducing unemployment, poverty and crime, and put them into an article for the 'Hackney Gazette'. The Tory candidate Tim Miller responded with an accusation that I was a modern-day Robin Hood; by redistributing wealth, said Miller, "nothing is done to increase the size of the cake." The 'Gazette' could hardly refuse me the opportunity to make a reply:

> Hackney does not suffer from the inability to create prosperity. There are prosperous people connected with Hackney, who make their money in Hackney, out of the work of the people of Hackney, and promptly export their financial gains to the 'prosperous' areas where they live. Take a look at these 'prosperous' areas: there is no industry there, no business – so where does their prosperity come from? It comes from areas like Hackney, which are systematically milked of the wealth they produce....
>
> Our problem is not the one that the Tories suggest, that is the size of the cake; it is the problem of a more equitable sharing of the sizeable cake we already have....
>
> I am not trying to rob the rich to give to the poor, but simply to give to the people of Hackney what is theirs by right.

The CLP activists were surprised, to say the least. They had grown accustomed to regarding the 'Hackney Gazette' as a paper which would ignore Labour issues and promote Tory ones. They had virtually stopped sending in reports of Party activities. I proved, and continued to prove, that the 'Gazette' would print material that was well-presented, and I have had little need to complain of the coverage the paper had given me, since I invariably had the right of reply.

Law and order, unemployment, public speaking; the usual issues commanded a lot of attention in the election. But whenever the Tories went to press, the issues of the day earned much less attention than my past history. The campaign looked like being a carbon-copy of Stockport South, with Tories and Liberals trotting out the witch-hunt for the benefit of 'Gazette' readers. The Labour and Tory candidates met in a debate which denigrated from a discussion of local problems into an effort to see who could dig the knife the deepest into me. When the Tories again tried to force a debate, I declined. I could not see why Labour should give the

Tories a platform for expressing their views and, in any case, while I would not have objected to a **genuine** debate, I did not relish being put up as an Aunt Sally for Tom Miller and his friends to knock down. Miller responded in the press by saying that Labour had 'gagged' their candidate; my opinions, claimed Miller, were left of the Communist Party's. The 'Gazette' then printed a statement in reply, headed "Call me a Communist and I'll sue".

The local Tories were not the only ones in the mudslinging business. The national press took up the challenge of an imminent election with gusto, and their chief object was to discredit Labour by convincing voters that Callaghan was only nominally the head of a Labour Party which had been infiltrated and taken over by the extreme Left. The right-wing of the Labour Party fell for this ploy, and by the time of the election the Labour Left was under attack almost as much from its own right-wing as it was from 'The Sun', the 'Express', and the 'Telegraph'.

The London 'Evening News' was one of the first in the field after the election was called, with its article on 7th April 1979 "By the Left....lurch!" which picked me out for special attention:

> What makes his selection the more surprising is that Roberts.... was for most of the post-war years banned from Labour candidacies. The reason.... was that (the NEC) considered Roberts' brand of Socialism had too little in common with that of the Labour Party. So what has changed? Roberts has not.

The 'News' regretted the imminent demise of Labour-as-we-know-it:

> To the late Herbert Morrison, socialism meant anything which a Labour Government does. I doubt if Jim Callaghan would dissent from that interpretation.
>
> To Ernie Roberts and his friends on the Left, it means changing 'society' and the human beings who compose it....
>
> It means treating more than 20,000 Soviet tanks in Europe as if they were toy tractors in a children's nursery.

Douglas Eden, a right-wing Labour member since defected to the SDP, took up the argument in the 'Daily Telegraph' on 11th April. The 'Telegraph', not noted for its Labour sympathies, must have greeted with glee this opportunity to show the Labour Right at the throats of the Labour Left. Hackney North was one of eleven constituencies earmarked by Eden as being too extreme for the 'legitimate Left'.

Woodrow Wyatt chipped in with a scare-story in the 'Sunday Mirror', followed up by 'The Sun's "How many Reds in Labour's bed?" (the Reds they named included "some pretty odd fish indeed, such as Ernie Roberts"). A week before the election the Social Democratic Alliance joined hands with the Tory press to secure Labour's defeat in the election by warning electors not to vote Labour in 59 constituencies, of which Hackney North was one.

The campaign was evidently going to be a difficult one. Nobody expected me to hold the 10,553 majority of David Weitzman, as he had all the disadvantages of a new candidate, as well as the vociferous opposition of national and local press to contend with, plus the natural antagonism towards a Labour Government which had failed to deliver the goods. The only question was, by how much would the Labour majority drop?

The constituents displayed a discouraging mixture of apathy ("I'm not voting this time") and reaction ("I'm not voting Labour this time"), and Hackney's record of the lowest turnout in the previous General Election (52 per cent) looked like being repeated.

The electors had two main complaints: they had just received their rates assessments, and objected to paying more money for less service; the 'less service' element was symbolised by a social services dispute which meant that for several weeks refuse had not been collected, nor had the streets been swept, and this was the second major complaint. With the settlement of the dispute, services should have returned to normal, but they had not, and the residents were understandably angry, their anger being directed at Labour, who controlled the council.

I led a deputation of councillors to the street-cleansing officials at the Town Hall. The officials excused themselves with tales of lorries broken down and inadequate staffing. The councillors received these explanations politely and sympathetically. I did not. My experiences on Coventry City Council had prepared me for situations like this. I made it clear to the officials that they were the servants of the elected councillors, not their masters; if the councillors said the areas was to be cleaned, then it must be cleaned. The following day, the clearance of the rubbish began. The 'Gazette' printed a long front page article about the rotting refuse, with irate quotes from the

Tory and Liberal candidates; they had not asked me for my opinions. The refuse problem was so serious that a week was not enough to shift the backlog, and on the day before the election, I was met by angry residents of King's Crescent, who threatened that they would not only refuse to vote, but would fill the polling station with refuse unless it was removed. It was removed in time, after another altercation with Town Hall officials.

Many organisations canvassed candidates on a wide variety of issues ranging from abortion reform to Esperanto. I replied to every one, and even responded to a request from workers at the 'Evening News', who asked for the support of successful London candidates in saving the 2,200 jobs threatened by the closure of the newspaper; ironically, the 'Evening News' had only three weeks before been encouraging its readers **not** to vote for me.

My campaign closed on a low note. It was until four days before the election that I heard the rumour which was circulating in the constituency that I was anti-semitic. I did not know where the rumour had originated, but it had already travelled pretty far afield, since I was first warned of it by a friend, John Lebor, who was a councillor in the borough of Brent. Two days later I picked up a similar warning from the Jewish Labour candidate in Hackney Central, Stanley Clinton Davis, but it was too late to do much about the accusations, and I had to be content with a letter of denial printed in the 'Gazette' just before polling day.

The result of the election was a win for Labour, but with their majority halved in a 60.2 per cent poll:

Roberts (Lab)	14,688
Miller (Con)	9,467
Gates (Lib)	3,033
May (NF)	860
Goldman (TM)	418

There were three factors involved in the loss of votes – the national swing against Labour, the protest vote against rates and rubbish, and 'scare tactics' – and it was impossible to say which factor accounted for what proportion of the nine per cent swing to the Tories.

Chapter 9

Wise students will not all of them too readily forget the desolating sentence of Gibbon, greatest of all literary historians, that history is indeed little more than the register of the crimes, follies and misfortunes of mankind.

1   Representing Britain's poorest borough in Parliament
2   Maiden speech
3   Hunger strike unto death
4   Messages from the H blocks
5   Bill to end Britain's rule in Northern Ireland

Nevertheless, there I was: Ernie Roberts MP. There was only one hurdle left to jump, and the National Front was all out to make sure that I fell at it. Throughout the campaign, I had been scrupulous about expenses, ensuring that every item was accounted for in my election returns. Yet it was through expenses that the NF hoped to bring to bring about my downfall. An NF candidate wrote to the Director of Public Prosecutions, asking that legal action be taken against me, Neil Kinnock and Martin Flannery, who were all executive members of the ANL. He declared that the ANL had distributed election literature, the cost of which was not included in the expense returns of election agents, and that Kinnock, Flannery and I – though principally I, then ANL Treasurer – were responsible for this breach of the law. I had myself used ANL leaflets in my campaign, but the cost of these was included in my agent's returns; I had no means of knowing what had been done in other constituencies.

The DPP judged that criminal proceedings were not justified, but in January 1980, NF member Sydney Chaney wrote to the Speaker of the

House of Commons, asking him to intervene, since the DPP had said there was no case to answer. A year later, Chaney again put pressure on the DPP, threatening private prosecutions if no public action was taken, but these private actions have not yet materialised.

Once over the election, I settled down to the thankless task of being a backbencher. For the first few weeks of the new Parliament, business was conducted in a variety of odd places. Secretaries were consulted on benches in corridors or at tables in the tearoom; constituents were interviewed publicly in the Central Lobby. Facilities for new Members consisted of a coathanger (embellished with a loop of tape on which to hang a sword) and – a week or so later – a locker in a corridor. New recruits had to wait until the pecking-order of old Members had been satisfied in respect of office accommodation before being allowed to share out what was left. One of my first activities in the House was to put pressure on the Leader, Norman St John Stevas, to hasten the procedure so that each MP, however lowly, would at least have the basic minimum of a desk and a telephone.

My secretary had a substantial share of a large office. I myself got a desk in the Cloisters, a long corridor which I shared with eleven other Members. It was a historic place, one of the oldest parts of the Commons, and reputed to be where the death warrant of Charles I was signed, but the history did not compensate for the poor facilities.

The facilities in the constituency were even worse. The Party rented premises on Stamford Hill which were in a deplorable condition. David Weitzman had held his 'surgeries' there, and I continued to do so, until eventually pieces of the ceiling began falling on my head while I was interviewing constituents, and each surgery began with the sweeping up of rubble which had accumulated on the floor since the previous one. After eighteen months, I rented premises which were owned by a Housing Association, who agreed to let me hold surgeries there until they were ready to renovate the house. It was no palace, but it was clean and dry. At Stamford Hill, constituents had been horrified that an MP should have to work in such terrible conditions; in the new premises, they were horrified that rooms as good as that should be used as offices instead of for housing a family!

Housing cases formed a large proportion of the cases brought to me, with immigration a close second. At first I followed David Weitzman's pattern of a fortnightly surgery held on Sunday mornings. This soon proved inadequate, and I began to hold surgeries every week. The surgery lasts from 11am until the last constituent has gone, three or often four hours later, and there is sometimes a meeting in the constituency after that, which means a seven-day working week.

A surgery can be a harrowing experience. It is commonly thought that Britain in the eighties is a place where no one need live in poverty. Hackney is living proof that this is not so. In a constituency where an old lady can die because she has nothing to eat but cardboard; where a mother has to let her baby sleep in a drawer in a damp basement, knowing that she has already lost two babies in similar conditions; where a young woman is persecuted by local children because of her mental condition and barricades herself in a room for weeks on end, and no place can be found for her in a hospital because of overcrowding; in an area where these things happen, the more ordinary kinds of poverty are commonplace.

I used my maiden speech, during the debate on the Budget on 27th June 1979, to outline the effects of the Tory measures in Hackney, where there were:

- 5,000 one-parent families;
- 1,000 children in care;
- 12,000 homeless;
- the largest percentage of low-paid workers in London;
- the highest infant mortality rate in Europe;
- above average unemployment;
- starvation of investment.

I continued:

This degree of poverty is even more glaring when you see adjacent to Hackney the constituency represented by the Honourable Member for the City of London and Westminster, where you can find the Stock Exchange, the Bank of England, the joint stock banks, Lloyds, the commodity markets and so on. In fact, over the portico of the Royal Exchange it is spelled out, "The earth is the Lord's and the fullness thereof". It is true! I am sure many noble members in the other place will say 'Amen!' to that! But all this wealth adjacent to so much poverty in the East End is indecent....

It was announced in the press on the day of the Tory victory in the General Election, that share values increased by £2,000 million within hours. If they can provide wealth so easily, so massively, so quickly, then surely we should build more stock exchanges and solve all our economic problems....

The national cake is very big, but still only the crumbs fall from the rich man's table for the working people, and this Finance Bill will ensure that this situation remains, because it ignores the vital point about our national cake, which is – not just the size of the cake, but who owns the bakery.

....Mr Speaker, I spent twenty years as a national trade union officer, facing over the negotiating table hard-headed men of business, whose aim was to keep a tight grip on what the workers had earned for them. Looking across this carpeted divide, I see what is in effect the same Executive of Big Business, facing me over a new negotiating table, the floor of the House.

My job here will be the same as it has always been, Mr Speaker, to fight for a just share of the wealth of this nation for those who created it.

I quickly reached the conclusion that speeches in the House are almost valueless. With a large Government majority plus the fact that, as in Gilbert & Sullivan's 'Iolanthe', most Honourable Members "always voted at their Party's call, and never thought of thinking for themselves at all," I felt that speaking in the Chamber would be a waste of time which might be better employed elsewhere.

Although I have spoken on occasions in the House, therefore, most of my work took place outside it. In this respect, I was fortunate in having a London constituency, which made it possible to maximise my time with the constituents, and still get back to the House in time for a vote.

With between five and six thousand letters a year to deal with, plus constituency meetings, and a constant stream of meetings in the House which alone could fill up a Member's diary for the week, it seems incredible that some MPs manage to carry on running lucrative businesses alongside their jobs in Parliament. I have always believed that an MP's job is a full-time job, and in my case that is indisputably true.

I always made it my business to be present at the monthly meetings of the Executive Committee of my CLP, and at the monthly meetings of the General Management Committee, where I presented a report covering all my activities during the previous month – the number and type of constituents' problems I had taken up, meetings I attended, organisations I sponsored, joined or initiated, any press coverage I received, 'early day motions' I had put down or signed in the House, in fact anything and everything an MP's Party ought to know. The GMC was then able to commend or criticise my actions, and to recommend any future developments.

Undoubtedly the major issue for me outside the constituency during 1980/81 was Ireland. I had long before my association with Hackney been campaigning for British troops to be withdrawn from Northern Ireland, and in this I was at one with my CLP. In April 1980, the Hackney North party joined forces with Islington CLP to form the Labour Committee on Ireland, based on the 'Troops Out' demand, and received considerable support from many CLPs opposed to the bi-partisan policy followed by the Labour Party.

Only a few months later, a hunger strike – "to the bitter climax of death if necessary" – began in the Maze prison in Belfast, where the prisoners were demanding the same conditions which had been accorded to those previously convicted of similar offences, conditions known as "special category status". Both IRA and Loyalist prisoners were involved in the hunger-strike, although press reports made it appear that this was a demand for political status by 'IRA murderers'.

I founded, with the aid of sponsors, MPs, TU leaders, artists, etc, and became the chairman of an ad hoc group with the unwieldy title 'Don't Let the Irish Prisoners Die Committee' (DLIPD), whose founding statement made clear its principles:

> No one wants anything but a basis for peace and progress in Northern Ireland. But all that will result from the deaths of any of the hunger strikers is violence and misery now and fuel for violence far into the future.
>
> They will strengthen the hand of all those who favour force rather than democratic political campaigning. The people of Northern Ireland, both Catholic and Protestant, need a new chance to break out of the spiral of tension, terror and death.
>
> A serious move by the government to negotiate an agreement with the hunger strikers from both sides on the basis of a humanitarian approach to the prisoners' five points would create such a chance.
>
> We urge the government to make such a move for three reasons:

Justice: because more than 300 prisoners of the same type already enjoy more favourable conditions than the hunger strikers are demanding.

Compassion: not only for the hunger strikers but for their anguished families and all who stand to suffer if violence continues.

Understanding: of the history that has given rise to their passionate convictions, whether or not we share them.

We as for an imaginative breakthrough, not on behalf of one section of the community only, but for all the people of the province for whom the current deadlock offers only a prospect of looming catastrophe.

Throughout the DLIPD campaign, the Committee made it clear that the campaign was for both Catholic and Protestant communities, and above all that they neither approved of nor condoned violence as an answer to the political problems of Ireland. Press reports distorted the campaign to such an extent, however, that I received letters from all over Britain, condemning my support of the murderous IRA. Interviewed on a number of radio programmes, I declared bluntly that I did not support violence by either side; this statement was almost invariably edited out of the broadcast version, resulting in another shower of letters from outraged members of the public. I replied patiently to each letter, making five points:

1 there were both Protestant and Catholic hunger strikers making the same demands;
2 they were not all 'murderers' – many had been convicted on minor charges which in England would have meant no more than a fine, but in Ireland led to a 14-year prison sentence;
3 they were convicted in special courts, without a jury, which undoubtedly made them 'special' prisoners, yet as soon as they were convicted, they suddenly became 'ordinary' again;
4 they were asking only for the same conditions which previous governments had granted to other prisoners, and which those prisoners still had;
5 the Committee was trying to prevent prison deaths from leading to further violence against innocent people.

In return for my efforts I received many replies from those who had first written angrily, or even abusively, thanking me for taking the trouble to explain, and making the point that they had been unaware of the facts which I had put before them.

During this campaign, I received letters from some of the hunger strikers and some of their fellow prisoners. The method used to deliver these letters was ingenious. They were written on cigarette paper in very small handwriting; they needed a magnifying glass to read them. They were often folded small and wrapped in silver paper. The prisoners put them into their mouths and passed them to their visiting friends when kissing them good-bye.

The government remained intransigent, and the press gave them every support. The venom and hatred expressed on all sides by those who called themselves 'Christians' was beyond belief. John Junor, writing in the 'Sunday Express' on 3rd May 1981 about the imminent death of hunger striker Bobby Sands – who had been elected as MP by the 30,000 electors of Fermanagh & South Tyrone – criticised the Pope for pleading on behalf of Sands, and then went on:

> I will shed no tears when Sands dies. My only hope is that if and when he does every other IRA terrorist will go on the same sort of hunger strike in sympathy. And stay on it until they are all in wooden suits.

> I would rejoice if Mr Neal Blaney and Mr Ernie Roberts added their own stinking names to the list.

Neal Blaney, Eire MP and Member of the European Assembly, had come to England at the request of the DLIPD Committee to take part in a press conference at the House of Commons. This was one of a number of such conferences arranged by me during the hunger strikes, each one arousing the fury of the press, who denounced DLIPD for inviting Irish murderers and criminals into our Parliament. In vain did the Committee point out that those invited were neither murderers nor criminals, but members of the public; that is, unless you hold the families of convicts guilty of the same offences as the convicts themselves. Nor did the media allow that it was incomparably better to settle the issue by argument than by bombs and bullets, and where better to state a case than in the Mother of Free Parliaments?

The Thatcher Government issued a pamphlet called 'H Blocks – the facts'; giving a one-sided view of the real situation. Friends of the H Block prisoners produced a pamphlet in reply called 'H Blocks – the truth'. I was asked to write the foreword; I wrote:

Throughout the centuries patriots and martyrs have been the political prisoners of their oppressors. They have been castigated as Terrorists and after the settlement of the conflicts have become respected statesmen. The solution to the Irish problem is political. It is a United Ireland.

After the death of Bobby Sands MP, the 'East End News' was the only paper to quote me without distortion, repeating my demands for removal of British troops, and the uniting of Ireland, with compensation for those who wish to leave and live on the British mainland. As 'East End News' pointed out, tacit agreement between the political parties at Westminster meant that Sands' seat would remain empty, and "What better way to convince the Irish electorate that they can't win by the ballot box?"

When under pressure from Dafydd Thomas MP and myself, the writ was moved for the Fermanagh & South Tyrone by-election in August 1981, the electorate had not changed their minds: they elected Owen Carron, who had been Sands' agent in the previous contest. His first act as representative of the constituency was to request a meeting with the Prime Minister to discuss the continuing problems in Ireland. Mrs Thatcher refused to meet him.

During 1984 I had the opportunity to put a Bill before Parliament. In consultation with my constituency I chose a Bill to terminate British rule over Northern Ireland. It was supported by Tony Benn MP, Denis Canavan MP, Denis Skinner MP, Jeremy Corbyn MP, and others. It was a short Bill, based upon similar provisions in the 'Withdrawal from Palestine Act'. I gave the parliamentary authorities instructions on the printing and date for the distribution of the Bill. However, I received an apology from the Public Bill Office for printing and distributing a few copies of the Bill before I gave them permission. A further difficulty was presented by the Northern Ireland Minister's office which said the Bill would need the consent of the Queen before it could go before Parliament. Later I received a letter from Douglas Hurd, the Minister, stating the Queen had agreed that the Bill could go before Parliament. Nevertheless, the Tory Government's supporters decided to block the Bill. On the occasions I tried to move and speak on the Bill, they cried out "Object" to the Speaker. This stopped me speaking on the Bill and so it fell.

So much for parliamentary democracy!

Chapter 10

Is not diplomacy, called by Voltaire the field of lies, as able as it ever was to dupe governments and the governed alike by grand abstract catchwords, veiling obscure and inexplicable purposes and turning the whole world over with blood and tears to a strange Witch's Sabbath?

1   Work as an MP – housing, unemployment, transport, smoking, and South Africa
2   Re-nomination – big majorities
3   De-selection
4   First black woman MP
5   Special Award of Merit

The vast majority of parliamentary business is much more low-key than the Irish situation. I found myself fighting exactly the same battles as I fought as a councillor in Coventry, meeting the same arguments and responding the same way as I did thirty years before.

On the question of rates, Hackney is faced with the same choice that faced Coventry. With a Tory Government cutting back spending and penalising 'high-spending' authorities, do Hackney residents want better services or lower rates?

On civil defence, the Government is again trying to con the public that there is a defence against nuclear attack. This is, I said, even less possible than it was thirty years ago. The Tories would yet again have us believe that they are anxious to provide 'defence', yet at the same time they are killing off the services on which conventional defence relies – hospitals, ambulances, fire services, etc – by starving them of cash.

The same old arguments are raging on housing, poverty, racism.... the more things appear to change, the more they remain the same. After a lifetime of fighting the same battles, I am still coming back with the same answer: Socialism. And when critics say "It can't work," I reply "It's never been tried!" So I found myself fighting on a new battlefield – the House of Commons.

I was asked to summarise my experiences and views of the Tory Government by the editor of the AEU Journal – on the Tory Government's record from 1979–1985, in support of the union's political fund campaign. I replied with:

The first week in which Thatcher was elected as Prime Minister in 1979 she stated in the Conservative News, "My troops are ready," and since that date she has conducted a class war against the trade unions, the pensioners, the unemployed, the sick and school children.

Unemployment has increased from 1.3 million in 1979 to nearly 4 million in 1985. The number of supplementary benefit claimants has risen from 2.9 million to 4.5 million, whilst the rich have become richer and the working class poorer.

Since 1979 millions of workers are worse off.

A third of the full time workers – 2 million men and 2½ million women receive less than ⅔ of the average wage. A further 3 million part-time workers are also on low pay. Actions taken by the Tory government to reduce pay were:

- Repeal of Schedule 11 of the Employment Protection Act – which gave workers the right to arbitration and fair wages.
- Repeal of the Fair Wages Resolution which guaranteed fair wages for those employed under Government contracts.
- Refusal to make suitable amendments to the Equal Pay Act to ensure equal pay for work of equal value.

The Tories determination to scrap Wage Councils will remove another 3 million workers from legal protection of their wages. But those who Thatcher represents on £50,000 pa have gained over £150 pw. Tory Tax policies have benefited only those getting over £20,000 pa. £3,000 million have been given to the rich in tax concessions since 1979.

The Sunday Telegraph stated (5 Feb '84) "The strength of shares.... has produced a new issue boom that has created more than 200 new paper millionaires.... the rich clearly do get richer.... sometimes it is just a question of sitting back and let the actions of others enrich them."

But Karl Marx puts it much clearer: "It is the exploitation of man by man."

In addition to the exploitation of working men and women the burden of taxation has been placed more and more on their backs. The Tories in their Election Manifesto in 1979 said, "We shall cut income tax at all levels," but in 1983 the Tory Chancellor of Exchequer admitted in the Financial Times (7 Sept) that, "We have had over the past 4 years to increase the level of taxation overall."

Since 1979 they have increased the tax burden on working class families:

- Doubling VAT from 8% to 15%.
- Increased their National Insurance contribution rates in 1980, '81, '82, '84.
- They have forced up local rates by cutting the Rate Support Grant to local councils.
- Prescription charges have been increased by 1000% i.e. from 20 pence to £2.00.
- Fuel Taxes increased – Gas prices have gone up since 1979 by 130%.
- Electricity prices have gone up by 90%.

They have forced up the average Council house rents by 130% since 1979. The Tories have increased many other taxes on the working people whilst at the same time reducing taxation on the Employers.

Since 1979 they have introduced 5 Social Security Acts, each one to cut expenditure and so undermines the Welfare State.

- The Old prior to 1979 had their pensions linked to rises in prices and earnings, the Tories have stopped that. Pensioners are worse off, Earning-related Pensions are under attack.
- The Sick benefit has been abolished for the first 8 weeks of sickness. Employers now have the duty to pay the sick. Industrial injury benefits were abolished altogether.
- The Unemployed have had their benefits reduced and brought into taxation. The earnings related supplement has been abolished.

The Butchery of the Health Services

Thatcher has stated at Tory Party Conferences that: "The NHS is safe only with us." The Tories have destroyed the basic principle of the NHS i.e. a service free at the point of use and funded out of the general taxation – we now have a two class health system – a private sector catering for the healthy and wealthy and a drastically cut and undermined NHS for the working class. Since 1979 nearly 200 hospitals have been fully or partly closed with a loss of nearly 10,000 beds, further hospitals are threatened with closure.

The British Kidney Patients Association estimate that 3,000 kidney patients die each year, due to Government refusal to provide funds and equipment. Whilst Government attacks the NHS there are 670,000 patients waiting for treatment.

Housing since 1979 has borne the main Tory attacks, building houses for rent by councils has been savagely cut by the Government. There are:

- over 1 million on the housing waiting lists;
- 1¼ million unfit dwellings;
- 1 million dwellings lack basic sanitary provision;
- 2½ million dwellings affected by dampness;
- 800,000 families live in overcrowded conditions.

But the Tories are increasing public expenditure in one area – the arms business. They have spent £65,000 million on arms since 1979. They are to spend a further £18,000 million this year on nuclear and other arms. All of this is at the expense of the unemployed, OAPs, the sick and homeless.

In order to get away with such policies, Thatcher has had to attack the organisation of the workers – the trade unions, many anti-trade union laws have been passed since 1979:

- Massive fines up to £25,000 can be imposed upon unions: for instance on the National Graphical Association, also heavy fines on the NUM.
- The Employment Acts of 1980 and 1982 have curbed:
  1 The right to organise industrial action – increasing sympathetic action.
  2 The right to be informed and consulted on Company decisions.
  3 The right to be protected against unfair dismissal and to maternity leave.

The Tory anti Trade Union Act of 1984

- Interferes with union rule books, on elections.
- Imposes ballots before strike action which prolongs disputes and undermines negotiations.
- Curtails the freedom of unions to hold 'Political funds'.

In 1984 the Tory Government outlawed Trade Union membership at the GCHQ. They used mass police cordons to prevent picketing during the Miners dispute. All these attacks on the working class and their unions are the reasons why we need a political fund to defend our political interests. So be certain you vote 'yes' in the ballot for a political fund.

All the trade unions who conducted a ballot to establish a political fund voted overwhelmingly in favour. Since I wrote that article, the situation on all those issues has become worse. The Tory Party, in 1994, continues to prove that it is a class party.

I found that being an MP can be a depressing business. There is no sense of power in the job, only an awareness of limitations. There is always a strong feeling that a backbencher is virtually powerless in spite of occasional successes. There was the time when I was able to persuade striking dockers to release a consignment of special flour in time for the Hackney Jewish community to make their special bread for the Passover although that success was due, not so much to my position in Parliament, as to the previous good relations with the Transport & General Workers' Union over almost half a century of trade unionism. And there was the time, in November 1980, when I joined a 'picket line' of angry MPs to prevent Black Rod from entering the Commons to start the prorogation ceremony. As a result, the Tories were forced to withdraw a document on rent rises for council tenants which they had intended to push through discussion before the Christmas recess.

However, the comparative rarity of successful backbench action is the reason why the Left continues to fight for the Parliamentary Labour Party to operate on a more democratic basis: to give **all** elected Labour MPs a part to play in the running of the Party inside the House. Until pressure was applied from the Left after the 1979 election, meetings of the PLP took no votes on the issues they discussed and so the strength of any opposition to 'official' policy was an unknown quantity. The next step, in my opinion, is a recorded-vote system in the PLP meetings so that constituents can make sure that they are being honestly represented.

This is not a popular viewpoint among the right-wing of the Party and even among some on the Left. Just how much resistance there is to recorded voting can be gauged by the vociferous annoyance of many MPs who did not wish their votes in the Deputy Leadership election to be made public lest their CLP should disapprove. I believe that many CLPs would be disgusted by the stand taken by their MPs 'off the record' and that a recorded-vote system would allow the electorate to be better judges of their representatives.

On one occasion in the House of Commons, at 1am, when most of the MPs had gone home to their comfortable beds, I was fighting for the homeless and healthless by opening an adjournment debate on this shocking situation. I stated:

> Many people for whom I speak in this debate have already gone to their beds on park benches, in shop doorways, disused factories, empty or derelict properties, on

the pavements or are squatting. The rest are still wandering about seeking shelter and a place to rest their bodies.

It is estimated that there are about 100,000 such people in the United Kingdom. About 600,000 of them are in hostels or lodgings each night. In London, on any night about 2,000 people sleep out. In Hackney, there are about 3,000 single homeless people. They are homeless, rootless and healthless.

Not many people care about the single homeless. They say that they smell, that they are ragged, drunk or mentally ill. People are embarrassed by them. They cannot get medical treatment when they are ill. General practitioners, who are legally bound to give treatment and are morally bound by the Hippocratic oath to serve the sick, reject the down-and-out single homeless for fear of offending their respectable clientele.

The single homeless are driven to hospitals and casualty departments for primary treatment. Generally, they are received sympathetically by overworked casualty staff. The homeless come to rely on them to provide treatment for ills brought on by their homelessness. Complaints such as bronchitis, tuberculosis, dietary deficiencies and foot problems are suffered by people who sleep rough or who are turned out of hostels at 9am to tramp the streets and search for food and work.

Today I saw a heading that is in most of the national newspapers. It says: "Charles to pay £1 million for country home?"

He is a single person who certainly will not be homeless but who will spend a considerable sum of money to provide himself with another home. He is quitting Chevening House, which is a 115-room mansion near Sevenoaks, Kent. Perhaps he or the authorities can be persuaded to allow the young, single homeless, healthless of London to occupy that property.

Of course, they turned a deaf ear to that request. Several months later, the housing problem was discussed again by Parliament, Hackney having one of the most serious, so I took part and said that:

Three of the most important things in life are a job, a home and good health. They are all related and everyone has the right to them.

My philosophy is that rented housing is not a matter for private profit. Housing should be a service to which all people should have the right. They should have a decent home in which to live.

There is a massive problem of empty houses in London. About 129,000 empty dwellings exist in the capital. Of those, about 49,000 are in the public sector and almost twice as many, over 80,000, are privately owned.

In my constituency, over 300 families are living in bed-and-breakfast accommodation, some of them with four children living in one room. In the past week, 100 of them were put on to the street by an owner of bed-and-breakfast properties but he was compelled to take the back following action by the local authority.

There are tower blocks in Hackney which are not fit to live in and should be pulled down, and the Minister has under consideration blocks which require millions of pounds spent on them to keep them habitable or to have them taken down and the land used to provide decent accommodation. I would rather they were taken down.

In fact they were brought down a few years later by controlled explosion. Nevertheless, in 1994, the housing situation is as bad as ever.

International problems have always been of great concern to me, particularly the situation in South Africa and when the country came up for discussion in the Commons I referred to British investment there. I started by saying:

I want to declare an interest in this matter as the Chairman of the British Trade Union–South Africa Congress of Trade Unions Liaison Committee. We are trade unionists whose employers have branches in South Africa, where black trade unionists are used as cheap labour to undercut the wages, conditions and trade union rights of workers in Britain.

As British industry is the biggest outside investor in South Africa, we have demanded from the British employers, the multinationals in South Africa, that they concede the same trade union rights to organise and represent black workers as exist in their companies in this country. We insist that they pay at least the same wages for the same work as are paid to British workers.

If the Government and the Opposition want the facts, then read the book 'Organise and Starve' by the South African Congress of Trade Unions. It says: It must never be forgotten that apartheid and racial discrimination in South Africa, like everywhere else, has an aim far more important than discrimination itself. The aim is economic exploitation. The root and the fruit of apartheid and racial discrimination is profit. Migrant labour, pass laws, poverty wages, victimisation at the workplace, unemployment, repression, imprisonment, banning orders, death – these are the ingredients of exploitation that shape the lives of millions of African workers from the cradle to the grave under apartheid.

These statements were met with grunts and groans of opposition MPs. They did not like the blunt remarks of a trade unionist and of course they fell on stony ground.

Another international issue of grave concern was the so-called special relationship with USA. The British people's views as expressed through such organisations as the Campaign for Nuclear Disarmament were concerned about the threats of nuclear war between the superpowers and the basing of American missiles in Britain. So, when Thatcher gave Reagan an invitation to speak to a meeting of Lords and MPs in 1982, many MPs, trade unionists and peace-loving citizens opposed this invitation so a reception was organised by them called 'Reagan Reception Committee'. I was chosen as Chairman and it was sponsored by 100 MPs, Lords and trade union leaders. In our published statement we wrote:

> We will be asked to welcome the man who has insisted on the production of the neutron bomb, the weapons of biological warfare and who is foisting Cruise missiles on Britain.

We urged a picket of the American Embassy on the arrival of President Reagan. A message to the American people was printed in which it said:

> We call upon the American people to join us in a world-wide might peace campaign that will compel the Superpowers – the United States, the Soviet Union and their military-minded supporters in Britain, Germany and other countries – to commence genuine disarmament negotiations and so really protect the lives of the common people.

Thatcher was stopped from holding a joint meeting of both Houses of Parliament for President Reagan to address in Westminster Hall because she had not consulted the other political parties in Parliament. She had to resort to a meeting in a House of Lords chamber.

By these actions we were able to show the American and British governments that we were against any 'special relationship' which led to nuclear arms confrontation and build-up. We were struggling for a nuclear-free, peaceful world.

At about this time, I wrote to Thatcher complaining about the massive arms expenditure and the sale of armaments to other countries for use against their own people and other countries. In her reply on 3rd June 1982, she concluded with:

> The Defence Sales Organisation was set up in 1966 under a Labour Government, and successive Governments have acknowledged the useful role the DSO plays. The Government firmly believes that there are both political and economic benefits to be derived from defence sales, and the DSO, by providing a wide range of assistance to industry, is promoting equipment and negotiating contracts

with overseas customers. The Government does not, therefore, believe that it would be in the national interest to close the DSO.

We do not, however, permit arms to be exported indiscriminately. There are strict controls over the export of arms and a wide range of other military equipment. All proposals for defence sales are scrutinised very carefully and an export licence is only granted if we are satisfied that the equipment is required for legitimate defence purposes. An export licence would not be granted if we thought the equipment was likely to be used for internal repression.

We now know the truth after the conflicts in Africa and the Middle East including Iraq, which have resulted in the Lord Justice Scott inquiry in 1994 as well as the arms sales linked with financial aid to Malaysia.

The arms industry is a terrible business but it is a terribly profitable business. We continue to expand expenditure on armaments including Trident nuclear submarines. In the 1994 Tory government budget, £24,000 million is to be spent, whilst the health and welfare services are cut in real terms.

The transport problems in London cause anger and frustration for the working people whether they use the trains, buses or their own cars. So when the Parliamentary Standing Committee for London Regional Transport was set up, I agreed to serve on it. During the many sessions of the committee we held I made the following comments and demands:

The most important aspect of transport is that it runs regularly and people can rely on it. For that to happen, it must be well organised. It must be organised centrally and not by independent transport companies endeavouring to provide a transport system in London because that will not result in an organised and reliable service for people to get to and from their businesses.

The question of traffic congestion has been raised and those who live in London or who use the roads know that is a problem. Hon Members have only to look out of the Committee Room window to see the evidence.

The Government's logic is: if it makes a private profit for someone, do it. If it makes a private profit to take traffic off the railways and stick it on the roads, do it. The Government put private profit and private interests before the interests of the public. That is clear in any service that we may care to examine and certainly in transport. The Bill will provide an opportunity for private operators to make a profit out of transport despite the chaotic conditions that may be caused. The multiplicity of independent transport operators in London will mean that conditions will become archaic and worse than they are now.

It has often been said during our debate that London cannot afford any more chaos and disintegration. We need more integration. We already have some but not enough. We need ever greater integration of London's transport services. Then, the transport that Londoners require can be provided at an economic cost because there will no longer be uneconomic competition with different companies trying to cater for the same restricted market.

There is an urgent need for greater investment in public transport – new trains and rolling stock both above and underground. The tracks need repairs and upgrading, but in spite of all the criticisms, London transport services in 1994 are worse than ever. The government is too busy preparing the system for privatisation.

I was disturbed about the serious effects of smoking upon the general public. My father died as a result of heavy smoking and my brothers also suffered chest complaints from the same habit although I had never smoked nor drunk alcohol myself. However, I put down an Early Day Motion in the Commons in November 1984 which read:

Royal Warrants and Tobacco. That this House, noting that the British death rate due to smoking is running at 2,000 per week and that 150 honourable Members have signed a petition requesting the withdrawal of Royal warrants from all tobacco products, would welcome withdrawal of those warrants by Her Majesty the Queen and urges the Secretary of State for Social Services to do all in his power to make the public aware of the dangers of smoking.

I followed this up with a letter to the Queen referring her to the 100,000 of her subjects who die each year as a result of smoking and to her sister, Princess Margaret, who is a heavy smoker, asking for the withdrawal of the Royal Warrant from cigarette advertising. I received the following reply dated 5th February 1985:

Your letter of the 15th January 1985, addressed to the Queen, has been passed to this Office as matters concerning the Royal Warrants of Appointment to Tradesmen are within the aegis of Lord Chamberlain.

Her Majesty had already received a copy of the Early Day Motion which was handed in at Buckingham Palace in November.

Your concern over the health aspect of smoking is well understood and, of course, as you no doubt know neither the Queen, the Duke of Edinburgh, Queen Elizabeth The Queen Mother nor the Prince and Princess of Wales smoke and it is only for the supply of cigarettes to official guests at Royal Residences that the Grant of Warrants of Appointment to Tradesmen have been given.

This policy is under review and I am grateful to your bringing to our attention the concern of Members of Parliament. This will be taken into account when the individual Warrants are reviewed.

I sent a further letter to the Queen a year later on 4th December 1985, pressing for the withdrawal of the Royal Warrant on cigarettes which read:

Your Majesty

In January 1984, a petition, an Early Day Motion signed by MPs, and a letter from me were sent to your Majesty asking you to withdraw the Royal Warrant from cigarette manufacturers.

We drew your Majesty's attention to the facts produced by the British Medical Association that 100,000 of your subjects were being killed each year by smoking cigarettes. We received a letter from The Lord Chamberlain's Office saying that the issue of Royal Warrants would be reviewed by the Royal Household Tradesmen Warrant Committee.

It is now December 1985 and, according to a detailed report named 'The Big Kill' issued by The British Medical Association and the Health Educational Council, a further 100,000 persons have been killed by smoking.

Enclosed are copies of Press statements with signatures, a copy of the foreword from the report and a letter from The British Medical Association concerning the advertising of cigarettes.

I beg your Majesty to stop the use of the Royal Warrants on cigarettes and so help save the lives of the young and the old from smoking.

No action has yet been taken to withdraw the Royal Warrant. So much for the concern about the health of her subjects.

My constituents in Hackney North were plagued by the problems of prostitution and continually raised the matter with me. So when the Government set up a Standing Committee on the Sexual Offence Bill in 1985, I agreed to serve on it. I told the committee that I had had many meetings with residents over a number of years about the problems in the Brownswood, Finsbury Park and Manor House areas. We had taken action to try and prevent the problem but that action had caused a great nuisance. We had put gates across the roads to stop kerb crawling. We did it on one road, which stopped the kerb crawling there, but then there was a demand from the next road and so it went on. We continually pushed the kerb crawling out but we did not get rid of it. Therefore, the problem had not been reduced.

Mothers and young women had complained to me about the insulting attitudes of motorists driving along and soliciting them in the areas that I have mentioned. Every day and, particularly at night, these women went about with the ever present fear of attack.

At that time there had been a heavy police presence in the areas I mentioned, resulting in many more prosecutions, but the problem still existed. Only the night before, a deputation of young women had come to see me and urged me to speak out on this problem of kerb crawling and soliciting by motorists. I was in favour of some legislation to deal with the problem but I know that many of the women who are involved in prostitution are driven on to the streets to get money because of unemployment and poverty. When unemployment increases as it has done, prostitution increases. It is no coincidence that we were discussing this problem at a time of mass unemployment. I asked the Government to look at this aspect of the problem and take steps to alleviate unemployment which drives women onto the streets to get a living.

I wished to draw attention to the fact that people selling their bodies is not the only kind of prostitution with which society is plagued. People sell both their brains and their principles often for immoral purposes and sometimes that can do more harm to society than sexual prostitution does.

When the order about unfair dismissal from employment was to be discussed by Parliament, I was determined to speak in this debate because of my numerous experiences of being sacked. I told them that I spoke not as a lawyer but as someone who had been a shop steward for 25 years and as a national trade union official with some experience of dismissals and protection against dismissals.

The order would remove the right of a worker to go before a tribunal and appeal against unfair dismissal if he had been employed for less than two years.

I was opposed to the order being sneaked in at a late hour because it could not stand the light of day. The order was absolutely irrelevant to job creation. Its aim was to make sacking easier and cheaper. I went on:

I know from my experience that shop stewards, workers and trade union representatives generally are always under the threat of victimisation by their employers. It happens continually. There was far better protection under the 1940 essential works order. It often protected me when I was at work. It operated at a time when the country needed the workers' labour and was prepared to give them protection in their jobs.

Directors and top management – there are some representatives here – are well protected against unfair dismissal. They are protected by contracts with companies which provide massive golden handshakes. Those who own and control the means of production, distribution and exchange will use their power to hire and fire as they please. Their only concern will always be to make as much profit as they can and to squeeze as much work as they can from people they employ.

It would be far better if this Government introduced an order on the right to work rather than on the right to sack. They should pay more attention to that.

The Tory government has gone on to make workers even more insecure in their employment. Workers are being dismissed by government departments as well as private employers and today there are four million unemployed.

Unemployment has always been a major concern for me as I had personal experience, at one period being unemployed for three years. During the 1930s I was active in the National Unemployed Workers' Movement with Tom Mann and Wal Hannington. When unemployment began to grow again in the 1970s, I wrote a booklet entitled 'The Fight Against Unemployment'. It began with two songs:

Work boys work and be contented,
As long as you've enough to buy a meal;
For if you will but try, you'll be wealthy by and by,
If only you'll put your shoulders to the wheel.
(Music-hall song, about 1910)
Oh, why don't you work like other men do?
How the hell can I work when there's no work to do?
(International Wobblies' Song, USA 1930s)

My opinion is that of the disastrous results for the working class of the international concentration of finance capital, is growing unemployment due to mergers and closures of industries; also, the various countries' capitalist governments' efforts to solve their economic problems by financial manoeuvres and other protectionist policies against foreign competition. This means that the burdens are increasingly put on the backs of the working class. Unemployment and attacks on wages are the means the employers and their governments use to do this.

Mass unemployment has fluctuated widely over the years. The number of workers denied the right to work in 1920 was 691,103, but within a few months, by March 1921, this number had increased to 2,171,288. The numbers of unemployed workers varied during subsequent years but, by 1933, they had reached dramatic proportions. British Labour Statistics published by the Department of Employment and Productivity gives the registered numbers of unemployed workers in the United Kingdom as follows:

January 1923	1,460,400
December 1929	1,565,300
December 1930	2,725,000
September 1931	2,897,000
January 1933	2,979,000

In the concluding paragraph of the booklet, I quoted this poem by Thomas Irving James, the son of an unemployed miner:

Will they stand in groups again
shabby hungry broken men,
coughing, cursing, pacing .... pacing,
smoking, talking football, racing,
hands thrust deep in trouser pockets,
fingering their pitmen's dockets,
wishing it had been a shilling,
killing time, while time is killing –
killing body, killing soul,
dying slowly on the dole?

I argued:

The slogan of the unemployed in the past, 'work or full maintenance', is not the answer. A redundancy payment and dole money are no substitute for a wage and the right to work.

Unemployment was increasing rapidly again in the 1980s and Parliament decided to discuss the problem in December 1982 and, during this debate, I took up the cudgel again on behalf of the unemployed. I said:

When the Tories came to power in 1979, unemployment in London was 132,000. In 1982 it is nearer 390,000 – three times as many. One eighth of London's workforce is unemployed.

In 1994 the number was 500,000. If it were only admitted, the real national unemployment figure is nearer four million. More than one person in eight is unemployed in the United Kingdom, chasing some 100,000 vacancies – 40 workers for each vacancy.

In 1945, the Labour Government had a policy of full employment. In 1951, under the Tory Party, that policy became a high and stable level of employment. In the 1960s, Governments began to talk about an acceptable level of unemployment. From 1970 onwards, we had an unacceptable rate of unemployment. All parties and Governments admit that Government policies are responsible for employment. Therefore, this Government must take responsibility for their employment policies.

During the economic crisis of the 1930s, the unemployed believed – because they were told to believe it – that unemployment was the result of the economic climate. The same is said today. It was said that the climate was bad but that, like the weather, it would change if people would only wait long enough. It was said that the economic climate had nothing to do with the Government. No doubt it came from outer space. It was also said – just as it is today – that the economic climate was caused by the world recession. It was as if unemployment was not the result of Government policies.

There is no doubt that the present unemployment is caused by the Tory Government's policies. To add insult to injury, Ministers call those who are unemployed and who are on social security, scroungers. There are Ministers, such as the Secretary of State for Employment, who do not understand what employment is all about. The unemployed are told to get on their bikes to look for work.

What has suddenly struck the capitalist world, of which the United Kingdom is a part? Why are 30 million people unemployed among the Western nations? Why are there massive food mountains and why are prices for that food so high when there is poverty and unemployment? Why are the storehouses full of manufactured goods? Why is food destroyed while people starve? Why are the majority of workers in Britain and in other countries poor? Such absurdities exist only because of the private ownership of the means of production, distribution and exchange in Britain and in other countries. Profit comes before the needs of the people.

During the early 1980s, the 'Right to Work Campaign' was set up by the Socialist Workers' Party and sponsored by hundreds of trade union and Labour Party organisations. I was the national treasurer and, together with John Deason, the secretary, spoke at their many meetings. On one occasion, Deason was arrested in Blackpool during a Labour Party conference. I was informed and I went to the police station to get him released. A national march of the unemployed, dressed in orange-coloured jackets, marched from Scotland to London. They were attacked by the police. A particularly savage attack took place near Hendon and many protests were made by the Labour movement. After a few more demonstrations outside the Tory and Labour Party Conferences and also outside the TUC, the 'Right to Work Campaign' folded up due to lack of support from the millions of unemployed.

'Hackney Gazette' reported in May 1983 that a call had been made for me to stand down in favour of a black candidate by a 'Black Representation Campaign', which were putting forward seven black candidates including Diane Abbott whom the Black Campaign finally decided to support as their candidate. The 'Gazette' reported that I had got off to a flying start in my reselection battle. "He has won all the early nominations including a dozen unions, the Trades Union Council and the first two wards to make their choice – all by big majorities." I said that several organisations of black people had written supporting me including a letter containing several hundred signatures.

"I will continue to fully represent all races, colours and creeds in the community," I told the 'Hackney Gazette'.

At the end of the selection fight, I was nominated by 15 Trade Union branches and six of the nine ward branches. The selection result looked to be a foregone conclusion. I was certain to win. My speech to the Selection Conference referred to:

- accountability of representatives;
- support for principles before loyalty to leaders;
- no racist immigration laws;
- no sexist inequalities;
- no deals to keep nuclear weapons;
- no witch-hunt in the Party.

I issued the following statement to the delegates:

Since I was elected as MP for Hackney North & Stoke Newington in May 1979, I have reported to and consulted with the Hackney North party, the General Management Committee and the Executive Committee each month. These reports have concerned my daily activities and the great variety of problems I have dealt with, both in my weekly surgery and in the 20,000 or so letters I have written on problems such as housing, unemployment, DHSS benefits, immigration, education, Ireland, police, racialism, etc.

I believe it is right and proper for a Constituency Party to mandate its MP on all major issues. Furthermore I am of the opinion that the National Executive of the Labour Party is elected by the Annual Conference of the Party to be the custodian of the policies decided by Conference. Therefore the Executive should support these policies when deciding the Party's General Election Manifesto with the Shadow Cabinet.

The Parliamentary Labour Party should be more democratic and open: the way that MPs vote in their meetings should be recorded and made known to the constituency parties, so that members can see how they are being represented in Parliament.

The Labour Party has existed for 77 years. Our philosophy is Socialist. The Party has been elected as the Government in Britain six times, yet we have not made much progress towards Socialism. This has been because of the refusal of the right-wing leaders to carry out the policies decided by the members, and their lack of accountability to the members of the Party for their actions. Accountability within the Party by all its representatives is vital.

Throughout all my activities I have maintained a close liaison with the members and the Party, inviting their comments/criticisms and promoting the kind of relationship which I believe to be essential between an MP and CLP.

In spite of the overwhelming support I received with the majority of nominations, some of the delegates to the Selection Conference failed to carry out their accountability to their branches and switched their branch's vote to Diane Abbott. They said that they wanted Hackney to have the first black woman Member of Parliament. I lost by four votes. There is pressure in the Labour Party to have black candidates only on the shortlist in some constituencies.

I have often quoted my friend, the black Jacobite leader, CLR James, who, during an interview on Race, said: "I am against the conception of race. The people who are opposing you are of the same race. The division is class or the social position you are in. If you make it purely race, that means you have a lot of people, black people who are oppressing black people too." He went on to say, "The people who suffer from race are usually people in the middle or lower orders of society, therefore, for them it may begin as race, but they soon find out it is a question of class too.... You never put race before class."

During my time in the House of Commons, I was revolted by the 'club' atmosphere. I deplored the fraternisation which goes on across party boundaries, and the first-name matiness that characterise the gentlemen's agreements, such as pairing, which turn government into a game. I did not fraternise with other parties; indeed, there was precious little fraternisation with members of my own party, many of whom felt threatened by the impetus towards democratising the PLP and making its actions open to public scrutiny.

At a meeting between the AUEW Executive and the union's parliamentary group, I rose from the table along with the others when the division bell rang, and as they all went off to vote, Ken Gill (General Secretary of the AUEW Draughtsmen's Section) commented that the Commons was the only place that had ever got me jumping through a hoop. He was wrong. I might file meekly through the lobby on occasion, but I was far from being tamed.

As I walked through the division lobby one night after listening to the same arguments coming from both sides of the House, I said to Joan Maynard MP – in my opinion one of the best workers' representatives in the House – "I'm going home – I can't find the Labour Party in here." The same sense of bewildered frustration emerged after a meeting of the London Group of Labour MPs, when I said:

I just don't connect with them at all – we're not talking the same language. They're talking about how to make capitalism work better, and I'm talking about how to replace it.

I was out of my element in the House, and my colleagues know it. Raymond Fletcher MP, entertaining some American guests, was explaining that the character of the House was changing, as there were fewer ex-military types and more real workers' representatives than ever before. Just then, I passed through the lobby close by the group, and one of the Americans pointed me out as "a typical ex-colonel". Fletcher replied: "You couldn't have picked a worse example; there isn't anybody Left of him in here."

After I had ceased to be an MP in 1989, I again set about building an organisation of unemployed workers and called it the 'National Organisation of Unemployed Workers' for which I had the support of a number of Labour MPs, MEPs and local organisations. In the 1990s I sent out several statements to the unemployed and employed, one of which read as follows:

> The Voice of the Unemployed. An appeal to all the unemployed, and Trade Union, Labour Party Workers' Organisations. Dear Friends, please read on: it concerns YOU!
>
> Unemployment continues to rise, no jobs are secure, who will be the next victims? Soon there will be 3,000,000 registered unemployed (the true figure of the Unemployed is 4,000,000). Don't you think it's time a stand was made against unemployment? The misery caused by unemployment must and can be ended. But to do that, a UNITED effort is needed by the UNEMPLOYED and the Trade Union organisations. The silent acceptance of UNEMPLOYMENT over the last 13 years has permitted the TORY Government and the employers to continue with sackings and attack living standards. Will you be next? We have been tolerant too long. It is time to make a UNITED stand. Action is needed.
>
> The NATIONAL ORGANISATION OF UNEMPLOYED WORKERS together with other organisations of the unemployed and some MPs have been urged to convene a conference to consider what kind of action is best to deal with this disastrous situation. UNEMPLOYMENT must be a top priority.
>
> The RIGHT TO WORK; PROPER TRAINING; ADEQUATE MAINTE-NANCE; END UNEMPLOYMENT must be out aims.
>
> The NOUW is sponsored by the Socialist Campaign Group of Labour MPs, MEPs and local leaders of the Unemployed.
>
> You and your organisation are invited to a conference to be held in the HOUSE OF COMMONS in the near future.

Several conferences of representatives of the unemployed have been held up to 1994 but we have not achieved the unity which the unemployed built in the 1930s. The NOUW is still striving to unite in action the millions of unemployed.

The question has been asked of those that have known me for many years, "What kind of man is Ernie Roberts, apart from his politics?" They reply that there isn't any Ernie Roberts apart from his politics. He has a one-track mind, and whatever the subject at the start of a conversation with him, after a couple of minutes it will be politics. He is invariable convinced that he is right. he never says, "I think so," but "It is so." How, he asks, can he convince anybody else if he is not sure himself? He will never be a 'statesman' because of his inability to compromise; whatever the subject in hand, he never forgets that the ultimate objective is Socialism, therefore he finds it difficult to accept "papering over the cracks" as a political remedy.

In personal conversation I am said to be mild and soft-spoken, but on a platform I can change to a loud delivery which is sometimes aggressive. Some say I am without doubt better at answering questions than at making speeches, where my elementary-school grammar and lack of logical ordering of my material sometimes prove to be drawbacks. But in argument, I can tie an opponent in knots, and because I keep my cool my opponents often get irritated beyond measure.

It has been said that my 'youthful' appearance is exaggerated by my taste in clothes, described as 'elegant', 'terrible', 'adventurous', or 'distinguished' according to which paper you read. I have often found that people who cannot find any meeting-point with me in politics will comment on my clothes instead. I have been described as "a typical Tory" because of my clothes, although my choice is anything but conservative. From my youth, I have taken the attitude that Socialism means 'levelling up' not 'levelling down', and that applies equally to dress, although I am certainly not extravagant, buying clothes in sales and nearly-new shops.

My hobby is listed in 'Who's Who' as politics. For relaxation I indulge in political criticism − switching on the TV and talking at it non-stop. Given a choice I will watch a political programme in preference to anything else.

Nevertheless, I am not without a sense of humour. I incline towards wit rather than smut, and enjoy a good political joke, even if it tells against my own party. I can see the funny side of most situations − afterwards. At the time, I am inclined to think the worst of everything and everybody, particularly if they belong to one of those groups against whom I am most severely prejudiced − businessmen, lawyers and top entertainers.

My hallmark is easy to define. It is either 'single-mindedness' or 'bloody-mindedness', depending on your political colouring. People have said that you either love me or you hate me. You can't be indifferent.

My life's work has been directed towards helping to establish Socialism in Britain. For me, Socialism means that working people must have certain fundamental rights: the right to work, and to have a decent home; the right to educational opportunities, to develop the personality, to enjoy literature and the arts; the right to peace.

Above all, I believe in the right which I have so often been denied: the right to criticise and question, and to challenge. The right to reply to charges and accusations.

In order to achieve these rights, I believe that it is essential for the working class to organise, to understand its own strength and its ability to change society through the twin levers of the trade union movement and the Labour Party.

To this end, I have lived a life of unusual intensity, and consistent struggle. I live, in the words of the poet Bailey:

in deeds, not years; in thoughts, not breaths;
In feelings, not in figures on a dial.

During September 1993, I felt ill and short of breath, so I went to Manor House Hospital of which I have been a member for over 40 years in order to get a check up. X-rays showed that my right lung had collapsed. The consultant sent me to Harefield Heart and Lung Hospital where tests were carried out. I was also taken to Mount Vernon Cancer Hospital for further checks. After a few days in Harefield Hospital, I was told that I had a secondary cancer in my lung and there was nothing they could do for me. I was referred back to Manor House Hospital where the consultant carried out periodic checks on my development but offered no treatment for cancer. Therefore, I decided, as I have done throughout my life, to fight back against the disease by continuing my usual activities and trying alternative medicines.

In April 1994, the EC of the AEEU decided to present me with a Special Award of Merit in Coventry for services to the union over a period of 60 years. The Lord Mayor of Coventry, learning of this, decided to arrange a civic function for the presentation:

After a lifetime of struggle one experiences the ebb and flow of the fight-back of the working class, learning slowly from our past mistakes and building on our victories. When divided, we are defeated, but united, we win. As Karl Marx has urged us: "Workers of the world unite, you have nothing to lose but your chains and a world to gain."

Finally, listen to Shelley:

Rise like lions after slumber
In unvanquishable number
Shake your chains to earth like dew
Which in sleep had fallen on you
Ye are many – they are few.

Photo of myself on taking up office as Assistant General Secretary of the AEU in 1957.

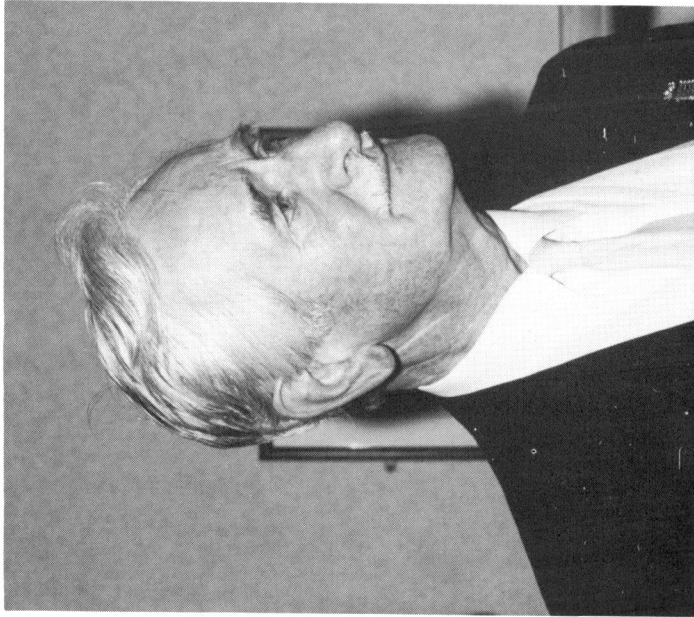

Photo taken at the celebration of the 50th anniversary of the West Midlands Regional Council of the Labour Party, December 1992.

Myself in 1929 on arriving in Oxford to work for Pressed Steel Co.

AEU delegates to the 1946 Labour Party Conference.
I am standing behind Jack Tanner, with Ben Gardiner and Sir Robert Young on the front row.

Clement and Mrs Attlee at the eve of poll rally, Stockport 1955,
supporting candidate Muriel Nichol and myself.

Nye Bevan being congratulated by me upon his election as Party treasurer after
many years in 1956.

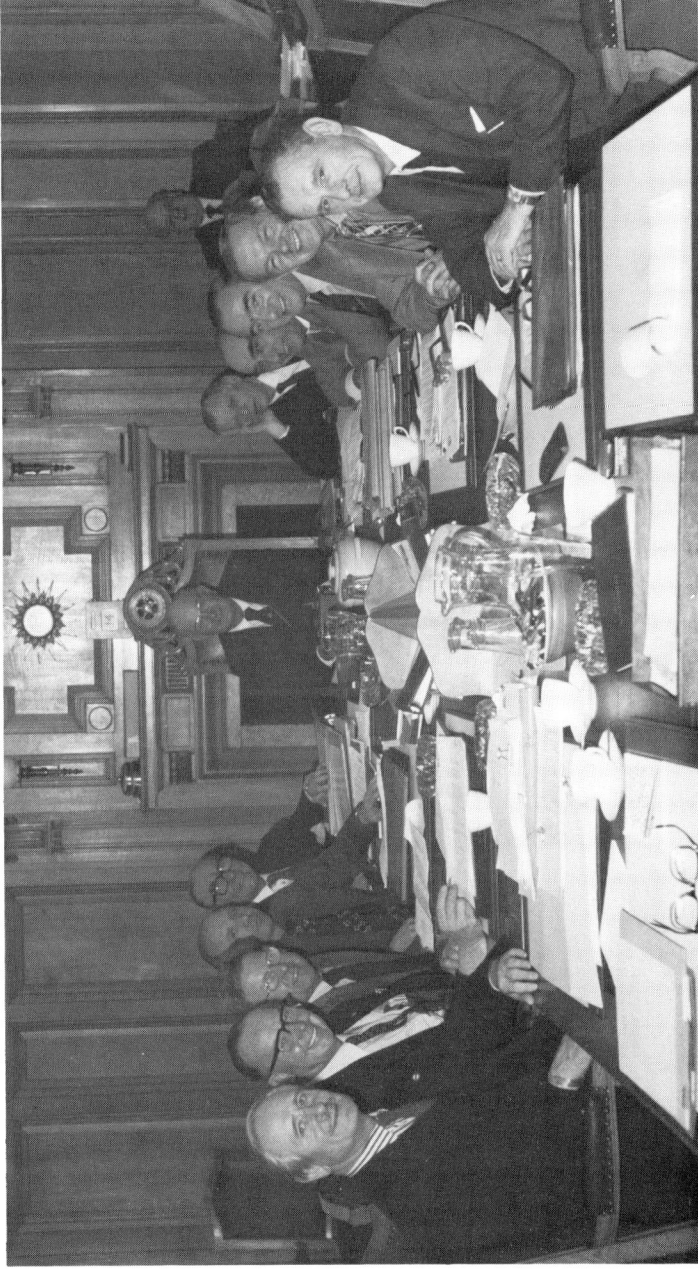

AEU EC, 1977, in session. Pictured are (from right to left): Ken Brett (AGS), Terry Duffy, Les Dixon, Bill Johns, Reg Birch, Hugh Scanlon (President), John Boyd (General Secretary), Gavin Laird, Gerry Russell, Len Edmondson, and myself.

Joyce, Ernie and daughter Joy campaigning in 1979 General Election in Hackney.

Presentation of Special Award of Merit (9th April 1994) made by Bro John Allen, EC member AEEU. On the left of the photograph is the Lord Mayor of Coventry who hosted the function, Councillor Alex Boyd.

The Anti-Nazi League carnival and demonstration of 150,000 in London, May 1994.
Photograph: Mark Campbell.